TAKING RELIGION
TO SCHOOL

TAKING RELIGION TO SCHOOL

CHRISTIAN THEOLOGY
AND SECULAR EDUCATION

STEPHEN H. WEBB

Brazos Press

A Division of Baker Book House Co
Grand Rapids, Michigan 49516

Published by Brazos Press
a division of Baker Book House Company
P.O. Box 6287, Grand Rapids, MI 49516-6287

Printed in the United States of America

Library of Congress Cataloging-in-Publication Data

Webb, Stephen H., 1961-
    Taking religion to school : Christian theology and secular education / Stephen H. Webb.
        p.   cm.
    Includes bibliographical references.
    ISBN 1-58743-002-9
    1. Religion in the public schools–United States. 2. Theology. I. Title.
LC111.W43 2000
379.2'8'0973–dc21   00-040381

For current information about all releases from Brazos Press, visit our web site:
http://www.brazospress.com

CONTENTS

99816

ACKNOWLEDGMENTS

Rodney Clapp, Bill Placher, Jim Spiegel, David Cunningham, Brad Stull, Raymond Williams, and Diane Timmerman read this book with care and diligence. I could not have asked for more friendly criticism. They taught me to listen more carefully to what I was trying to say. Peter Frederick, professor of history at Wabash College, first tried to persuade me that talking about teaching is not only intellectually interesting but necessary for my survival in the classroom. Although it took many years, this book is my response to his proddings. Most of all, Raymond Williams, director of the Wabash Center for Teaching and Learning in Theology and Religion, has supported steadfastly all of my struggles to become a better teacher and to write about why I think it is so important to be open and honest about faith in the classroom. He has done more than anyone else I know to bring pedagogy to the forefront of religious studies. A generous grant from the Wabash Center—which is funded by Lilly Endowment Inc.—for the 1999–2000 school year gave me the time to write this book.

I draw from several previously published essays. All of this work has been significantly revised to be integrated into my thesis. I am grateful to the editors and publishers of the following books and journals for permission to use this material.

"Teaching as Confessing: Redeeming a Theological Trope for Pedagogy," *Teaching Theology and Religion* 2/3 (October 1999): 143–53.

"Teaching Religion Religiously: A Dialogue Between Stephen H. Webb and William C. Placher," *Teaching Theology and Religion* 3/2 (June 2000): 81–87.

"Recalling: A Theologian Remembers His Church," in *Falling Toward Grace: Images of Religion and Culture from the Heartland* (Bloomington: Indiana University Press, 1998). This is a revision of "Sons and Heirs of Salvation," *The Christian Century* (April 17, 1996): 428–30.

"The Voice of Theology: Rethinking the Personal and the Objective in Christian Pedagogy," *Journal of the American Academy of Religion* 65/4 (Fall 1997): 763–81.

"Theologizing the Postmodern Classroom," *Encounter* 55 (Summer 1995): 229–39.

"Rhetoric, Pedagogy and the Study of Religion," with Richard B. Miller and Laurie L. Patton, *Journal of the American Academy of Religion* 62 (Fall 1994): 819–50.

Review of Peter C. Hodgson, *God's Wisdom: Toward a Theology of Education,* in *The Christian Century* (December 15, 1999): 1236.

Review of Warren A. Nord, *Religion and American Education,* in *Teaching Religion and Theology* 2/2 (June 1999): 122–23.

Review Essay of Bill Readings, *The University in Ruins,* in *Teaching Theology and Religion* I/3 (October 1998): 187–90.

Review of George Marsden, *The Outrageous Idea of Christian Scholarship,* in *Teaching Theology and Religion* I/1 (February 1998): 65–6.

I also need to thank the leaders and participants of several workshops who have listened to my ideas with both cheerful and critical attention. They showed me that talking about teaching is one of the practices that sustains friendship in the academy.

The first Lilly Workshop on Teaching Religion, directed by Raymond Williams, met at Wabash College during the Summer and Fall of 1991 and the Spring and Summer of 1992. I especially want to thank W. Lee Humphrey and Mary Kay Kramp for their inspiration and friendship during this workshop. This experimental workshop was the first to draw together teachers from every field in religious studies to talk about teaching religion. We had the advantage of not really knowing what we were doing, so we could make it up along the way.

The Wabash Theology Consultation, directed by Bill Placher, met at Wabash College in July 1996, '97, and '98. This group laughed as vigorously as it argued, making it a delightful forum to talk about teaching.

And the AAR/Lilly Conference on Teaching Religion, directed by Raymond Williams, met in Santa Fe during April 1997.

Finally, this book is dedicated to my colleagues (past and present) in the religion department at Wabash College, who have given me lots of room to practice the art of teaching religion and have listened as I have tried to develop my religious voice, and to all of my students at Wabash, who have patiently taught me how to teach by showing me how they learn.

INTRODUCTION

TEACHING RELIGION RELIGIOUSLY

I can remember the exact moment, in the fall of 1987, when I realized that I did not know how to teach. I was fresh from a graduate school that taught me to regard teaching as something not worth thinking about, precisely because nothing was ever said about it. As graduate students, we no more would have talked about teaching than we would have admitted liking a Bruce Willis movie. We thought we were training to become thinkers, not teachers, and as a result, we had no preparation whatsoever for the professional challenges we would soon encounter. This pedagogical silence implied that true knowledge naturally overflows from the mind of the scholar. All you need to be a teacher is students with their empty hands extended in gratitude. My first semester of teaching had been going on long enough for me to discover that this model of teaching did not work, but I did not know how to replace it with something else. I had told my students everything that I thought I knew, and they did not seem all that impressed or grateful.

So I was a bit annoyed when I was asked to co-teach the senior humanities colloquium one evening. The colloquium met once a week, always with a different pair of teachers leading the discussion on a classic text. My co-teacher was Eric Dean, longtime chair of the religion department and the humanities division, one of the pillars of the faculty who had been at the college almost forever, or so it seemed to me. He began the class with a blistering demonstration of the Socratic method, building on student comments with a series of questions that led students from their set opinions to a myriad of complex issues that threatened, I thought, to drown them in confusion, if not despair. I was threatened, too, as I watched his performance in awe. I had come to class with a topic or two that we might explore, and here I was with my head spinning faster than those of the students. After a succession of leading questions that seemed to force the class toward the brink of exasperation, he turned to me and paused. I looked him straight in the eyes and said nothing, trying to mask my dread. It was as if I were a student all over again. "Well," he said, with a smile, "now it's your turn."

Eric was a great teacher, and he knew that this group of seniors could handle this forceful barrage, which he did not use in other situations. What he did not know was how terrified I was of teaching in front of him. Teaching is the most private of professions. Teachers rarely see each other teach, and they rarely even talk about their teaching to each other. Each classroom has its own personality, and pedagogical problems are so personal, involving our innermost vulnerabilities and limitations, that teaching is something we share more often with our families and closest friends than with other teachers. Besides, there always seem to be more important things to talk about at faculty lunches, like byzantine school policies and typical administrative bungling. We teach in private, with students who share stories about us with each other, but there is little public awareness of what we do and how we do it.

As a college student, I had been compelled to study religion because I felt my life depended on it. I needed to learn how other people put faith and reason together, and I needed to place my religious experiences in a context that would make them look less unusual and irregular. I could not clarify the various levels of my typical adolescent unhappiness without trying to make out the underlying larger patterns of faith and doubt that my life was tracing.

In graduate school, I had discovered that learning about religion was supposed to be the same thing as learning about any other topic, mastering a set of methods and a body of information. When I returned to my alma mater to teach, however, I knew that I had to figure out how to bring my religious life and my professional development closer together in order to survive. Discovering that I really did not know how to teach provided a great impetus to sorting through my priorities and reflecting on why I had wanted to teach in the first place. Every semester, before a new set of classes, I would begin to feel anxiety swelling up inside of me, signaling that something was not quite right in my sense of myself as a teacher. Although I used to dream that once I had mastered enough material in religious studies my classroom jitters would vanish, I now know that such dreams are more like fantasies, because fear is a fairly normal condition of the teaching vocation. I came to the point where I could manage, if not eliminate, my anxiety about teaching by probing the conflicts I had about religion and authority. I had to listen to my anxiety to find out where my passion was coming from and what my voice sounded like in the halls of academe.

I decided that I could not teach religion without figuring out where I was religiously, for the simple reason that who I was determined what I did in the classroom. Moreover, I needed to let the students see my internal struggles so they could have a model for their own, or at least so they could see that their struggles were relevant to what they were learning. This book, then, is the record of my quest for integrity in the classroom. That quest forced me, over and over again, back to a simple lesson I am still learning, that is, how to teach religion religiously. I could not teach religion any differently from how I had learned it—as an aspect of my search for God and as a way of taking the measure of the state of my soul.

Teaching religion religiously was something I needed to learn not only for my own spiritual growth but also to become an effective teacher. Religion is a phenomenon that involves many dimensions—psychological, sociological, historical, political, literary, ethical, philosophical, and on—but I learned that only by taking religious *faith* seriously could I do justice to this topic and involve the full range of my students' passions in the classroom. I could not have learned this lesson without students who were patiently open to my stuttering attempts to teach them and without a religion department that believed in me more than I believed in myself.

Religion classes should be dramatic, reflecting all of the pathos of the religious quest. Like good theater, the study of religion should let students decide for themselves the level of their participation, allowing them to try on roles, witness moving spectacles, and then go home to ponder what they have learned.

Teaching religion should also be a joy and a privilege. This, too, I learned from Eric Dean. A few weeks after that humanities colloquium, Eric stopped by my office on the way back from class. He was near the end of a remarkable career devoted to teaching, and he wore the smile of a novice having just made a discovery. "Can you believe that they pay us to do this?" he asked. "We must be the luckiest people in the world. We get to sit around with eager young people and talk about the most important issues imaginable. I hope they never find out that I would do it all for free." Sometimes I still cannot believe that I am a theologian, paid to introduce students to the richness of the Christian faith, charged with helping them through the intellectual phase of their spiritual journeys.

Although it has taken me a long time to learn it, teaching is always and only a matter of grace. To be vulnerable to the demands of students, honest about one's weaknesses, and open to the mystery of the community that classrooms can become requires a sensitivity to the higher power that sustains all that we do. This book is, in part, a meditation on the ways in which the teaching of religion can be distorted by the strategies teachers use to prohibit the expression of religious passion in the classroom. Chief among those strategies are specialization and compartmentalization—the idea that teaching religion is a matter of a passing on technical information and can be done in

14

ways radically distinct from the practices of churches, mosques, and synagogues. This book is also a meditation on the movement of grace that occurs when people begin to listen to and learn from each other as they open a book and ask a question. Teaching religion is not always explicitly about God. However, attending to the power of the Almighty in the hopes and fears of each student is not a bad way to think about how the teaching of religion should be done.

I follow a simple, threefold argument throughout this book. First, the teaching of religion is a religious activity. What a teacher believes about God makes a difference in how she teaches what others believe about God. No teacher of religion can be absolutely neutral toward the topic and be an effective teacher. True, the study of religion is part of a common human search for wisdom and understanding, while the practice of religious faith is a more specific response to God's gift of salvation. There are good practical reasons to keep the two somewhat separate in public education, but it is impossible to ignore the ways they overlap and interpenetrate. The study of religion derives much of its power from the exercise of faith, so the two activities can be competitive and antagonistic but also can converge to the point where the study becomes one necessary component of *being* religious. When we ask students to think about God, we are not inviting them to worship in a formal way but to attend to the mystery that is the ground of existence, and it is inevitable that such attention blurs the boundary between church and school, faith and reason, meditation and study.

Second, if teaching religion is a kind of religious activity, then it is of the utmost importance that teachers think through the intersection of theory and practice, reason and faith in their own lives. Many religion teachers have religious affiliations but often look at teaching the subject as being only indirectly related to their religious lives—a vocation that grows out of but is clearly differentiated from their beliefs. In reality, of course, the effective religion classroom blurs the boundaries between the public and the private to the extent that teachers cannot leave their attitudes toward religion at the door. Consequently, teaching religion is never completely free from the language and practices of religious faith. What religion teachers do in the secular classroom might be more careful, diverse, and complex than what is done in religious institutions, but it is a version of the latter nonetheless. Even when teachers try to define the religion classroom as the opposite of the church, a space where students are encouraged to criticize and denounce the idea of faith, they are still acknowledging the power of religion, and thus the most antireligious classrooms are derivative of that which they reject.

Our culture tries to restrict religious belief to the private realm in order to liberate civic discussions of political questions from religious controversy. While some benefits result from this strategy, I will argue that the silencing of religion in education is as harmful to the democratic pursuit of pluralism as it is to those whose voices are never heard. If people of faith are to learn how to participate in public discussions with their most cherished values intact, then they must be encouraged throughout the educational process to bring their faith to the table rather than learning to act as if it does not matter. Religion teachers, then, should model ways in which students can discern how faith can become a part of the learning experience rather than be regarded as something awkward to avoid.

Many teachers of religion have so much at stake in their topic that it is not an exaggeration to say that teaching religion is one mode of being religious. To the extent that this is true, teachers of religion have the obligation to try to integrate their personal and professional lives. Such integration raises all sorts of issues about personal identity, integrity, and subjectivity in the classroom. Rather than developing a specific theory of personal identity, I will try to address the ways in which teaching religion religiously allows teachers and students alike to explore the dimensions of faith in nonthreatening ways.

Third, if teaching religion is a religious activity, high schools, colleges, and universities need to give more scope for religious voices in the classroom and among religion faculty members. If there is no neutral position with regard to religion, there is no higher plane upon which religious discussions can be neutralized. Public education, then, needs to invite and welcome religious discussions that are led by people of faith, even to the point of religious passion and disagreement. Public education also needs, now more than ever, the discipline of theology, which tries to make sense of religious conflict without abandoning the notion of religious truth. Theology cannot provide all the answers to the academic study of religion, but theologians can help keep the discussion going by demarcating the limits of religious agreement and outlining what is at stake in the study of religion.

We live in a postmodern world where all levels of education are experiencing a legitimation crisis, so that the source of teachers' authority to make judgments about and evaluations of their students is increasingly unclear. Without the Enlightenment narrative of rationality that undergirds so many discussions of religion, religion teachers are forced to be more attentive to the religious narratives of their students. There is no one way to bring together faith and reason, passion and critique in the study of religion. Teachers cannot dissolve those tensions by developing some general theory of religion or by abdicating their role as spiritual guides in the classroom. If theology is the name for the project that tries to sustain and explore the classic tensions between faith and reason, then we are all—those of us who teach and study religion—theologians now.

Theology, in other words, is just another name for the holistic approach to the study of religion, in which students and teachers come together to probe the mysteries of the divine and seek a public discourse on the many passions that divide us. Discussion of religion in the classroom will range from rejection and critique to defense and reconstruction. The theological classroom will not foreclose on any of these possibilities, especially the possibility that students and teachers alike will draw closer to God and experience something of the power that leads so many people outside of the classroom to places of worship.

The religion classroom is not the church, mosque, or synagogue, but there is no reason why the former should not point, no matter how provisionally and awkwardly, to the latter. Indeed, the religion classroom that does not so point beyond itself cannot claim to be addressing its topic in any adequate way. Rather than trying to take the place of lived faith by mas-

17

tering religion with some reductive theory, the religion class-room should leave students unsettled and disturbed, motivating them to continue their educational journey well beyond the confines of the academic study of religion. One way to measure the success of the study of religion, then, is to gauge its failure to offer final answers and its stimulation of students' desire for something more.

I offer my pedagogical autobiography in chapter one not to draw attention to my idiosyncratic experiences but because all of the issues I deal with in this book emerge from my struggle to be a Christian theologian in a secular educational setting. I also hope that my story of how faith influences pedagogy will serve as an example of my thesis on the blurring of the boundaries between the subjective and objective study of religion. My story concerns the struggle to give a voice to both faith and intellect in the classroom, thus illustrating my contention that the goal of religion teachers should be to listen to their students and call forth their best religious voices.

Chapter two addresses the fears and concerns many educators have about the role of religion in the classroom. It explains why teachers often feel unprepared when it comes to religion, and it deals with controversial issues such as evolution and character education. It also develops two pedagogical models for helping teachers deal with those concerns.

Many recent books on teaching have tried to recover moral and spiritual dimensions to pedagogy. Dealing with several representatives of this argument in chapter three, I argue that it is a mistake to construe education as a whole to be a religious phenomenon. When that happens, religion often is reduced to a psychologically helpful motivation for education, so that the various religions and their differences are not adequately addressed. If the argument is made that education *in general* is religious, then only the most general forms of religious faith will be taught and encouraged in the classroom. The result will be a religious relativism that leaves little room for particular beliefs. It is better, I suggest, to promote the study of actual

18

religions in the classroom than to defend the idea that education is an essentially religious enterprise.

Chapter four deals with the question of religious confessions in the classroom. How can we teach religion without asking our students to talk about themselves and, moreover, without being honest about ourselves? Yet what do we do with personal opinions in the religion classroom, when the appeal to subjective experience often is used to insulate the individual from external comment or critique? In this chapter I delve into the history of confessional practices, arguing that we need to fully understand what confession is in order to utilize personal experience in the classroom in pedagogically healthy ways. In the Christian tradition, confession is not a brazen publication of personal deficiency but a communal statement of shared values and commitments. Confession enables individuals to acknowledge those traditions that make the moral life possible. Likewise, religion teachers should enable their students to connect their personal histories to the larger contexts of traditions, rituals, and beliefs that make religion worth studying in the first place.

Chapter five tackles the difficult question of how universities have changed with the onslaught of postmodern philosophy. If moral and epistemological relativism rule the day, then what does the university stand for? What is the goal of education when students want practical skills and there is little agreement about widely shared cultural ideals? I make the case that in the postmodern university the study of religion is needed more than ever before. Moreover, precisely because notions of rationality are changing, there is an opportunity for religion to return to the classroom in more direct and assertive ways.

Many recent books on education have lamented the decline of religion's influence over the schools. The history of religion and education in North America really comprises two stories, the attempt by scholars influenced by the Enlightenment to study religion without the benefit of religious conviction and the struggle by religious believers to shape education according to the virtues and values of faith. Ecumenical Protestants were able to represent both groups by identifying the virtues of mainline Protestant churches with the civic faith of the nation. Liberal Protestants were tolerant, inclusive, and learned. They were able to set the terms for the study of religion and succeeded in promoting religion from the campus ministries to the classroom. However, when America became increasingly diverse and mainline Protestantism no longer could make the case that it embodied the faith of the nation, the study of religion became fragmented. The ensuing crisis means that there is no longer a consensus about how to teach religion in public education. Chapter six is a case study in the changing fortunes of religion in higher education. It examines the role of religion at Wabash College, where religion has evolved in order to adapt to changing circumstances but remains very much alive as an intellectual and personal force for student learning.

Chapter seven consists of a dialogue with a theologian, William C. Placher, who combines a traditionalist's concerns about the heritage of Christianity with a passion for reading the Bible in progressive and creative ways. Bill is my mentor and friend, and our conversations have shaped much of my thought. More important, he disagrees with me on some fundamental features of my idea that religion must be taught religiously. Those disagreements are too important to be excluded from this book. Rather than summarize Bill's position, I let him speak for himself.

The last chapter surveys the development of religious studies departments in North America, addresses the renewed popularity of reductionistic and materialistic studies of religion, suggests how theology is different from and yet essential for religious studies, and argues that theology in the classroom is a necessary component of every attempt to learn something about religion. Religion is such a contentious issue, and the study of religion is such a personal enterprise, that I argue that all religion teachers are theologians to a significant extent. Everyone who enters the religion classroom comes with deep beliefs, and these beliefs inevitably shape how religion is taught and learned. Rather than avoiding the potential conflicts that arise in the study of religion, the religion classroom should teach these conflicts as the very stuff of public debate and religious concern.

The study of religion is, in part, an attempt to figure out how far reason can go in illuminating the mysteries of faith. Asking students to study religion is an invitation based on the trust that teachers can model ways for reason and faith to come together. After all, religious belief should be brought into the public realm of education only with its integrity intact. Thus, theology must be a primary component in the preparation of religion teachers and in the curriculum of religion classes.

Although I teach in a private, independent, liberal arts college, I think my experiences and insights are especially relevant for those who teach and learn in public schools, whether at the collegiate or secondary level. My college is intensely secular, so I have had to figure out ways to teach religion in a diverse environment that is sometimes indifferent or even hostile to considerations of faith. Fortunately, my college also has given me the freedom to explore and expand the boundaries that usually separate faith from the classroom. I have been able to experiment with integrating faith and reason in my teaching, and I think what I have learned is applicable to all who study and teach religion, even in contexts significantly different from my own. Indeed, I see little difference between teaching religion in public or parochial schools, college or high school. The same issues are raised, and the same challenges need to be met. Moreover, I believe the real battle over religion and education is being waged in public high schools. If religion is to become an ingredient in every student's educational development, public schools will have to be pushed to be more sensitive to theological concerns. Educators will need to be convinced that religion can be taught in ways that are sensitive to and supportive of the life of faith. Thus, I have directed many observations and arguments toward public high school teachers, as well as those in postsecondary education.

Finally, though my perspective is from Christian theology, my arguments also would support the inclusion, in appropriate ways, of other religious perspectives in public education. Indeed, I do not think any religious tradition can be taught well without a highly trained sensitivity to the internal logic of its claims to truth.

ONE

CONFESSIONS OF A THEOLOGIAN

HOW I LEARNED WHY I TEACH

I began thinking seriously about theology and pedagogical issues when a student came up to me in a church history class and asked, "This is great, but why haven't I learned any of it in church?" The question pleased me to no end. My own turn to the study of religion had enabled me to make sense of my evangelical upbringing and provided me with important continuities during a period when I was trying to break free from my past. Modern theological scholarship was as serious and sober as the devotional material of my church, but it was more challenging and complex, and thus it seemed more real. I had come to see myself as exploring the kinds of issues and saying the kinds of things that would have kept me in the church of my youth, if only my ministers and Sunday school teachers had been more probing and better read. My teaching, then, was a re-creation of the religious education I had never had, or a redemption of the one I did have. It was also, of course, a way for me to take the place of those figures of my youth who held me with such power that I did not want to let them go. My idealized student would be somebody who understood the sacred space of my classroom, somebody who came to church when coming to my class. My pedagogical fantasy was that I could recapitulate my past while saving it from intellectual confusion and that, consequently, my students could become, well . . . *me*.

I am no longer so confident about projecting my life narrative onto my students, but I remain convinced that all teachers of religion must think back to their earliest experiences with religion to understand why and how they teach. I was drawn to study and teach religion because I was surrounded by religious authority from my earliest years. When I was young, I did not distinguish between preaching and teaching or faith and scholarship, and I still cannot afford such neat categories and compartments. Thinking about religion was never a luxury for me; instead it was a way of surviving the intensity of my conservative religious upbringing. Even during my darkest years, when I tried to gain some distance from the faith of my parents, I knew I was still thinking their thoughts, sending their ideas in directions that would never completely escape their orbit. All thinking about religion is born in some relationship to religious faith, so the study of religion is never entirely free from the worship that makes it possible.

More than just shaping my world, the church *was* my world when I was growing up. This was due not only to the time we spent there—twice on Sundays, Wednesday evenings, Saturday activities, and vacation Bible school in the summer—but also to the dinner table conversation, which circled around church gossip and earnest talk about building funds and attendance figures. Englewood Christian Church (an independent church in the Stone-Campbell tradition) was located on Rural Street, which at one time was appropriately named, but Indianapolis had long ago rolled over this tract and moved on. Many of the people who ran the church had lived in that neighborhood during better times, and now they had a reverse commute, driving for half an hour back into the city to worship. Englewood was full of the poor and the disadvantaged, the very people who kept appearing in the Gospel stories themselves. It did not take me long to realize that most of my friends at church were very different from my friends at school in the suburbs. I did not fully understand just how strange a place it was until I visited a friend's church near my home, with its modern building, green lawn, and smartly dressed members. Englewood's building was old and functional, surrounded by small houses with no yards. Its huge parking lot was its most potent symbol of growth and prosperity.

Englewood was never fundamentalist in today's sense of that term. The idea that the world needed Christianizing would have meant that the world needed recognizing, that there really were two worlds after all. Instead, there was talk about building up the body, contributing to the building fund, and buying more buses. To grow meant to absorb some of the surrounding world into our own, without surveying the boundaries that separated us. The buses would circle the poor neighborhoods encompassing the church, picking up children by offering prizes and thus boosting Sunday school numbers. Every Christmas these kids would be rewarded with apples and oranges. I never took any home, although I did help my father pass them out, feeling a bit ashamed to be giving away what I myself would not accept as a gift.

My best friend at church, Andy, was the p.k., the preacher's kid, and my dad was the chairman of the elders, and I guess we thought we owned the place. Englewood was the architecture of our spirituality, the shape, touch, and feel of what we were supposed to become. We were heirs of authority, brothers battling for the birthright. We realized from the beginning that we had to conform ourselves to this place by becoming characters in its drama if we were to make it our own. We learned how to mythologize the church with our games, fears, and laughter. There were no boundaries, only our versions of a sacred grove or a magic stone: the yellow stairs, the boiler room, the dark hallway, rooms we were not supposed to enter and places we created on our own. Climbing to the top of the fire escape, we could imagine Moses on Mount Sinai or Jesus being led by the devil to the pinnacle of the temple, and the devil saying to him,

"If you are the Son of God, throw yourself down!" We knew that the religious life was not possible without the power of temptation. Andy and I thought we could outrun Englewood by racing through its halls or leave it behind by climbing onto its roofs. The irony is that by trying so hard to master it we ended up becoming such a part of it that we could never let it go.

On a wall in my house hangs a picture of our congregation taken in that huge parking lot with a panoramic camera that captured the entire half-circle of the more than one thousand people in attendance that day. When I show friends this photograph, I cover up the date, because the thin black ties and wide lapels on the men and the stacked and layered hair on the women seem to come from the fifties rather than from 1970. I was not the only one who seemed oblivious to the Vietnam war, the counter culture, student protests, and cultural revolutions. At age nine I was clutching a Bible, one knee on the pavement, full of innocent sincerity. One year Andy's dad ran behind the crowd after the camera began panning so he could be on both ends of the picture—the alpha and omega of the church.

That world was insular but complete. Soon enough, however, it began to crumble. My religious confusions and doubts began with my public schooling. School was a world even more intense and comprehensive than church because I spent more time there. It was also a world that ran mostly on tracks parallel to my church life but rarely crossing it. Although some conflict between the two existed, I would have welcomed even more, instead of the apparently unbridgeable gulf that separated them. Ordinarily, my school life just disdained, rather than bothering to deny, my church life, which is always more devastating. And if school was where I began to feel the tattered and fraying edges of my religious upbringing, school was also where I would eventually try to find some resolution for my increasingly split personality, rendered double by the different languages of religious and secular education.

We are taught from the beginning of our schooling that religion is not a part of education. The message to Christian children is that we should keep religion to ourselves, because it cannot be discussed properly in the classroom. Schools teach everything from sex education to how to be polite, but the mystery of faith is evidently beyond their reach. Among the educated in our culture, religion is not something you talk about in personal ways, so much so that it seems one of the main purposes of education is to produce a class of people who will not let their religious passions overrule their sense of citizenship.

The politics of the civic repression of religion are reproduced in the classroom at the cost of disconnecting many students from the very source of their motivation to learn. The existence of religious studies programs in colleges and universities hardly solves the problem. Students who take religious studies classes are trained to recognize trends, patterns, and themes, rehearsing the various skills they need to manage the sheer complexity of religious phenomena. They practice talking about religion with great sophistication. They are seldom given the opportunity, however, to speak religiously with confidence and depth. Teachers at all levels of education need models of pedagogy that will allow them to teach religion in ways that honor religious faith. Without such models, religious passion just seems too dangerous to most teachers, so they draw invisible but effective boundaries around what is acceptable when it comes to religious speech in the classroom. As a result, religious voices frequently are excluded from education altogether.

Many stories substantiate these claims. Recently, the media covered the case of a first grader who wanted to bring a children's Bible story to class for reading day. Like me, the student associated learning to read with Bible stories, but the teacher, worried about separation of church and state, forced him to take the book home.

My realization that I would have to compartmentalize my faith and my studies came at the beginning of my teenage years. I remember nearly every face at my seventh grade lunchroom table. We ate together every day of the year, and we argued about religion with every bite we ate. One student was a Jehovah's Witness, and he was well versed in the Bible, challenging me to back up my criticisms of his interpretation of the end times. I am certain that we exuded more intellectual energy over that lunch table than I experienced in any of my

27

classes throughout all of junior high school. I suppose we were exercising such intellectual daring because we were talking about something that all of us actually cared about deeply and completely.

Those debates came to an end one day when a teacher who was patrolling the cafeteria came up behind us and heard only part of the conversation—my side of the argument about heaven and hell and the fate of humanity. He reprimanded me harshly in front of my friends. He was clearly angered by what he had heard, and he told me in a shaking voice that I had no right to be telling others they were wrong about religion and that I should not even be talking about religion at school. At the dinner table that evening I related the incident to my parents, sharing my embarrassment over having been publicly scolded, feeling humiliated and confused. My parents shared my anguish, but I could sense their frustration at their impotence. What could they do? The schools were controlled by the authorities, they were a secular space, and what we believed was not welcome there. My parents did not consider sending me to a private school, but the incident makes me think it is no wonder that religious conservatives are leaving public schools in droves and fighting back through the courts.

My problems were hardly unique. Many scholars now see secularization as a product of liberal Protestantism and thus as one moment within the history of Christianity, rather than as the inevitable and necessary outcome of Western history. However, I grew up in a period when educators adopted a European indifference toward religion as the norm, not the exception it is proving to be. Secularization was simply assumed as the basic framework of education. Schools were religion-free zones. Consequently, I carried my faith as a burden that was too heavy to take to school. It was easier to leave it at home, so I began developing two lives with little connection between them.

Surely we have so much rhetorical conflict in our society over religion precisely because nobody learns how to talk about it in school. This leads to some strange results. Most important, the exclusion of religion from the public square forces Christians to engage in distorted social practices to get out their message. Every time we went shopping one summer, I put tracts behind windshield wiper blades in an eager but misguided attempt to connect with the world around me. Now evangelicals are much more confident about arguing the merits of faith for a wide range of social and political issues, but in the sixties and seventies, evangelicals had no political experience and no hope of reforming American public policy. Our focus was on personal conversion, the authority of the Bible, and the cross of Christ, issues that were not easily assimilated into public discussion. The cultural elite talked about the grave social issues of the day; we were left with that region known as the things of the heart, the personal piety that was fueled by our warm and glowing church services. We witnessed to people because our own little world was the only world we knew, so we could not imagine other people finding their worlds to be better and happier places. And we could not imagine how others perceived us because we had no experience in public discussions of religious identity, tradition, and history.

The exclusion of religion from education also meant that I identified my religious belief as the emotional aspect of my character, a desire for salvation that was separate from and even at odds with my intellectual development in the classroom. Religion could thus set the emotional tone of my life, providing a dramatic background for the mundane duties that filled the time in between church meetings. Unfortunately, this drama often turned out to be melodrama, because only unhealthy consequences can flow when religion is reduced to one aspect of personal development. I wavered between an emotionalism that sent me off in extreme directions and often ended in depression and self-hate and an intellectualism that alienated me from my family and classmates.

The fact that my religious friends and I had to bottle up our religious passions also meant that we often released them in irreverent and reckless ways. I am always surprised at the incredulity of secular people when they find that people of faith—especially when they are young—can have an impious side. I was never shocked when, eating dinner with Andy, his

29

father would mimic and parody members of the congregation until we roared with laughter. My most religious friends were also the ones who dared to be the most transgressive, perhaps because we thought life was shaped by competing powers of good and evil, and we felt secure enough in our faith to make furtive excursions across the boundary between them. Moreover, we lived in such a religiously intense world for most of the time that, when we felt compelled to test that world, we could gain distance from it only by doing precisely those things that were most forbidden to us. Thus, I lived in a tumultuous zone of conflicting tendencies where the coexistence of good and bad deeds made perfect sense to me, even if it left most people utterly confused.

My confusion was exacerbated by social trends that drove a wedge into the infrastructure of the family. The sixties and seventies witnessed the rapid acceleration of a burgeoning economic class, teenagers, who were supposed to spend their money on commodities that would win their complete separation from the world of parents. My older brother was just old enough to be persuaded by the idea that a new world was coming, so while I was struggling with traditional religious belief, he vanished into the new "religion" of leftist rhetoric and drug music. He was certain that only a revolution could save the world, and thus he sought peace outside of all institutions and authorities, a view I was to run into in the academy over and over again. I was just young enough to find his disappearing act both enticing and troubling. Like most teenagers coming of age in the seventies—that confusing decade between Woodstock and Reagan, which mainstreamed the culture of the sixties, producing both innocent and outlandish fashions and behavior—I never quite knew in what direction I was heading. The result of these cultural forces was that people of my generation had a hard time taking the religion of their parents seriously, and our teachers, many of whom were shaped by the more reticent conventions of the fifties, when it was not polite to talk about religion in public, could not offer us much help.

I could not quite put the idiosyncrasies of my faith and the conforming demands of a public education together until I saw that it was possible to turn one's private passions into a subject of intellectual endeavor. I was always afraid that thinking too hard about religion would make it disappear, spun into thoughts that would carry no weight, but I seemed fated to think about nothing else. This constant tension between faith and reason swirled within my soul and led to many lapses and revivals, apostasies and conversions that recycled like a bad made-for-TV-movie, leaving me exhausted but bracing for the next collision. These battles were private rituals (what Freud would call neuroses), which enabled me to find some meaning in the increasing polarization of my two selves.

As I grew older, I noticed that many of my religious friends were becoming more conservative in their outlook and behavior, so that I had to make friends with non-Christians to share those times when I was trying to disentangle myself from the church. Some of my friends only knew one side or the other of this struggle, and I tried to keep these groups separate, spending time now with my wilder friends and then with my religious friends. I worked hard to keep them—and thus the two sides of my soul—from meeting each other. But there were always leaks, and one history teacher in high school was so surprised to hear about my wild side that he passed on to me what he had heard with the assurances that he did not believe a thing. He just wanted to let me know how ungrounded rumors could be.

I took advantage of the debate team—which had its own room that served as a place to go when I skipped classes and took weekend trips where privilege could be abused—to flaunt my freedom from religious authority. It was easy to succeed in debate by scoring points with scattershot zeal because that is how evangelicals learned to argue—aggressively presenting the evidence that demands a verdict. In debate, however, I was rewarded for arguing any and every position regardless of merit, so the tools of rationality seemed increasingly empty and formal. Debate became a futile game, a hollow exercise devoid of any purpose other than to use the combative drive to win points against the competition. The more debates I won, the looser my morals became. One morning I got a little bit drunk with a friend in the parking lot before classes began. Fortunately, my first period Latin teacher told my debate coach, who spirited me away to the debate room to sober me up before I could attend any more classes. The "ungrounded rumors" my history teacher had warned me about must have passed into greater circulation, because I did not make it into the National Honor Society due to my low character, even though I gave the commencement address at my high school graduation—evidence of my two worlds living simultaneously but out of sync.

During my senior year of high school I discovered the work of the evangelical writer Francis Schaeffer. His christological reading of the history of philosophy would hardly pass muster in any accredited college today, but his courage in engaging and criticizing the great philosophers opened my eyes not only to the world of philosophy but also to how theological arguments might work. Schaeffer was a new kind of evangelical who stood up for his beliefs by engaging modern culture on its own terms. Even though his scholarship could be sloppy and his criticisms of other philosophers were often *ad hominem* (he argued, with exaggeration but not without some truth, that Nietzsche's mental breakdown at the end of his life was a result of his iconoclastic philosophy), he was important to many of us at the time who were trying to break out of the isolationism of pre-Reagan evangelicalism. Later, during my freshman year in college, I said one word about him to my religion professor and quickly learned that Schaeffer was not a person to be taken seriously in higher education, so I promptly forgot all about him. But reading his work during my senior year in high school, along with the much more academically respectable work of C. S. Lewis, Dietrich Bonhoeffer, and Paul Tillich, made me hope that someday I could learn to fuse my trajectories of faith and reason.

I also discovered some friends who shared my plight. Tom and I began talking about religion when I saw that he had brought a Bible to our chemistry class. Later we met Steve in the mall, and we knew he was a Christian by the big "Jesus" buckle that kept his belt in place. When we nervously approached him, we felt like Christians in the days of the Roman Empire, exchanging secret symbols to discern a friend or foe. None of us knew how to say who he was at just that time in adolescence when being able to identify yourself seems to be the only power you have. Because we were so anxious about our faith, we went overboard in proving our certitude to the world. We did not know how to be a group of friends in any other shape than the church, so we founded a weekly Bible study with twenty or so regular participants. I often led the study part of the meetings, but just the act of getting people together to share our plight had a significant impact, because it satisfied a basic need for belonging at a time when you did not exist if you were not in an identifiable group. We also started a modest Christian newspaper, called *The Dove,* that my mother would duplicate at work. With a mixture of excitement and embarrassment, we distributed it in the high school before classes started. Communists in the fifties could not have been more secretive or impassioned. The principal of our high school was a Christian, so we got away with it.[1] Although I belonged to many school groups and wrote for the school paper, I felt forced to create these educational outlets because I had no saner alternatives. The only other option was to keep my faith quiet and sequestered in the church, which I knew I could not do.

Looking back at these experiences, I am struck by how important it was for me to talk to people about religion. I was always attempting to become a teacher of religion, trying out various contexts for spreading the gospel and engaging the issues. None of them fit until I went to college and sat at the feet of professors who were as firm in their faith as they were respected for their scholarship. When I interviewed at Wabash College for a prestigious scholarship, the committee members ran through my resume, talked about my major activities, and then asked if they had left out anything. In the flash of that moment, I thought about the Bible study and *The Dove,* which had been much more important to me than all of my other awards and accomplishments, and I realized that my religious faith constituted another world that could not be mentioned in such proximity to the new world of higher education I was about to enter. So I said nothing, and I left that old world of religious passion and enthusiasm behind when I graduated from high school in 1979.

33

As a student at Wabash in the early 1980s I knew that the college was a very secular place, but the religion department gave me a home where I could work out my faith with dignity and respect. I suppose if I had gone to a large, secular university, I could have separated completely my religious and intellectual development, but such an operation would have left me spiritually depleted and moribund. On the other hand, I was not sufficiently secure in my identity to attend a Christian college, where I was afraid my questioning nature might be prematurely stifled, so that I might have continued in my spiral of rebellion and revival. (I had let it be known at church that I did not want to register for the draft, which the government required of all eighteen year olds just as I had reached that age, and the elders took me aside and insisted that I must not break the law. That experience led me to be suspicious of the alliance of church and state and made me think that I needed some distance from the church in order to find my own political reading of the Bible.) At Wabash the atmosphere was very secular, but the religion department was very supportive of my faith. Once a week I attended a communion service led by department members, and worshiping with my teachers meant the world to me, as my world was otherwise being colonized by all sorts of new ideals and ideologies.

Spending so much of my time in the religion department allowed me to acquire a theological perspective on my educational experiences, but the fraternity life I returned to after classes reminded me that I was not at a church-related college. Most Wabash students live in fraternities, but they are not primarily party houses. My fraternity was just as proud of its grade point average as its weekend activities, which helped me to see that my wild side did not have to be opposed to classroom achievement. Nevertheless, fraternal life promised a well-structured community that was profoundly secular, so my sense of belonging to it was filled with not a small amount of anxiety and confusion. Once I figured out that the fraternity was like a church in miniature, with its muted politics, good-natured gossip, and ritualized bonding, I was able to manage my ambivalence about the place by applying the social skills I had learned at Englewood. As a result, I won election as house president during my sophomore year. But I never felt truly at home there, because I knew that, for all the forced consensus about pride in our particular traditions, the fraternity was a pretty poor imitation of a truly religious society. Besides, I was more interested in arguing with fraternity brothers about religion and philosophy than in planning house budgets and enforcing the rules.

The freedom of college life exacerbated my mood swings between piety and partying, but the discipline of my studies also began the healing process of finding some middle ground from which to grow. That middle ground, however, had little room for my evangelical upbringing. In the summer after my freshman year, Steve (who had by then discarded his "Jesus" belt buckle) and I served as interns for Englewood, living right next to the church and running the youth programs. We became friends with the urban poor who attended Englewood, and we experienced firsthand the powerful role a church can play in disadvantaged neighborhoods. We hung out with people like Darryl, who was always looking for bags of money hidden in trash cans, confident that one day he would strike it rich. I preached my first sermon that summer, but most of our focus was on organizing activities for the neighborhood kids. Many of our attempts to reach out to them were awkward. At one point I gave my high school trumpet to some poor kids, perhaps as a feeble attempt to compensate for the Christmas gifts of apples and oranges that I had handed out with my dad years before. It was a quixotic gesture that even then I knew was more about my fumbling need for self-divestiture than any real plan to help the poor. It didn't do them any good (I didn't, after all, offer to teach them how to play it), and it made me regret my impulsive behavior. By the end of the summer, Steve and I both had decided that there was just too much distance between us and them. We did not know how to share their lives when we were so busy trying to figure out our own. It was a good summer, but it was a conclusion rather than a start to my dream of becoming a minister, and it was my good-bye to Englewood.

I probably could not have abandoned Englewood so decisively without the quasi-religious atmosphere at Wabash. All colleges, especially private liberal arts colleges with religious roots, can be a lot like churches. This is due not only to the historical connection between the churches and higher education but also to the way educational institutions shape space and time. To separate students from the world as well as to make holy their own mission, colleges create a sacred order. Colleges are intense places because faculty treat them like churches, where learning is a matter of ultimate concern, a righteous and transcendent cause. Wabash College, an independent school with historical ties to the Presbyterian Church, is no exception to this rule. Indeed, Wabash, as one of the last all-male colleges, has an especially significant number of rituals and traditions that keep the student body busy and brotherly—rituals that, for me, echoed the tight religious bonding of my earliest years. In many ways, Wabash looks and feels like a religious school, which gives it what charm it possesses.

On my best days I could be fooled by such charm into thinking I had found a new temple, a place to worship free of any feelings of guilt or conflict, a place to bring my best gifts. The traditions and rituals of Wabash let me rationalize that I was hardly changing paths as I let go of my religious past for something more intellectually stimulating. Every day on the way to class I walked by the chapel, the tallest point on campus and the first thing you see when you enter the college. It is a good symbol for the role of religion at Wabash because, although we began and ended our college careers there in hallowed convocations, we did not spend much time there in between. Gone are the days of daily chapel services, so, except for special events, it is usually an empty space. Only the basement is busy with printing activities, a useful reminder that the Protestant Reformation was made possible by the printing press. The underutilized chapel is part of our tradition, giving our historical narrative a distinctive flavor, but its emptiness reminds us that it is not something that should be taken too seriously. Wabash is not, after all, a church college.

The chapel is at the end of a long mall, a public space that is at the center of the campus. The openness of the mall is an appropriate counterpart to the chapel, a symbol of the college's commitment to rational inquiry and independence from church and state. The mall is surrounded by red brick Georgian buildings that hark back to the New England architecture that conjures tradition and learning to midwesterners. In one corner of the mall are three small houses, the oldest buildings on the campus, homes of the earliest Wabash faculty. They were moved to this spot to constitute a kind of colonial town in miniature. Beyond the mall is the arboretum, a reminder of the primordial forest out of which Indiana was carved. This edenic bit of nature is a nice counterpoint to the stress of studying, and it recalls, for me, the idealistic mission of the college's founders to bring both religion and learning to the frontier.

Wabash uses not only space but also time to initiate students into the world of higher education. One of the appeals of Wabash is the use of rituals to structure the educational process, giving rhythm to the school year. My immersion into Englewood was marked by many ritualized activities, but my departure from it, and my struggles to find my own religious voice, took place in a cultural vacuum, where I had to create my own community and traditions. At Wabash, especially in my fraternity, with its own religious roots, I found a substitute for my high school Bible study. Wabash was every bit as set apart from the world as was Englewood, and equally demanding. The students were proud of its anachronism as one of the last all-male colleges, and as such, the school needed to be rich in tradition, a cloister of monastic gravity, to justify the sacrifices male students make to give up a coed environment. Most men's schools went coed in the late '60s and early '70s due to well-founded political pressure, but they also could not sustain the traditions necessary to make all-male education work.

There were many rites of passage my freshman year, but the one that stands out the most is Chapel Sing. Fraternity freshmen shout the school song, which tradition claims to be the longest in the nation, on the Chapel steps. The pledge class that shouts the loudest without missing any words wins. It is a sublime spectacle of a sea of sound. For me, it came right at that autumnal moment when we had been in classes long enough that they were becoming routine, and I was beginning to despair that the semester would never end. The seasons were falling toward winter, the days were getting shorter, and yet summer was still in the air. Shouting at the top of our lungs was one way of calling nature's bluff. Facing my first Indiana winter away from home, I needed to proclaim that I still had a lot of life left in me. It didn't matter what I was singing, only that my voice was mingling with dozens of others' as they echoed down the college mall.

Chapel Sing was a true rite of passage. It did not mean pledgeship was over, but it did mean we had passed a test that put our unity on trial. After all, Chapel Sing was not a one-day event. We had to stand on the patio practicing the school song nearly every day. Singing together is a great way of establishing community, especially when the active brothers taunt you and the song you are learning is so long. My fondest memories of church were of the evangelical hymns we sang. I knew the words to many of them before I knew how to read. I remember believing I was finally grown up when I realized that you follow the written lines along with the music rather than reading them straight down the page. These were songs you could march to, with their strident beat and proud rhetoric. Some of their tunes had been borrowed from the riotous songs of tavern life, so I should not have been surprised that the drinking songs in the fraternity sounded oddly similar. If much of my college education seemed to come from another world, more sophisticated and genteel, at least these fraternity experiences made me feel right at home.

Rituals such as this made my journey through Wabash seem less disruptive to the many transformations of my faith. On good days I felt that, even as I was losing, changing, and regaining my faith, I was on a path that essentially was spiritual, that Wabash was taking me to places that would not replace but instead ultimately strengthen the very ties that college ordinarily stretches to the breaking point. On other days, the intensely masculine atmosphere of the college made me suspect that my religious nervousness and constant spiritual malaise were seen by my fellow students as forms of feminine hysteria that were as out of place to them as women in the classroom.

I expected more of this tension between the drama and the content of religious education in graduate school but quickly discovered that the higher you went in education the less religious you were expected to be. The Divinity School at the University of Chicago is located in Swift Hall, as close to the physical center of that campus as you can be, and the faculty members there worked hard to correlate the location with their sense of the centrality of religious studies, confident in their attempts to show the relevance of the study of religion to nearly every topic and discipline. The Divinity School defined its students strictly by the quality of their minds, not by the state of their souls. This narrow focus on intellectual development meant that I could afford to put my religious doubts and conflicts on hold. As long as I could perform academically, I was accepted as an apprentice to the study of religion. It did not matter that I was losing my way religiously, having traveled so far from my religious roots that I was in danger of not being able to see where I had been and thus where I needed to go.

At a meeting of religion professors a few years ago, a friend from those Chicago years presented a paper about gender and graduate school education. It let loose a flood of memories. To substantiate her own narrative about how hard it was to find her voice in the rigorous climate of graduate school, she had interviewed several female students who had attended the Divinity School, and their experiences were not pleasant. The ensuing discussion was like a group therapy session in which everyone was eager to tell a horror story. Some of the participants said they had never told these stories before, indeed, that they had tried to forget all about them. We decided that gender was not such a crucial factor, because all of us experienced the Ph.D. pursuit as an exercise, to a great extent, in mortification and humiliation. There was little grace in the graduate study of religion, and much castigation, penance, and asceticism. It is no wonder, then, that professors often are hesitant to be vulnerable in the classroom. Teachers, like parents, reproduce their training in ways of which they are hardly aware. We teach as we have been taught, for better or worse.

What saved me were two theologians who, while representing the highest intellectual achievement, nevertheless expressed their faith in the very act of teaching. Langdon Gilkey was the theological voice of my graduate education. He wrote as he spoke, and hearing him made it much easier to read his work, which is true of few academicians today. He was his voice: a deep baritone, rich and melodious, as authoritative as his dress was bohemian. He looked like a prophet, with wild, unruly hair and a bandanna around his neck. For his students, this thundering was what thinking about God sounded like. He did not lecture; instead he preached. And in his last years at the University of Chicago his voice often would crack under the pressure of emotion, as if he were giving us the very sounds of a theologian trying, with his last gasps, to offer us God. The result was that his teaching always had a sacramental quality. If theology has a sound, just as a place can be conjured in one's memory by the hint of a certain aroma, then to this day it sounds to me like Langdon Gilkey's beseeching voice.

While Gilkey was the voice, David Tracy was the embodiment of theology, and he opened himself to me just as he did to every struggling, young theologian. As a Roman Catholic priest, he was heir to all the riches of the Christian tradition, and he evinced no anxiety in sifting through that tradition to construct a modern vision for the church. Although he occupied all the space in a classroom, and his mind reeled off ideas with an intimidating fecundity, he always managed, by opening intellectual doors a student never knew existed, to provide room in his thoughts for the student. His interests were so catholic that he was a walking medieval cathedral, with a wide and inviting atrium leading to so many subsidiary altars and private chapels that one could never run out of room for exploration. His capacity for generous affirmation is truly astonishing. The older I get, the more I appreciate this gift for its rareness in intellectual life. He has an exceptional ability to rise above rancorous debates about religion, perhaps because his talent is such that he surveys the religious scene from the vantage point of an

40

upper room that he gladly opens to all. When he asked me to be his research assistant, I experienced a windfall of grace and felt like my initiation into the world of scholarship had begun.

Pluralism was the key word during my graduate years, which occurred before deconstruction became so popular with its emphasis on differences that cannot and should not be reconciled. Tracy looked for the analogies that made conversations among the religions possible, while Gilkey was sensitive to the sharp edges of ideas that kept them apart. But even Gilkey, through his command of dialectical formulations, sought to find patterns in the midst of competing traditions of thought. Consequently, we approached pluralism as an intellectual problem that could be solved heroically, rather than as a condition of humanity that must be tolerated tragically and endured. We were in search of a unified theory of religion that would explain religious diversity by connecting all religions to one experience of faith. We thought theologians were the heroes of the new age of pluralism, pushing religious boundaries in new directions, rather than mere clerks of the traditions, preserving the past by making modest comments on the margins of sacred texts. With the passion of Gilkey and the optimism of Tracy, I returned to Wabash to teach religion in 1987 as a convinced liberal pluralist, ready to convert my conservative students to the good news about the transcendental unity of all religious experience. Pluralism had become my religion, a convenient substitute for my evangelical faith, allowing me to defend the value of all religions while neglecting my own religious roots.

Like all faiths built on purely intellectual commitments, my pluralism was destined for disillusionment. That process began in subtle ways when Bill Placher, my college teacher, became my mentor and guide. Bill was trained in a more conservative theological tradition at Yale University. He was a leading member of a movement known as postliberalism, which was trying to find the inner, logical flaws in liberal theology in order to retrieve more traditional accounts of faith. Nevertheless, he never tried to change my theological views. Instead, he taught by example, showing me how to maintain one's theological integrity in the secular academy. Bill gave me the hands to do

41

the work of theology, the tools I needed to complement the voice and the body I had received at the University of Chicago. Bill's calm demeanor and avoidance of conflict was a necessary counterbalance to my impulsive behavior and passionate need for argument and conflict. He always has time to read what I am writing and to listen to my complaints, and his wise counsel is born out of an ability to attend with a quiet intensity to what the other person is saying.

At the end of my first year of teaching at Wabash, the giants of the religion department (for that is what they were to me then and how I still see them) put on a lunch for me that I will never forget. David Greene, Eric Dean, Hall Peebles, and Raymond Williams (Bill was on sabbatical) wined and dined me as if I had given them more than they had given me. It was a bounty of a meal, and I felt overwhelmed and undeserving. I felt disoriented that such graciousness was coming to me—that the department that had shaped me as a student of religion was now honoring me as a teacher, as one of its own. Such tokens of support put me in their debt to such a degree that I believed I would never be able to pay them back.

Such a gracious act, however, was not enough to make me feel completely at home. After returning to Wabash, I had been impressed with the religious commitment of many of our students, but I also had begun to find out just how secular Wabash really is. Getting to know faculty outside the religion department, I had begun to learn how to dissimulate my faith in order not to come across as "too religious." There was the art professor who, when I told him I was on my way to the chapel to preach, asked why we needed a chapel at all, let alone a sermon during the week. Then there was the colleague from the English department who, when I told him that a class that day had had a particularly exciting discussion about God, mumbled something about Sunday school and turned away in disgust. Once, while the religion faculty were away at a conference, a philosophy professor, who thought that we were too Christian, made a motion at a faculty meeting to abolish the department. In the aftermath of this fiasco, a political science professor told me that the only purpose to studying religion was to show students how irrational it is, and that anything short of this was not intellectual.

That such comments were a shock to me was evidence of how naive I was about the role of religion in higher education and how sheltered I had been from the worst forms of secular prejudice. Once, when I was at a workshop on teaching, the leader asked us to draw a picture representing how we felt about the institution in which we taught. I drew a lonely stick figure on a deserted island with one tree and a stack of books, surrounded by a flock of birds. The tree was meant to symbolize my department (and also, given the obvious symbolism, my faith), the books my vocation, and the birds my students. Wabash was doing me the favor of forcing me to reconsider whether religious pluralism was the good news that public education so desperately needed. I was learning that not everyone thought religion was the exciting, central topic I had been trained to assume, and that no matter how pluralistic and liberal I may be, I was branded as a teacher of religion who took his subject matter too personally and was thus someone to be held in suspicion. These experiences made me resolve all the more to try to reconnect the two halves of my life, the intellectual and the religious.

Some of my alienation from my colleagues stemmed from my different understanding of the teaching vocation. Most teachers enter their profession because they like to talk a lot. They master early on the expectations of the classroom, and move from reward to reward through the educational system and never leave it. My educational experiences were quite different. Education was such a personal and painful quest for me that I never liked to talk in classes. Looking back, I'm not sure why I was so successful academically, because I don't see myself as having been the kind of student I so much enjoy encouraging today. I was too critical and too scrupulous in my introverted consciousness to contribute easily and readily to the classroom. I wrote good papers instead, and kept the classroom conversation going back in the fraternity where I lived. When I could engage friends about the truth of Christianity or the power of religious faith, I couldn't shut up, but somehow my full self never emerged comfortably in the classroom.

Even today I am not a good discussion participant when talking with my secular colleagues. This is not just the case of a typical introvert who thinks too hard about what he is saying before he says it and analyzes the flow of the conversation rather than looking for a place to join in. As a student, I brought a lot of anger to education. I would get frustrated in conversations about religion and jump in at the wrong time or with the wrong tone. I deflected the disapproval I felt from others, which resulted in a mixture of self-righteousness and self-doubt. In a way, I represented the typical evangelical attitude toward the life of the mind, which oscillates between intellectual arrogance and alienation. The root of these problems was that I had not been able to bring my deepest self into alignment with my classroom self. I know that one can never do that completely or truly. And I know that postmodern philosophers tell us that there is no deep self, only the play of the various masks we wear for our different roles. But my panic at not being able to talk in class, not being able to find the right words, was evidence that I did not know how to go from one role to another. Even when you play a role, you have to bring yourself to the part, or the acting is flat and false. Today, as a teacher who is open and honest about my faith, I can be myself with students as we grow closer during the semester, even as I assume various poses to challenge and nurture them. But as a student, I was afraid that bringing too much of myself into the classroom would rip off my mask and reveal more of myself than was appropriate for that role.

This self-portrait probably makes me sound a lot more pious than I was, or implies that I am seeking excuses through elaborate theories to rationalize my weakness and incompetencies. I was not always pious in the stereotypical sense, but I was adept at arguing and thinking, and it was precisely the lack of connection between my piety and my rationality that kept me silent. Teachers think a lot about why some classes go well and others do not, and the diagnosis often comes down to finding out why some students find it difficult to talk in class. All teachers have had the experience when, in the midst of a slow discussion, the students suddenly stumble onto a practical or contemporary topic that excites them and find they do not want to stop talking. When you hear students talking about sports, parties, or movies, you know there is a tremendous amount of energy that needs only to be tapped and channeled. If you spend years telling students that talking in class involves certain restrictions about what they can say, that there are rules that eliminate major parts of their lives, then is it any wonder they feel no connection to education and no sense of ownership of the classroom? Likewise, I find it hard to feel fully a part of most discussions with colleagues because, simply, I am not fully there or fully allowed to be there.

If I could not master the art of discussion in the public places of education, I could refine my voice in the written word. I had always wanted to be a writer. While in the fourth grade, I quit the track team to work instead on a "novel" during recess, much to the chagrin of my gym teacher. He was angry when, after he confronted me, I could not explain my choice to him. After that I didn't try very hard to explain my passion for writing to anybody. In high school I spent countless hours writing the history of the school, under the direction of a history teacher (the one who warned me of the rumors about my reputation). Nobody but him seemed to know what I was up to, and the resulting book was read by teachers and older alumni, not my friends— but that was okay by me. I wrote more for myself than anybody else. I reached a point in graduate school where I believed I could not write, because I was trying too hard to be a sophisticated intellectual but felt I had nothing to say. I could not write without passion, even anger, so it was fortunate when I finally found a subject that spoke to my own troubled religiosity.

Karl Barth was a formidable theologian, often stereotyped as a conservative who wanted to revive old-fashioned orthodoxy. This is hardly fair to his mature work, but it is even less descriptive of his early period. I was attracted to the theology of Barth's early period because of his anger. Without an advanced degree, he was an outsider to the academy, and with his evangelical roots, he was an outsider to the modern world. At first he was a preacher rather than a professor, but even behind the pulpit he had a way of alienating people with his

45

insistence on the otherness of God and the depravity of all human attempts to penetrate the divine mystery. Hardly anybody had written on Barth for a doctoral dissertation at the University of Chicago Divinity School since my own Wabash professor, Eric Dean, had compared Barth and Calvin back in the early 1950s. In a way, I wanted to get back at my education by writing about Barth. I could write with such passion about how Barth shook the foundation of liberal theology because I was fantasizing about my own relationship to academic theology. By placing Barth in a postmodern context I could suggest that his attack against modernism actually was even more appropriate in today's intellectual climate, and thus I could make it my own.

Similarly, when I fiercely defend my religiously conservative students at Wabash, I am defending myself, or at least what I once was. I gave up a bit of my faith to conform to the standards of secular education; I am now trying to teach in such a way that my students can keep theirs. Being a theologian is thus a kind of revenge for me. I want to keep others from having done unto them what was done to me. But the situation is not nearly so negative as that. Theology saved me from my public silence, so I guess it is only natural that I think it can save others as well. If I had not seen the way clear to putting my faith and intellect together, I'm not sure how I would have survived the educational system. In high school, it was the debate team that engaged me and provided an outlet for my intellectual energy, an outlet I found nowhere else. Debate assuaged my religious anxiety because it so closely imitated the ways in which I was used to arguing the finer points of Christian doctrine. High school did not sanction such arguments outside of the debate team, but in college I could return to theology, which had all the liveliness of debate and the substance of life's deepest passions.

Theology was a way of survival for me, of self-recovery as well as self-discovery. The discipline of religious studies is for students who have not been immersed in a religious tradition, privileged students who can pick and choose religious themes and discuss them from the "higher" vantage point of the finicky consumer. For students still stuck in the throes of religious devotion, anxiety, and decision, the study of religion must be theological. Both are needed in the religion classroom, because students have both sides to them, but theology is more often neglected. Children are natural theologians, asking questions about topics ultimate and trivial alike, with a simplicity that is lost when they learn to be skeptical and coy about their faith. The media equate faith with fanaticism, and students don't want to stand out, be noticed, or, worst of all, be ridiculed. Through religious studies, students can parlay their interest in religion into socially acceptable channels so it does not overflow the boundaries of middle-class decorum or academic rigor. The study of theology entails the harder and more transformational work of taking students back to those childhood questions that seemed so bewildering and mesmerizing. To ask students to theologize is to draw them back into their experiences so that the gap between theory and practice is closed, and what they learn becomes a part of who they are.

It took me years to say, when asked what I did, that I was a theologian. I would often say I taught religion or, better, philosophy (which is true), because I was afraid of the responses. (Many religion departments appear to be similarly embarrassed when they label contemporary theology courses with the euphemism "Modern Religious Thought.") Inevitably, people would think I was a minister, or that I was a Holy Roller out to convert them. Or the very mention of theology would conjure images of such needless and unfathomable speculation that they would be reduced to silence and even confusion, perhaps in surprise that there were still people in the world who made their living from practicing such an ancient art. In my anxiety to prove that I belonged in the academy, I would overwork and overpublish, pushing for institutional affirmation and sometimes creating conflict, just to know somebody up there was aware of me. I have heard similar stories from many friends who teach theology and feel they have to work twice as hard, since their field is on the boundary of what is considered acceptable by academic standards. My rush to publish was another way of saying that I could be more productive, more scholarly, more academic than anybody else at Wabash and still be a

47

Christian. I felt I had to try harder because I teach in a field that is under so much suspicion, but it was also my way of proving that faith and reason could keep each other company after all. My publications were my way of saying, "See, I am reasonable after all, aren't I? Don't I belong here too?"

But it wasn't just my vocation that made me feel marginalized in the academy. Because I was raised in an evangelical church, I often thought I spoke a different language, or at least had a different accent, from nearly everyone else. The style of theological discourse we employed at church and home was argumentative and aggressive. When we talked about religion, we knew somebody's salvation was at stake. I cannot shake this sense of gravity, and as a result, I often find myself communicating with my colleagues today in ways they find to be impudent and arrogant. There is a certain civility in the academy that I can never quite muster, and I only remember it is there when I violate its unwritten rules about how to talk quietly and politely about religion. For me, such conversations never seem real, because they seem to turn religion into a game or a matter of indifference, but when I am being my most real self, others often are taken aback and find me too brash and blunt.

I wish I could say that teaching religion has taught me to be true to myself, but that would be a good-hearted lie, because I am not sure I have one deep self that is unitary and unchanging. I know that all of the conflicts I feel will never magically disappear, no matter how much integrity I try to muster in the classroom. Teaching religion has taught me to see these conflicts as gifts from God, part of the struggle that shapes my fallen and thus fragmented, yet graced, self. As a Christian my hope is in God, but as a teacher my only hope of connecting with students over the course of a long career is not to hide my conflicts but to utilize them as teaching tools, so the students can see that what I teach is real and that I am what I teach. By the grace of God, teaching religion keeps me honest about my faith, its strengths and, mainly, its weaknesses. This forces me to delve repeatedly into the tradition that upholds me, so I can even go as far as to say that becoming a teacher of religion has been my salvation.

It would be a mistake, however, to hold up the model of a more faithful and passionate religion classroom as a final answer to all the problems of pedagogy. Sometimes personalizing the classroom, an eagerness to hear the stories of our students, can be the source of teaching failures as well as successes. Jane Tompkins, an English professor who has written a moving memoir about her life in education, writes about the moment she most wants to avoid, "unconsciously reenacting on a public stage an inward drama of which I have no knowledge."[2] When our wounds are not healed, we tend to inflict our pain on others without even knowing it. We can be leading students down our own dysfunctional religious paths without being aware of what we are doing if we have not thought through how our past infiltrates our teaching of religion.

Indeed, our teaching virtues usually are also the source of our teaching vices, because our strengths lead us to overestimate the number of situations in which our most successful strategies are appropriate. Several years ago I taught a senior seminar that was full of the best students I had ever had. The fact that there were too many students in the class—and too many really good students—kept the class from becoming the community I was hoping for. There was a competitive atmosphere that was not healthy. About a third of the way through the semester, some students began making comments about the syllabus, the books I had chosen, and the order in which we were reading them. At first I was defensive, but then I decided to let the students run with their complaints so we could air their grievances and move on. The students also must have felt that things were not going as they should, because once they turned on the syllabus, they found their scapegoat. They tore it apart with the finesse and skill I had been expecting them to apply to the texts we were reading. Afterward, rather than the exercise having purged their frustrations and allowing them to return to the subject matter, there was a sense that the class really didn't work and thus there was not much sense in getting excited about it. For the rest of the semester, there was a continual metacritique going on in which the students distanced themselves from the material by arguing about why we were reading it. Normally I find such conversations helpful in the classroom, but I let this go too far and never did get this class back on track.

My worst teaching moments come when I start to speak too directly to a student, talking about personal, religious issues in a tone of voice that works in the office but not in the classroom. I have found that when I want too much from my students, I need to stop and think about what is missing in my own life. No matter how personal a classroom gets, there should always be mediating structures that allow students to try on roles and explore positions they might not take home with them. The text and subject matter should provide a place where students and teachers meet to reveal themselves only for the purpose of advancing a conversation that can carry them along to new insights. Otherwise, the personal becomes an end in itself, and once students realize this, the class can lose steam and direction. They put down their books and just start talking, thinking that whatever they say is significant simply because it is what they really feel.

I learned something about my limitations from a freshman in a course on religion and literature. He seemed to be enjoying the class and contributing, even though the class consisted mainly of older students. I had opened the class to their personal stories, and many students spoke on an intimate level about their religious experiences, which made me feel the class was a terrific success. For their long papers, I allowed them to write a piece of fiction or a memoir about their own religious lives. When it came time for this student to start writing his term paper, he asked me if he could write about the Book of Mormon, because he was a member of the Church of Jesus Christ of Latter-Day Saints. I cautioned him about how difficult it is to write about any text considered to be sacred scripture and that he needed to learn to appreciate the book for its literary aspects without diminishing his faith commitment. When he persisted, I told him he could do it as long as he took a literary approach. I asked him to use some of the tools and ideas we had developed in class to read his holy scriptures in a new and fresh way. Subsequently, I was distressed when I read a paper that was a basic and unapologetic defense of the literal truth of the Mormon faith.

At first I was angry, and I wrote some comments on the paper to the effect that this was not college work, that merely repeating church doctrine, any church doctrine, did not make for a creative and imaginative essay. Later, I softened a bit, realizing that he was just a freshman, and wrote some consoling remarks below my initial reaction. After a half-hearted attempt to contact him for a face-to-face talk, at the end of a very busy semester I put the paper on a table in the hallway where I knew he would pick it up. I didn't see him again. I had let him down in many ways, not least for not trying harder to talk to him, but mainly for not more clearly establishing appropriate boundaries in that class. My older students understood what it meant to write a personal paper that still had academic merit, but he did not. I gave him too much freedom, and he relied on what he had been taught—old-fashioned apologetics for Mormon truth. I needed to model for him the kind of essay I was looking for, and because I provided no models, other than our classroom conversations, he lapsed into his earlier religious training, something for which I could hardly hold him responsible.

Even with these limitations to developing a more personal and faithful classroom, I think the goal of teaching religion should be to enable students to become more immersed in their own religious traditions or, if they do not have such traditions or are in the process of leaving them behind, they should be brought to the point where they can see the power of traditions that they never fully considered. But I am aware that I am formulating what is best for my students on the basis of what worked for me when I was studying religion. Mark Edmundson, in a provocative reflection on the risks and dangers of education, makes the startling claim that "All good teaching involves some kidnapping; there's a touch of malice involved."[3] Teaching, like raising children in general, is inevitably about reproducing oneself, though in intellectual, not biological, terms. And just as parents struggle to give their children what they need, not necessarily what they want, teachers too risk push-

51

ing students further than they want to go in order to show them opportunities they did not know were possible.

Edmundson also observes that teachers need their students as much as their students need them. "As well as some sorrow, good teachers have many motivations, but I suspect that loneliness is often one of them. You need a small group, a coterie, to talk to; unable to find it in the larger world, you try to create it in the smaller sphere of a classroom."[4] Just as it is said that the urge to write a novel is born when one cannot find the perfect book to read, the urge to teach comes, at least in part, from a sense that we do not have the right people to talk to outside of the classroom.

For the teaching of religion, this observation points to a devastating failure. If our churches were better at religious education, perhaps there would be less need to teach religion in school. To some extent, then, the study of religion in school is a sign of the failure of not only our churches but also our society as a whole to inculcate a respect for religious traditions and a curiosity about questions of ultimate meaning. The tragedy (or comedy) is that we want the schools to do something that society as a whole no longer knows how to do, that is, to train our children in the ways of God. It is not an honest answer to this issue, however, to say that religion can be taught at church or home, because schools have a virtual monopoly on our children. The fact that education is public and mandatory suggests that parents should exercise a lot of local control over what their children learn. For many parents, this means that if churches cannot compete with schools for the education of our children, then schools should at least not belittle what churches have to say and should be expected to go a long way toward reinforcing and supporting much that the churches teach.

Edmundson's characterization of teaching as a form of kidnapping is a dangerous but provocative metaphor. What would it mean to kidnap kids not from their parents but from the larger culture today? To most teachers in the '60s and '70s and even the Reagan '80s, it meant trying to liberate students from stifling conventionalism and narrow traditions. It was assumed that going to graduate school in the '80s was at least in part a political statement against everything Reagan represented. But what do we do now that cultural relativism has triumphed and talk-show host David Letterman has made cynicism boring and irony banal? In an educational environment that promotes tolerance to the point of relativism, from what are we trying to save our students and for what are we trying to liberate them?

The density of my students' moral relativism overwhelmed me one night when I taught Nietzsche to a group of seniors in a humanities colloquium. My co-teacher was a physics professor who had studied Nietzsche for years with depth and appreciation. I once found Nietzsche liberating, but I had become increasingly skeptical of Nietzsche's skepticism. The students all liked Nietzsche, which bothered me more than if they had either loved or hated him, so I tried to probe the contours of their quick identification with him. To me, Nietzsche either could be avidly followed or rejected with repugnance, but liking him hardly seemed an appropriate response. I tried to push the students hard to criticize him, and in the process I had to reinvent his amoralism for them, because they saw nothing harmful in it. They did not find anything original or striking in it, either. For them, Nietzsche was so much a part of the background of their existence that they hardly noticed what he was really saying.

Of course, they had terribly domesticated him and their weaker form of his moral relativism had blinded them to his hyperbolic celebration of the strong overman and his condemnation of everything that smacks of weakness. They put a happy face on his nihilism, while I saw in Nietzsche the rage that not only would disturb his contemporaries but also, as Francis Schaeffer taught me long ago, begin his own descent into madness. They were shocked when I suggested that Nietzsche was jealous of Jesus and that much of his philosophy was an attempt to write a new sacred script that would replace the Bible. They saw Nietzsche as a moral realist who fit in quite well with the virtues of capitalism, and they thought I was pushing too hard when I wanted to portray him as a moral revolutionary who threatened everything most people, even today, hold dear. For me, it was not a matter of liking or disliking Nietzsche, because even those who agree with him should find him so threatening to their basic beliefs that they are forced to read his books with an outstretched arm, keeping him at a safe distance. By beginning with moral relativism as a premise, they could only see Nietzsche as predictable and banal, precisely because they no longer take moral issues seriously. They are not the children of Nietzsche's philosophy, because then they would be both excited imitators and troubled rebels. Instead, they are Nietzsche's grandchildren, who, having transformed his questions into presuppositions, take his challenges for granted and no longer see him as he saw himself—as a dangerous force upsetting millennia of moral argument. Nietzsche has become their common sense.

When class was over, a student asked me how the director of the colloquium happened to pair professors with texts. It was a nearly random process, I said, but why did he want to know this bit of information? "Well," he replied, "I think class might work better if they got professors to teach only those books they really liked." This student was responding to my obvious discomfort at not being able to shake my students loose from their tepid response to Nietzsche. My pedagogical technique failed that night because I let myself feel annihilated by students who could not experience Nietzsche from my vantage point. The class and I were in two utterly different spiritual places, and I allowed my pain to get the best of me. Instead of using that pain as a way of reflecting on how to teach Nietzsche, I tried to inflict that pain directly on my students, forcing them to feel the Nietzsche I felt. I had done what Jane Tompkins warns against. I had put my own drama on the classroom stage when I discovered that the students did not sufficiently appreciate the drama that is Nietzsche.

Kidnapping my students from their moral torpor by showing them just how radical Nietzsche really is involved defending the very values the students, but not Nietzsche himself, so blithely dismissed. That pedagogical experience convinced me more than any other that students need to be pushed beyond the common sense consumerism of capitalist culture to uncover the moral traditions they do not even know they have left behind. Leading students back into ancient moral traditions sounds harmless enough, but what about the religious beliefs that give those traditions strength and power? What kind of kidnapping does teaching religion involve—from what and for what reason? Certainly no parent wants to think of the study of religion in terms that raise the specter of cults that brainwash students into abandoning all they have been taught at home. It would be better to teach religion as an adventure in tourism than as some kind of hostage situation in which students are pressured to drop their national identity and go native.

Nevertheless, the choice is not between relativism and indoctrination. Indeed, my own defense of open discussions of faith in the classroom is not meant to extend to an apology for every kind of theology. Certainly, some forms of religious reflection are more appropriate in secular classrooms than other forms, and no religion teacher should be intolerant and condescending toward those with different beliefs. Such intolerance, of course, can happen regardless of what beliefs the teacher holds. Yet the assumption is prevalent in educational circles that there is a correlation between a teacher with strong theological commitments and a classroom with little room for diversity and religious freedom. My experience has been just the opposite—teachers with a strong faith frequently are the ones who are the most sensitive to the various religious beliefs of their students.[5]

The media frequently equate a strong faith with intellectual narrowness: the more passionate the faith, the more intolerant the treatment of others.[6] Such caricatures ignore the complex development of evangelical theology in North America. Many people make the mistake of equating evangelical theology with fundamentalism and the religious right, while in reality evangelical theology has made great strides in distancing itself from its more strident brethren and making creative contributions to theological dialogue. Evangelical theology is not so much a separate school today as it is a set of concerns and convictions that pervade much theological work in the academy.

Admittedly, evangelical theology still is too frequently stuck in battles against modernism and appeals to inerrancy.[7] Although they are often portrayed as irrationalists, evangelicals never abandoned reasoning, but they do cling to older forms of rationality. Against the current epistemological fashions, they insist that there is only one truth in the world, that truth claims can be objectively defended even as they must be subjectively experienced, that faith gives true knowledge through the infallibility of Scripture, and that truth is just as likely to reside with the common folk as with the experts and specialists. Their populism and revivalism made them a dominant force in the nineteenth century, but those very factors had a negative impact on evangelical thought in the twentieth. Recently, however, as documented by George Marsden, academic evangelicals have made significant gains in secular fields of study, showing how faith is relevant to economics, psychology, literature, and history.[8] Evangelical theology is also growing and changing, but it has to struggle to find the right balance between traditional concerns and critical reflection. Much evangelical theology is still more practical than theoretical and more emotional than intellectual.

Part of the problem is that Christian schools keep a closer grip on theology than any other field, so theology is sometimes the least creative of disciplines in evangelical circles. In fact, students who have taken required religion courses in private high schools, regardless of whether they are Protestant or Roman Catholic, often have no idea how exciting religion courses can be in college. Moreover, fundamentalists often fight to keep religion out of the public schools, because they are afraid that their children will be encouraged to think about their faith as one option among many rather than as a subjective certainty. Some of their fears are justified. Many Christians suspect that when religion is taught in school, the pedagogy reflects the liberal emphasis on the sacredness of individual preferences rather than the conservative attention to the weight of communal traditions. However, even when taught well, theology will challenge fundamentalist and evangelical assumptions and practices almost as much as it will challenge liberal and secular philosophies, and only through such challenges can students experience the excitement of intellectual growth.

Too many teachers, administrators, and policymakers in education, however, are afraid of theology precisely because they think it threatens to kidnap students and coerce them into adopting a religious worldview. They see religious studies, having an objective and comparative bent, as a better way to approach religion, defusing the passions that theology ignites. Does this mean, though, that the religion classroom must be a counterchurch or antichurch space, doing what the churches do not do, raising questions instead of bowing heads? Martin Heidegger, the German philosopher, once said, after all, that questioning is the piety of thought. Is that the faith of the secular classroom—questioning as an unconditional end in itself? Can the secular classroom make room for answers, too?

At their best, liberals strive toward neutrality in their treatment of religion in education, but religion has a way of bringing everyone off the sidelines and into the game. The religious studies classroom, no matter how objectively it tries to treat faith, inevitably becomes a holy place. Just as much as theology, religious studies, by asking students to explore new religions, can blur the boundary between polite invitation and conniving seduction. The study of religion is always a kind of advanced Sunday school, a place where faith can be entertained and religious ideas entered into in ways that are not permitted or encouraged elsewhere. Religion teachers advocate for their positions as much as other teachers. All teachers want followers to some extent, want a sacred space where a group of young people will take them and their passions seriously. This must be especially true with the teaching of religion, where discussions often are exciting precisely because there is so much at stake.

True, many of us teach religion because of how the churches failed to show us that doubt and faith exist together and how the life of the mind can be one expression of the life of the spirit. For those of us seeking to integrate mind and spirit, the religion classroom does not have to be antichurch. It can be a kind of suprachurch or hyperchurch space, where the intellectual heritage of faith traditions, so often tragically ignored in churches and schools alike, is brought to the light of day. That can be liberating for students, though it is not liberation *from* but a liberation *for* faith.

The intellectual life of a theologian can be isolated. Academics think you are a throwback to the Middle Ages, and churchgoers do not trust your questions and speculations. Caught in the middle, the theologian only has one audience to hope for, and that is the students. Increasingly, however, that is being taken away, as more church-related colleges turn away from their religious pasts and state universities continue to emphasize all things nonwestern, as if teaching Christian students something about their own tradition would be dangerous and deplorable. Those of us who teach theology should enter the classroom every day with gratitude. If we could do what we do in the churches, that would be all for the better, but catechism in the churches has been gradually declining to the point where even religious students know little about their own traditions. Teaching theology in colleges, universities, and high schools is a second best option, but those are the first and only places where many people will think seriously about religion. The academy is right to mistrust us, because our ultimate loyalties lie outside its halls. Yet we do what we do for our students. It is to them that we commit ourselves, to show them a way back home.

RELIGION LOST AND FOUND IN PUBLIC EDUCATION

Although many educators still worry about teaching any religion in public schools, the good news is that there is a growing consensus about the need to return the Bible to the classrooms. This is demonstrated by the recently published handbook, *The Bible and Public Schools: A First Amendment Guide,* which has the imprimatur of a variety of groups ordinarily on opposite sides of this issue.[1] This breakthrough guidebook is modest in its intention to help students understand the historical, cultural, and literary significance of the Bible. Scared away from the topic of religion by the 1963 Supreme Court decision to ban organized prayer in public schools, educators have taken a surprisingly long time to realize that religion still can be taught and studied in the classroom. Indeed, one wonders how nearly any topic can be taught without some background in the Bible and the various religious traditions it has produced.

Nevertheless, opponents of religion in the schools insist that teaching the Bible will raise religious issues that will extend beyond the modest goals of establishing the Bible's historical

59

significance. And they are right. What will happen when students disagree about what is historical and what is sacred in the Bible? Whose Bible will be read, and how will it be interpreted? Is not the Bible itself a product of religious tradition, so that it cannot be understood without exploring the factors that shape faith communities? Educators should be applauded for finally having the courage to bring the Bible back into the classroom, but they need to be ready to take another step. Teachers need to be prepared to teach not only about religion but also the religious issues that surface when reading the Bible. You cannot teach the Bible without teaching something about theology. Whatever else it is, the Bible is a religious book, and reading it raises religious questions that demand some kind of answer.

The Need for a New Pedagogy of Religion

We are in the midst of a national renewal of religion in the public realm. To take but one example, one-third of medical schools now have courses on medicine and the role spirituality plays in the healing process, and the number of such courses is growing. Increasingly, doctors are recognizing the power of faith in the hospital room and prayer as an aid to the healing process. Mixing religion and medicine now seems commonplace, whereas not too long ago it was seen as a threat to the medical establishment. Similarly, faith-based welfare aid for the poor is becoming increasingly recognized and supported by the federal government since Congress created Charitable Choice as part of its sweeping welfare reform in 1996. Both trends are part of a growing holistic approach to the art of restoring health for mind, body, and soul.

Somehow, however, mixing religion and reason in the schools, while a popular topic for reformers and the wider public, still is seen as too explosive by many professional educators. Indeed, a pervasive fear about the role of religion in education remains among many, if not most, educators. Learning is seen by some as a less spiritual activity than healing, a process that involves only the head and not the heart. The idea that prayer could help students learn would strike most educators as bizarre beyond belief, a throwback to the days of enforced prayer in schools, rather than a progressive recognition of the power of belief to effect positive change. Our educational system, therefore, is in danger of becoming the last institution in America with a closed door policy with regard to faith, immune to the ways that religious belief influences mental and physical well-being.

Some of those fears about religion and education, when voiced by those involved in public schooling, have to do with the Constitution's establishment clause, which is commonly interpreted as requiring the separation of church and state. In the 1963 case, *Abington Township School District v. Schempp,* the United States Supreme Court ruled that Bible reading and prayer in public schools violated the First Amendment and were unconstitutional. This was a tremendous blow to the Protestant establishment, which long assumed that what was good for the Protestant church was good for the nation. The *Schempp* decision did not, however, completely ban religion from public education. Instead, it enshrined the distinction between the teaching "about" religion, which is acceptable, and the teaching "of" religion, which is unacceptable. Religion was considered acceptable, and even essential, for a complete education, as long as it was kept within certain well-defined boundaries.

The difficulty is that this boundary is problematic and cannot withstand careful scrutiny.[2] Objectivity is certainly a useful pedagogical strategy in every classroom, but it is not the only method teachers use to motivate students. All teachers, not just professors, profess; if teachers were not enthusiastic about their subject matter, then they would be held in suspicion, not esteem. Articulating and recommending informed and thoughtful beliefs about matters that arise from the curriculum is what teachers are paid to do. Teachers of religion, like teachers of any topic, need to show the depth and power of their subject matter—and they need to allow for real discussions about personal issues—in ways that are suitable to the students' level of development and interest and to the nature of the material being taught. The Court's search for a boundary

61

between church and state should focus not on the question of how religion can be taught objectively but how religion can be taught responsibly. By that I mean to whom are religion teachers responsible? My thesis is that religion teachers need to respond appropriately to the religious lives of their students and the specific nature of faith itself. How teachers can do that is the central topic of this book, a problem that is certainly not solved by the simplistic distinction between "about" and "of."

In fact, Supreme Court decisions about education and religion have been complex and even confusing, but the wall that separates them is not nearly as high or straight as many people imagine. For example, the Court has allowed states to give tax breaks to people who donate money for scholarships at religious schools, and charter schools and voucher programs are giving parents more freedom in choosing the kind of education they want for their children. Furthermore, the Court has made it clear that schools should not go overboard in working against religion. Justice Hugo Black stated in the 1947 *Everson v. Board of Education* decision that "State power is no more to be used so as to handicap religions than it is to favor them." And Justice Tom Clark argued in *Schempp* that public schools should not establish a religion of secularism, which would privilege those who do not believe over those who do. The separation of church and state, then, should not be taken to mean that public institutions must be purely secular. Rather than policing schools to keep religion out of the classrooms, the government should adopt what political science Professor Frank Guliuzza has called an "authentic neutrality," which not only would allow religion in the classroom but would encourage its teaching in a manner that is appropriate to the topic.[3]

Unfortunately, secularism is precisely what we have in most schools today. Stephen Carter, a Yale University Law professor who has written extensively on the role of religion in the public square, recounts the story of the Colorado public school teacher who was ordered to remove his Bible from his desk, where students might see it. He was forbidden to read it silently while students were busy taking a test or working on a writing assignment. Moreover, he was told to take books about Christianity out of the classroom library, even though books about Native American religion and other religious traditions remained. The federal appeals court that upheld this decision opined that "the teacher could not be allowed to create a religious atmosphere in the classroom, which, it seems, might happen if the students knew he was a Christian."[4] Carter concludes that in our national zeal to keep religion from dominating politics, we have created a political and legal culture that forces the faithful to keep their faith to themselves. The subsequent message that schools send students is clear: Religion is an arbitrary and purely private choice that does not significantly affect anything as serious as education. Becoming rational means becoming reasonable about your priorities, which means not letting religion interfere with your career or your decisions about the important issues of the day.

Schools, therefore, are in danger of distorting the very subjects they teach in attempting to neutralize religious faith. Warren Nord, a noted authority on religion and education, has systematically reviewed dozens of high school textbooks in a variety of disciplines, and his conclusions are depressing.[5] Religion is rarely mentioned, even in anthologies of literature or historical studies in which it would appear to be impossible to avoid the topic. The history textbooks he examined do not mention any theological movements, from the development of the historical-critical interpretation of the Bible to the rise of liberal theology. Students studying history in American high schools would have no idea about the role religion has played in world or western history, let alone that religious ways of looking at the world are intellectually defensible and widely popular.

A respondent to Nord might suggest that the high school texts are merely practicing neutrality with regard to religion, but this view is naive. Disdain and indifference, as forms of hostility, are far more insidious and damaging than open and honest criticism. The more important point is that dismissing religion as a factor in any way of looking at the world limits student exposure to a huge portion of intellectual history and contributes to the alienation that many religious people feel with regard to the secular presuppositions of education. While historians and literary critics have worked hard to give a voice to many subcultures that western educators have traditionally ignored, most religious subcultures are still thought to be too far outside of rational thought to be included in a broad and liberal educational process. Rather than finding their voices in schools, evangelicals are forced to impersonate the voices of others if they are to have anything at all to say.

There is little doubt today that American schools promote spiritual superficiality, moral shallowness, and cultural relativism. But it is easier to object to educational policies on grounds that they are racist or sexist than that they are religiously offensive. Part of the problem is that educators too often think of children as being so sensitive to religion that they must be sheltered from religious controversy. Young people can be taught every other divisive issue in school, from race to gender, but somehow introducing religious issues might offend somebody!

Roman Catholics and Jews have long established private schools because they believed their religious values were being negated in secular schools. Protestants remained in public schools up to the period after World War II because public education—when it dealt with religion at all—often promoted a civil religion that reflected mainline Protestant values. At the heart of this civil religion was an inclusive theism that provided the theoretical foundation for tolerance and mutual understanding. Defining civility in this way, however, left little room for those who take a more confessional or evangelical approach to religious truth. After *Schempp,* as the civil religion of America began to move from a Protestant to a New Age consensus, Protestants too began fleeing public schools in order to have the freedom to transmit their traditions to their children. Enrollments are surging at Christian colleges, which provide a faithful environment for students who do not want to compartmentalize their faith from their careers.[6] Indeed, the weakening of the connection between mainline churches and postsecondary education beginning in the 1960s opened wide the door to the resurgence of fundamentalism, which had been discredited by the evolutionary debates of the 1920s.

64

It is easy for conservative Christians, who began to regain power and prestige during the Reagan years, to believe that the world is against them, but the problem for the most part is not an overt conspiracy against Christianity. Many teachers are well-intentioned about the religious beliefs of their students. They just don't know how to talk about religion in the classroom. And why should they? They didn't talk about it when they were students and when they were being trained to be teachers. Moreover, the media present no models for how religious discussions can occur in public places. Consequently, teachers are forced either to fall back on the safe ground of tolerance, which risks treating all religions as being the same, or to shove religious belief into the background, where they hope students will not notice it.

Teachers know that students—when given the opportunity to discuss religion—inevitably ask difficult questions about truth, authority, and faith that are fundamentally theological. Without any sense of the role of theology in the classroom, however, teachers are unsure of how to deal with religious faith. If educators can figure out ways to give voice to theological concerns in the classroom, schools can go a long way toward healing the religious conflicts that sometimes threaten to tear apart our social fabric. We might also begin to heal the growing divide between private and public education. Putting religion back into public schools would make them truly democratic institutions and significantly advance the restoration of parental confidence in public education.

How do we attend to religious voices in the classroom? What pedagogical models help us respond to the religious faith of our students as we try to teach them intellectual skills critical to their futures? How closely can we bring together religion and education without threatening our pluralistic society? My hunch is that we need to be more open to religious faith in the classroom, more attentive to the multiple ways it shapes individual and human history, and more receptive to the power of faith as a key component of academic learning and character development. The challenge is in finding a pedagogical vision that affirms the value of personal confessions and faith commitments while encouraging students to broaden their religious horizons by placing their faith in larger contexts.

How Classroom Context Works Against Religion

Before discussing ways in which religion can be introduced into the secular classroom, it will be useful to think about how even the most sensitive classrooms preclude faithful utterances. Arguably, the very conventions of the classroom can work against those students who take religion personally. When the professor sits or stands in front of the class, trying her best to sound intelligent and in control, the tone is set for what is expected and what is not permitted. Professors are distinguished from schoolteachers only because they have mastered a body of material in highly specialized and technical ways. What they can offer students is a kind of discipline, a way of showing that they are in control of an incredible amount of complex information. In college, disciplining students is not a major problem or even a main focus, but discipline continues nonetheless. Theories and analyses are used to discipline ideas and texts, and the message sent to the students is that they are productive members of the classroom only to the extent that they learn to bracket their personal lives and take control of complex intellectual issues.

Students learn that when they raise their hands, they are really asking, no matter what their questions are, Am I smart enough? They naturally want the approval of their teachers, so they learn to exercise the same kind of discipline over themselves that the teacher models in the classroom, thus censuring their personal interest in the material. As a result, the students who succeed most in the classroom and are most likely to go on to become teachers learn to compartmentalize their intellectual and spiritual interests. They know how to meet the expectations of authority, but they become lopsided in their total development and subsequently pass on to their students the same inability to draw together the various aspects of their experience.

Teachers who try to rebel against this system of education are criticized for being too soft, for substituting therapy for scholarship, and for sacrificing the high standards of the academy for cheap popularity with the students. Indeed, there is often a taboo in the academy against becoming too close to students, and teachers who are too popular with their students are thought to be insufficiently serious, because, it is implied, true teaching could never result in so much excitement and involvement. If students really love a teacher, then something else besides education must be going on in the classroom. I cringe when students get too loud in my classes, and I hush them when they laugh too much for fear that my colleagues will overhear us and suspect that we are not really learning. Most educators believe that teachers who are popular unfairly trade on their personalities. Surely, runs the suspicion, they are not getting across all the information and methodology students really need to know. How many times has a good classroom conversation been interrupted because more material needed to be covered? Even though good teachers encourage student discussion, they are still afraid that too much personal conversation will ruin the classroom, taking students on detours from the main road of pure knowledge for its own sake.

Strategies for Silencing Religious Voices

So far I have argued that classrooms tend to marginalize passion, emotion, and personal engagement in general. This is true in terms of all aspects of students' personal lives, but when it comes to religion, there is even more nervousness on the part of many teachers about maintaining discipline and control. Open any newspaper or visit any bookstore and you will find that most people, when their religious experiences are granted validity and respect, are hungry to talk about religion. Nonetheless, the religion classroom frequently shuts down the very conversations that could make the study of religion exciting and transforming.

Three basic strategies, sometimes unspoken but frequently made all too clear, keep religious voices quiet in the classroom.

67

These strategies utilize cynicism, scapegoating, and objectivism. The first is the cynicism that is frequently behind the charge of hypocrisy against religion.[7] I do not know how many times I have heard students say, when we are discussing a religious concept or value, that such ideas have no meaning because nobody lives up to them. A well-developed critique of religious ideals is much needed, but cheap criticism that stems from an uncritical acceptance of culturally pervasive cynicism is not only pedagogically unhelpful but also tends to shut other students down. When a student announces that all religious people are hypocrites, and when he does so thinking that he has made a deep point, there is no choice for the teacher but to digress from the classroom topic and directly engage the student on the notion of hypocrisy. The teacher might ask why Christians are expected to hold to their ideals more consistently than other groups. That question should elicit a good discussion about whether having a double standard for the conduct of religious people is appropriate. More important, the teacher should ask whether Christianity and other religions can explain why so many believers fall short of their moral goals. Finally, the class should be encouraged to think about the corrosive effects of cynicism. Too many students think that holding high ideals and absolute beliefs is unwarranted merely because it is difficult.

The second strategy is to use the "menace" of the religious right as a bogeyman to scare off any reference to religion. Since the religious right is equated with religious passion altogether, and religious passion is reduced to something intimidating and scary, religious students must either take a vow of silence or learn to don the guise of "good" religion—a kind of ecumenical relativism—which is acceptable due to its very modesty and timidity. Often, when the religious right is denounced, a scapegoating effect makes the class feel tightly bonded by being able to name an acceptable enemy. The difficulty of talking about religion is made easier when everyone agrees that "we" tolerant folk are not like "them," the narrow-minded religious conservatives. The result, however, is an artificially constructed boundary that makes it nearly impossible for many religious students to speak out and risk denunciation. When a student makes a scoffing remark about the religious right, the teacher must counter it by initiating a discussion of stereotypes and media representations. This would happen in any class with regard to a stereotype of any other group. In my experience, Christian fundamentalists (and evangelicals are often grouped with them) are easily the most publicly and consistently maligned group in postsecondary education. Academic culture has sanctioned their abuse, and it is a shame that little is being done to fight through these stereotypes to have a conversation about what religious conservatives actually believe and how diverse they are.

The third strategy is to treat religion always as an object, something to be viewed from a distance, rather than as a topic that can make demands on us and move us to change. Treating religion as an object is bad pedagogy primarily because it does not do justice to the topic. Religions embody moral values and absolute claims that cannot be approached in the way we approach topics of less significance to us. True, the religion classroom is a place where students should learn to expand their personal faith by participating in a more diverse and intellectual discourse, but this does not mean students must sacrifice the very passion that makes the study of religion exciting and stimulating in the first place. Objectifying religion does not allow religious students to enter the classroom as subjects themselves, because it forces them to assume a mask of alienation that keeps them from connecting with the very material that is at once the focus of the course and the foundation of their lives. At times a teacher must call a discussion back to the text or topic, but this should be done to avoid only the most irrelevant and useless digressions. Most personal stories and insights are not detours from the main road of knowledge but the material that paves that road and makes it passable.

Direct vs. Indirect Discussions of Religion

The problem of objectivity is worth closer examination. Pedagogical style is not just a matter of how information is communicated; it is also connected to larger social issues because institutions reward, privilege, reprimand, and reject certain

69

styles. Teaching religion religiously, as I am defining it, is a performative art in which the speaker is intimately connected to the subject matter. The goal of a theologically oriented course is a vulnerable journey through the material of religion in ways that involve self-discovery and self-creation on the part of all of the participants. The academy, however, values the disembodied intellect over a more holistic approach to education. Theologians can create a lot of anxiety among their colleagues because of their more direct involvement with specific historical traditions and their appeal to criteria of meaning other than, or in addition to, the analytical task of reducing phenomena to their smallest parts. Theology troubles secular education with beliefs that are regularly treated by an intellectual elite as superfluous and, at best, worthy of historical study but not suitable for empathic understanding or philosophical defense.

To avoid being overtly theological, most teachers of religion learn to talk about and around religion, rather than directly engaging students on the issues that spring from religious faith. This objective approach to religion, however, is just as rhetorically constructed as the more direct strategy of theology. Teachers who use indirect pedagogy talk about religion in a passive or tentative voice ("Some people might believe. . . ."). They also rely on figurative tropes such as irony to handle religious passion playfully and understatement to soften their observations about religion and to qualify gently student beliefs. Just as sitcoms use laugh tracks because audiences do not like to feel uncertain about whether something is a joke and fear laughing in the wrong place, teachers use irony and understatement to signal to students that they do not have to believe anything they are being taught. The study of religion can seem uncomfortably close to the practice of religion, and students do not want to be embarrassed by expressing personal commitments when everybody else is just toying with ideas.

Such pedagogical modesty or reserve can be healthy. It shows that religion can be talked about in the same way and with the same tone as any other phenomenon. When overused, however, these strategies distance students from religion. Talking about religion in a hypothetical voice can promote the attitude that the ideal classroom discussion of this hot topic is cool and controlled. Treating religion as an object of study in which direct and less restrained modes of discourse like personal confession are off limits teaches students that the subjective side of religion is too problematical to be admitted into the public realm. Indirect pedagogical methods also devalue the question of truth, depriving students of the opportunity to develop and practice strategies of making, evaluating, revising, and defending truth claims in a public and pluralistic environment.

The predominance of indirect strategies in secular education can make theologians self-conscious and cautious about the distinctiveness of their rhetoric. Indeed, the theological voice, which is implicated in belief systems in more dense and direct ways than are other methodologies within the field of religion, can seem uncivil and intrusive when it enters the academic arena. In a cultural situation that celebrates the proliferation of worldviews and privileges the complexity of ambiguity over the passion of assent, some forms of religious expression and articulation will appear to be contentious, stubborn, and regressive, regardless of intention.

By discussing theological style in terms of a direct, rather than indirect, voice, however, I do not mean to suggest that theology is necessarily confrontational or polemical. Indeed, a confessional style of teaching is advocated by many feminists, as exemplified in the popular text, *Women's Ways of Knowing*. This study articulates a maternal model of teaching that emphasizes connecting classroom material to personal and practical issues. In contrast to an adversarial style that trades on inducing cognitive conflicts that are resolvable only by an appeal to a hierarchy of authorities and a mastery of methods, this approach listens and attends to voices being born in the classroom. The search for mutual understanding in the classroom is possible only if all participants are encouraged to develop their own learning styles: "Connected teachers are believers. They trust their students' thinking and encourage them to expand it. But in the psychological literature concerning the factors promoting cognitive development, doubt has played a more prominent role than belief . . . On

71

the whole, women found the experience of being doubted debilitating rather than energizing."[8] The authors insist, moreover, that for students to find their voices, teachers first must find and speak their own. Teachers can do this best by showing how passion and belief intermingle with the finest attempts at clarity and professionalism, producing a view of rationality as "a human, imperfect, and attainable activity."[9] Like a postmodern architect, the theological teacher reveals the structure of the classroom as it is being developed, disclosing agendas and goals, theological and otherwise, for comment and reformulation.

Of course, speaking in a direct voice can be dangerous. Language is power, as postmodern philosophers like to say, so it is no wonder that religion teachers are nervous about transferring control over the language of religious faith to students. The problem of the power of language is especially pertinent to the teaching of Christianity, not only for historical reasons (e.g., Christianity's contributions to various forms of oppression) but also because of contemporary concerns (the present reality of impressionable students representing diverse religious and antireligious perspectives). Nevertheless, as ethicist Robin Lovin argues, teachers too often assume that their students come to them with ready-made and prereflective values to which the teacher, in turn, contributes analysis and critique. "We are unprepared for a new type of student who arrives without values and who is skeptical of all value claims."[10] Many students today have no practice in maintaining passionate commitments to ideals and traditions that can provide sustenance throughout their lives. Teachers thus need to give students direction as well as criticism; students need the courage to utilize moral vocabularies and the confidence to synthesize analysis and action, reason and belief. If we want students to take religion personally, we must risk the possibility that they will take it religiously. But can this be done in ways that respect religious pluralism and student autonomy?

72

The Worry over Christian Hegemony

Some teachers might conclude that, if language is power, the most powerful forms of language, such as confessional and apologetic rhetoric, should be censured in the classroom. Indeed, a caricature of Christian theology goes like this: Theology is dogmatic and authoritarian, barely disguising its proselytizing appeals beneath a scholarly surface that is, in reality, a special pleading for privileges that belong to a distant era. To counter this image, theologians often are among the most careful in the classroom about their own beliefs and positions, and theology as a whole is obsessed with legitimating itself according to the rigorous standards set by contemporary philosophical methods.

Indeed, the goal of objectivity can be a safe haven for all teachers of religion when so many conflicting traditions are represented by the students and so little consensus exists about how to reach methodological or substantive agreement on religious issues. Nonetheless, I am convinced that the more religious faith and passion are permitted in the classroom, the more opportunities will abound for the kinds of discussions our country needs to heal its religious and political divisions. Paradoxically, hiding behind objectivism only worsens the kinds of religious alienation that objectivity is meant to overcome. Teachers worry that introducing reflection on religious faith will lead to conflict in the classroom, but the inevitability of such conflict is precisely the reason students need to be trained in how to talk about religion in the first place.

Take, for example, the case of Jewish-Christian relations. Educators sometimes are afraid of Christian theology because they think it will make Jewish students feel unwelcome. In the past, Jewish university students often had a hard time finding courses that taught them their own traditions and history. This need is being met through a remarkably rapid proliferation of Jewish studies programs. The growing pains of this young discipline illustrate the tensions and anxieties that religion causes in the academy. Should Jewish studies help Jewish students find themselves or should it strive for intellectual rigor at the expense of personal quests for identity and self-understanding?

73

At one recent conference on the field, Professor Hava Tirosh-Samuelson complained that non-Jews take courses in Jewish studies to explore another culture, but Jewish students frequently look elsewhere for spiritual sustenance. "In our haste to make Jewish studies into a respectable academic profession, a career like all others, we have killed the very spirit that has legitimized the enterprise in the first place," she argued.[11] She warned against critique for its own sake, which can only breed alienation and self-hatred. Many of those at the conference thought her remarks inappropriate and unprofessional.

Clearly, Jewish studies, which gained footing in the academy in the aftermath of the Holocaust, is trying to find its way as an academic discipline with more than academic ambitions. It is a field of ethnic and cultural studies that cannot be separated from political and religious interests, though many are pushing for more objectivity and less ideology. Nevertheless, the focus of many courses in Jewish studies is on Jewish identity, cohesion, and assimilation. The future of Jewish studies will be decided by practitioners with an intense and open stake in the religious and cultural formation of the Jewish people. It would be an uncanny fate for the field of Jewish studies to be forcibly assimilated into other, more specialized academic programs, erasing its own history and tradition.

The lesson here for the study of Christianity could be significant, but there is no Christian equivalent to Jewish studies in the academy. Thirty or forty years ago, religious studies programs amounted, for all practical purposes, to a Christian studies program, but that has not been true for quite some time. As the field of religious studies has become increasingly oriented toward non-Western topics, opportunities to study Christianity in colleges and universities have declined dramatically. Religion programs in public schools do not want to be accused of duplicating seminary curriculum, which means that their students learn little about church history and theology. Christianity is taught here and there in religious studies, but not in a systematic and comprehensive manner. Without a specific academic field of Christian studies, Christian educators have not been able to generate a debate about the role and purpose of studying Christianity that is as urgent as the educational developments in Judaism. Few educators would think it odd that Jewish professors take an inordinate interest in the survival and flourishing of Jewish traditions. There are special reasons for this, of course, given the tragic consequences of the Holocaust and more contemporary problems like high rates of intermarriage. The survival of Christianity is hardly at stake, so there is no parallel interest in Christianity's future in the academy.

Yet this comparison misses the point that many Christians believe their faith is marginalized by cultural centers of power like universities. Moreover, given the widespread homogenization of values in our consumeristic culture, all religions are in danger of becoming trivialized as religious literacy increasingly becomes a thing of the past. Religions become just another object to be bought and sold on the marketplace. If one religious belief does not meet an immediate need, it can be discarded for another. No religion is true, because all beliefs are useful at one time or another.

In response to these corrosive pressures, people of faith are finding out that they have more in common with each other than with the wider, secular culture. The study of religion, to the extent that it helps the faithful figure out ways to flourish in the modern world, should serve to help bring the various world religions closer together. Indeed, in schools with large populations of Christians and not enough Jewish students to sustain a strong Jewish studies program, one of the best ways to assure an interest in Judaism is to sustain and promote the Jewish-Christian dialogue that has become an integral part of Christian theology in the past twenty years. One of the best ways to introduce Christian students to Judaism is to have them study theology, because there they will confront their dependence on Judaism and have the opportunity to probe the complex relationship between these two religions, as well as the tragic consequences of Christianity's contributions to anti-Semitism. The result will be positive not only for the role of Judaism in the academy but also for the flourishing of Jewish communities in America. The more Christians know about

75

Judaism, and the more they have the opportunity for honest and open discussions about Christian origins, the better relations will be between these two groups.

Unfortunately, such dialogues are rare in public education. You cannot initiate discussion between two diverse religious traditions without giving students some framework for thinking through the complex philosophical and theological problems that arise, but such help is rarely forthcoming at any level of the educational system. Educators are afraid that letting Christian theology into the classroom will offend Muslim students or those of non-Western faiths, but theologians generally are the only scholars, along with comparativists, who are trained to deal with the clash of religious faiths. Unless religious differences are suppressed, the question of religious pluralism as it pertains to the truth of religious faith must be asked directly and honestly, and to do that, theological reflection is needed.

Of course, students become interested in thinking seriously about religion at different times in their lives, so no student should be forced to ask the hard questions about faith when the student is not ready. This does not mean, however, that questions of faith should be kept out of education, because for many students, religion functions as their motivation for learning in the first place. Frequently, educators use the notion of *diversity* to shun any explicit discourse about religion. They worry about making atheists or other minorities feel uncomfortable if religion is discussed in a Christian framework or if Christian students are too vocal about their faith. The problem is, of course, that diversity is a highly problematic term. Practically speaking, it is not possible to take with equal seriousness all viewpoints about everything. Tolerance can be an important means of ensuring a healthy educational atmosphere, but tolerance cannot be an end in itself for the educational process, because if everything is tolerated, nothing is taken seriously. Diversity is a fact of life, but it does not make for a sufficient life philosophy. Students need to learn how to find a place in the world, how to be rooted, how to follow visions that startle and inspire, and how to dream and hope. This is why, I take it, conservative ideologies are so popular across our campuses.

Students see a chaotic world, so they do not trust the intellect alone to make a cosmos out of this mess, and they are drawn to philosophies and theologies that emphasize community, tradition, and faith.

Religion courses at any level of public education can play a crucial role in motivating students to learn, as long as they are optional, local, and faithful. Although all students can learn to sharpen their thinking by plunging into theological reflections, the nature of the topic is sensitive enough that religion classes should be optional. In any case, students think best about religion when they are not being told that religion is good for them and that they must study it in order to graduate. (This does not mean that religion should not be a part of required courses in Western civilization or surveys of world cultures and traditions.) Religion courses also should reflect the concerns and issues of the school's students and local community. If religion is taught best by listening to the voices of students and giving them practice in making their beliefs public, religion courses should be under local control. Teachers need to know their audience—and educators must know their community—to provide them with religious reflection that will be helpful and challenging. Another way of saying this is that the study of religion should be faithful not only to the material under consideration but also to the faith of the students. It is their faith—or lack of it—that makes the study of religion exciting and transformative.

How Not to Sidestep Debates over Evolution

The conflict that immediately comes to mind when most people talk about religion and education is the debate over evolution. The scientific creationism movement probably has done more than any other issue to drive a wedge between liberals and conservatives on the role of religion in schools. Educators are afraid that the religious right will do everything in its power to get its views represented in the classroom, and they think they must fight with everything they have to ensure a religiously neutral education. Nonetheless, the issue will not go away, if only because the overwhelming majority of Americans

77

believe God created human beings, either directly or through the evolutionary process. The push for equal time statutes is a symptom of the discomfort the religiously faithful feel when their views are not represented in education. At the very least, most Americans want a truly pluralistic approach to this issue, which would honor science and faith. Unfortunately, such pluralism too frequently degenerates into polarized debate. The controversy over evolution, then, represents a national pedagogical failure of enormous proportions.

The theory of evolution itself does not say anything positive about the ultimate questions concerning the meaning and purpose of human life. The mechanism of natural selection does not reflect a higher purpose, because it has little, if any, direction. The growth in complexity and intelligence of species is by happenstance, a random process rather than a progressive development. Humans, according to evolutionary theory, resulted from a cosmic accident and are the incredibly unlikely product of an impersonal sequence of events. Evolution provides no spiritual consolation, although its portrait of an indifferent universe leaves many people turning to religion for an account of how our hopes and sufferings might not be in vain.

The problem is that the question of the origin of the universe and the growth of life is not merely a scientific issue. You cannot teach evolution without raising, no matter how inadvertently, metaphysical questions about the ultimate origin of all things and the nature of human beings. Most scientists confine their speculations about such questions to the empirical method, but religious conservatives are right to anticipate that when biological teaching crosses over into philosophical issues, the emphasis of evolution on the unplanned advance of nature favors agnosticism or atheism. Moreover, some scientists use evolution to promote a secular worldview, combating what they see as the dark forces of religious superstition. When such scientists insist that they are merely promulgating good science, they are not being honest with themselves. In response, creationists, who find it hard to have their views taken seriously in any part of school curriculum, try to cloak theological arguments in the language of science. Both groups obscure the fact that these issues are fundamentally religious, not scientific.

The teaching of evolution, then, is a delicate business. The study of evolution naturally and inevitably leads to a series of questions about the meaning of life that most scientists are ill-prepared to answer. Scientific teachers can hardly be expected to be well-trained in the ways and means of theological reflection. There should, however, be room in the educational process for teachers who are theologically sensitive and competent. If we moved the questions of ultimate origins and human nature out of the biological classroom (as far as that is possible) and into the religion classroom, we could let science be science while still giving voice to the great majority of students who want to think about the mystery of God and the uniqueness of humanity. In other words, we need to take the pressure off evolution so it can be treated as the theory it is, without expecting it to provide the answers to all of life's mysteries. Evolution would be much less controversial if it were not expected to carry the whole weight of the demand for religious perspectives in the curriculum. Teaching more religion in public schools will not solve the problem of evolution, but it will provide an alternative forum for the discussion of the relationship between religion and science, and it will make room for religious voices that are not so easily raised in the biology classroom.

Religion and science can never be absolutely separated, but there should be places in the curriculum—from high school through college—where both can be taught according to their own norms and principles. Liberal theologians, for example, have developed sophisticated theories of hermeneutics to reinterpret the religious language of Genesis and allow for the integration of evolution within the framework of divine creation. These theories provide intellectual accounts of how symbols and metaphors work, and they should be discussed in any school that teaches evolution. Indeed, if schools are going to teach issues that seriously challenge and even threaten to undermine their students' faith, the schools must provide students with the tools that will allow them to make sense of their faith in new ways.

79

Unfortunately, the liberal solution to this problem tends to allocate the public world of rationality to science and the private realm of feeling to religion. The basic move of much liberal theology, beginning with German theology in the nineteenth century, equates religion with the cultivation of the individual's subjectivity. Religion is thus an irrational response to the world based on the needs of the heart, which means theology is a soft discipline that can complement or supplement the hard sciences, which appeal to the head. Religious language, according to the classical theories of liberal hermeneutics, refers to the inner life of the spirit, not the external and verifiable world of nature. Science tells us what objective reality is, while religion illuminates the subjective realm of faith.

Fundamentalists insist more strongly than liberals that faith is built on rational principles, even if their principles now seem a bit old-fashioned. Fundamentalists argue that religious assumptions should guide scientific research, because religion provides objective information about the natural world that is essential for scientific progress. They are committed to a strong form of natural theology, one that is almost on equal footing with revealed theology. Both natural and revealed theology demonstrate how God's purposes are embedded in the very design of the world. Fundamentalists, therefore, are hardly as antiscientific as the media like to portray them. Instead, they look back to the days when rationality was thought to be one coherent whole, including scientific and religious belief under its broad umbrella.

Fundamentalist students who ground their arguments in the Bible as a sacred text that is more authoritative than empirical observation or scientific inquiry should be given the opportunity to make a case for a rationality that is more deductive than inductive. Their appeal to authority, after all, is common in all rational argumentation. Like most people, they reject the testimony of experts when their most cherished values are called into question. As a result of their belief in biblical inerrancy, they are labeled fanatics, but they are challenging traditional educational authorities in much the same way that other groups in the multicultural debates have tried to overturn accepted assumptions in order to get their voices heard. Fundamentalists raise serious questions about the nature of science and the role of authority in reason. That discussion must take place in religion classrooms if students of faith are not to feel that they are being condescendingly dismissed. The only alternative—trying to silence religious conservatives—will only lead to more of the problems we now have as fundamentalists try to utilize direct political action to force schools to respond to their concerns.

The purpose of teaching religion in secondary schools, then, is not to persuade Christian students to tone down their beliefs so they will not challenge the hard evidence of evolutionary theory. The point is to introduce students to the complex ways in which scientific and religious beliefs come to be formed. Fundamentalists who treat the Bible as a scientific textbook and liberals who treat religion as a private matter of the heart are on opposite ends of a wide spectrum of positions on how science and religion interact. Most religious students do not base their faith on a literal reading of Genesis, yet they also do not want to compartmentalize their faith outside the world of science. They need help in understanding how religious language works differently from the theories, symbols, and equations of science. Likewise, they deserve to know the full range of theological options when it comes to thinking about nature as both governed by universal laws and driven by divine purpose.

An Aside on Character Education

A happy compromise for many groups that want more religion in public schools is what has come to be called character education. This is no passing fad. Character education is here to stay in our schools because of the increasing pressures on fragmented families. The very term has become a symbol for restoring schools to their traditional role in society. When many people hear talk about character education, they imagine old-fashioned schools doing what they did years ago: giving students the moral foundation for a lifetime of learning. Such sentimental responses might explain why politicians of both parties are so attracted to this idea. The reality, however, is quite different from what educators often promise, so there needs to be a careful examination of the benefits and limits of this seductively simple reform.

Religious conservatives today are not alone, even though they are the most vocal, in expressing nostalgia for a time when facts and values, knowledge and morality hung together in a holistic vision of learning. Indeed, there was a time in American history when the connection between education and morality seemed obvious to everyone. Learning was a moral enterprise; advancing in knowledge meant becoming more responsible for your conduct and more responsive to the world around you. In the nineteenth century, for example, American educators were heavily influenced by the thinkers of the Scottish Enlightenment, who considered morality to be the exercise of a basic human capacity for perception. As historian Julie Reuben explains, "Just as people could sense the hardness of an object, they could sense the goodness of an act or idea."[12] Educators believed in a moral common sense, which was defined as the ability of every individual to derive moral conclusions from simple, empirical evidence. Being moral was a matter of *knowing* the right thing to do, not a subjective feeling or personal preference. This connection between morality and knowledge meant that the "hard" sciences were not alienated from the "soft" humanities, because all knowledge led to basic moral truths. Consequently, natural theology was a necessary aspect of the sciences. God's nature and will could be discovered in the physical world, which is God's good creation.

As the sciences became increasingly specialized in the twentieth century, such views were hard to sustain. Evolutionary theory did much to break the bond between a moral and empirical approach to nature. Advances in biology seemed to reveal a universe ruled by hard, cold laws that left individuals to survive by their own competitive advantages. If natural history was the story of the survival of the fittest, then religious truths could hardly be derived from empirical investigation. Religion could offer a safe haven from a heartless world, but religious perspectives had little grounding in the study of the way the world actually operates. As religion lost its connection to the natural order of things, religious truths were increasingly looked upon as pious platitudes with little practical value. Fundamentalists resisted these trends, but most Christians made their peace with a denuded and attenuated faith.

Consequently, morality began to be portrayed as a subjective, emotional, and private aspect of individual preference. Moral decisions were perceived as a product of the individual's will rather than as a result of collective wisdom. Ethics, rather than being taught as an integral aspect of every subject, became a branch of learning all by itself. Furthermore, to be a respected part of the curriculum, ethics had to become more and more like a science, with its own laws and methods. Ethicists began examining abstract moral dilemmas, enshrined in case studies, that were far removed from the context of religious traditions and beliefs. The point of ethics was to find moral principles that were applicable to all relevantly similar cases, principles that were a product of intellectual deliberation, not religious faith. The teaching of ethics, then, is hardly conducive to religious reflection. It often serves as a substitute for moral truths grounded in ideas about God and the world.

Some ethicists are sensitive to the connection between morality and religion. Indeed, much of the character education in the past was nothing more than a version of Christian morality minus any doctrine—"Christianity lite," if you will. Drawing on religious traditions for their ethical wisdom while ignoring their theological claims to truth might be expedient in public schools, but it is hardly fair to either religious life or ethical deliberation. As the prolific theologian Stanley Hauerwas has tirelessly pointed out, it is arguable whether there is such a thing as Christian ethics, if by that we mean the attempt to extract general ethical guidelines from Christianity that would be accessible to all, regardless of what they believe.[13] An ethical system consists of a set of abstract principles and a theory about what makes certain acts obligatory, but Christianity has no such thing. Christian ethics is about nothing more than simply being a good Christian. Christian ethics, then, is just another name for Christian theology. What Christianity teaches

83

about ethics is nothing different from or more than what Christianity teaches about Jesus Christ.

Christian ethics is not only an empty idea, it is also a dangerous one. Trying to find something called Christian ethics risks separating the moral life from its religious foundation. If you start with the doctrines of Christian faith and think them through in a consistent and full manner, you will get Christian ethics. If you start with some general notion of ethical standards, however, it is unlikely that you will be able to find your way back to the specifics of Christian faith.

Nonetheless, a well-respected discipline in public universities is called Christian ethics, or sometimes, more inclusively, religious ethics. I have a friend who teaches religious ethics, and he has told me—a Christian theologian with ethical interests—that I could not teach at his state university because what I do is too parochial. He, on the other hand, does something that is more relevant and appropriate to a diverse student body. He assumes that in public education it is more acceptable to talk about generic ethical problems than concrete religious beliefs. But does not the former lead directly into the latter? Moreover, given the contentious nature of ethical conflicts in our society, why not begin with the role of religious faith in moral deliberations? It is surely not easier to talk about abortion than it is to talk about God—and you might need to talk about God to make any progress on debates about abortion.

Indeed, the problem with my friend's line of thinking is that he does something that does not exist. Either he must employ some intellectual contortions to hide the theological assumptions of the ethicists he teaches, or he must teach religious ethics as a form of theology. The former would be intellectually dishonest, no matter how convenient. (How can you teach Augustine, St. Thomas Aquinas, Gandhi, or even Kant without talking about their theological beliefs?) If my friend does the latter, he does the same thing I do, only with a slightly different emphasis.

His dilemma has been brought about by trends within philosophy, not theology. For many years now, philosophers have been backing away from the Enlightenment goal of defending a universal morality grounded purely in reason. This retreat has made room for a resurgence in theological ethics, since all ethical thought now is recognized as local, not universal. If ethics are rooted in our deepest and strongest beliefs, ethical reflection will be, for most people, thoroughly theological. You cannot teach ethics, then, without teaching theology.

Character education, if it is to bring about morality in the public schools, must go to the heart of these complex issues to resist the fragmentation of education and the ideology of scientific materialism. We must once again connect morality to knowledge, which means connecting morality to the religious traditions that shape our moral perception.[14] If not, character education will be treated as a matter of behavior, not belief. The result will be a trivialization of moral instruction. Teaching students to pay attention in class, respect teachers, and not fight on the playground is important, but students need to learn that morality is an aspect of every part of their lives, including how, why, and what they learn. Especially for older children, acting morally requires informed reflection, not just rote training in following school rules. In sum, character education cannot be used as a convenient way to teach values in the classroom while avoiding the controversial issue of religious faith. Christian morality cannot be separated from Christian doctrine. On the contrary, to move morality to the center of education would require a more thorough treatment of the religious foundations for ethical behavior than advocates of character education have heretofore acknowledged.

A Note about Pedagogical Models

What would it look like to teach religion more directly, and thus more theologically, in the secular classroom? Let me provide two models that are meant to prod, not restrict, the pedagogical imagination. Each is based on a metaphorical comparison. But first let me offer this caveat: No model can solve the "problem" of religious passion in the classroom. All teachers, after a particularly good day, have wished they could have a videotape of the discussion to unlock its secrets or show to another class and say, "See, I told you it is possible to talk about

85

these things with excitement and passion. Here is how a good discussion works. Here is proof that our boring discussions are not just my fault!" But a great classroom conversation, like all spontaneous products of the human spirit, cannot be repeated, and its essence cannot be captured by a simple formula or recipe. This is why teachers often find the first time they teach a topic to be both more difficult and more rewarding than subsequent classes, because they do not know what is going to happen, and that makes everything new and exciting. The point of a pedagogical model, then, is not to enable teachers to minimize the unpredictable aspects of discussions so they do not have to work at them anymore. The point is to help teachers to let down their guard so they can enter into discussions more fully and freely. With regard to religion, the point is to find a place in education where the perception that religious passion is a problem becomes problematic itself.

If teaching is a performative art, it is more like improvisation than a traditional play. What works cannot be rerun. The best the teacher can do is try to set the stage so something risky can happen. And when teaching works, it is often because students and teachers alike reveal themselves in passing, saying something provocative almost accidentally by letting something out that does not quite fit the prevailing topic. It is amazing how quickly the dynamic of a religion classroom can change when a student reveals a belief in something. Whether being truly revelatory or trying on a role, the student interjects a charged moment into the conversation that has the potential to break up old thought patterns and exhausted generalizations. Suddenly, something hazardous and real has been put into play. Anything can happen if the teacher lets it. Pedagogical models should facilitate these happenings by letting teachers imagine their classroom spaces in new and liberating ways.

How Teaching Religion is Like Teaching a Foreign Language

The first model states that teaching religion is like teaching a foreign language. If students are increasingly ignorant of religious tradition, learning about a religious tradition will be, to them, like learning all of the grammatical rules of another language. Many religion scholars recently have emphasized the ways religions actually resemble natural languages. The doctrines of a religion, for example, function like the grammar of a language, enabling believers to make religious sense. And each religion has its own internal cohesion, much as all languages generate their own rules about how words combine to refer to the world.[15] Teaching religion, therefore, should be more like teaching a foreign language than teaching history or English. The teacher immerses the students in a world that is strange and exotic, hoping, but not demanding or requiring, that some aspects of this world will speak to their old one. As the prominent philosopher Alasdair MacIntyre has written about the study of other cultures, "Learning its language and being initiated into their community's tradition or traditions is one and the same initiation."[16] Teaching a religious "language" is an invitation that can have weighty consequences.

Students gravitate to religion for many reasons, but surely French professor Alice Kaplan puts her finger on one of them when she writes, "Why do people want to adopt another culture? Because there's something in their own they don't like, that doesn't *name them*."[17] In her autobiography, Kaplan tells of an irresistible attraction to French language and culture that was born in family tragedy. She could hide in another language when life got too messy. Yet this other world was also, most fundamentally, liberating and exciting. Teaching French, for her, was a matter of immersing students in new situations that required them to figure out who they were and what they wanted. Teaching, she maintains, "is about generating words— other people's words. Making people change, making them make mistakes, making them care and not care, making them sensitive, but not oversensitive, to the nuances of language. Making them take risks."[18] Part of the drama of teaching French, for example, comes from the physical work of enabling the student to pronounce the "r" by feeling it deep in the throat and hearing in it a novel sound that suggests a different world.

87

Kaplan found her motivation to teach French in her personal experience of a self-discovery made possible by traveling far from home. Religion teachers also take students into a world that is removed from the familiar and yet rich with personal meaning to the teacher. But students cannot be forced to benefit from the study of religion as if the teacher were a tour guide returning with a group of first-time visitors to a distant place she dearly loves, pointing out all the spots they should adore, hoping they will have the same experience she did many years ago. The life of religion calls to us in different ways, and the religion teacher must respect those differences. In fact, it is the teacher's primary responsibility to help others listen to that call in the first place. If students do not leave a religion class with a sense of what it might mean to have their lives transformed by faith, that class has failed just as much as a foreign language class that teaches the rules of grammar, vocabulary, and pronunciation but never sufficiently enchants students with the whole way of life represented by the language or motivates them to pay a potentially life-changing visit to a far country.

Teaching Religion and the Metaphor of Passing

The second model relies on the phenomenon of passing, which has become a popular metaphor for pedagogy in recent scholarship.[19] Hiding one's membership in a minority community while pretending to be a part of the larger and more nondescript public is called passing. Passing means putting one's self-identification at risk by assuming a role that society has sanctioned as being more appropriate. This is in contrast to coming out, which means revealing one's true self, frequently hidden from public view.

Questions about identity and representation abound in higher education. Who has the right to speak for and identify with specific groups of people? How are voices mediated by texts and ideas? In religious studies, who speaks for the faithful, and how do "we" talk about "them"? Do we assume the identities of the religious beliefs we teach? When a Protestant teaches Thomas Aquinas or an atheist teaches Buddhism or a New Ager teaches

Roman Catholicism, are we telling our students that traditional boundaries no longer matter, that the study of religion consists of a series of border crossings, raids on othernesses, attempts to occupy foreign territory? Are we making a statement about our own fluid subjectivity, our lack of an essential, interior core, and our ability to mutate and dissimulate?

In its most specific sense, passing does not carry a favorable connotation in education today. Indeed, passing often involves politicized battles about how society defines and oppresses marginalized groups. Identity politics dominates the university, and most teachers believe there is a mainstream of public opinion and behavior that marginalizes minority groups. Passing is frequently criticized by those who want minority groups to claim their own identities, rather than trying to fit in with the mainstream.

More generally speaking, however, passing entails an implicit critique of the idea that there is a true self amid all the roles we play. According to the logic of passing, students can pass themselves off as whatever they want to be, and individuals are responsible for choosing their image and deciding the groups with which they want to identify. Passing, as a kind of performance, is a complex event of identity-testing that suits well the exploration of religion in the classroom.

Religious students need a voice in public education, but I do not want them to become stereotyped as yet another group of overly sensitive, defensive, resentful, and demanding students who want their voices to go unquestioned. Nevertheless, the study of religion does involve questions of self-identity in ways that cannot and should not be avoided in the classroom. Besides, passing is not always about minorities trying to act like those who belong to the mainstream. Members of dominant groups often try to pass as outsiders to gain distance from their family backgrounds, to experiment with new identities, and to enjoy the perceived privileges of living on the frayed edges of the social contract. The study of religion, I am arguing, is an invitation for students to pass themselves off in a multitude of roles. Whether students are seeking to inhabit or challenge religious faith, to hide or assert their religious identities, they are negotiating the ways in which religions themselves invite people to perform certain roles as evidence of changed and transformed lives.

In the multicultural classroom, where notions of identity are up for grabs, passing has become a necessary pedagogical strategy. It is often opposed to the notion of integrity. If passing denotes the self in transition, in search of new identities, integrity suggests the self at rest, secure in the knowledge that what others see is the real thing. It is important to note, however, that passing and integrity need not be seen as opposite ways of formulating selfhood. Passing does not have to be rooted in the anxiety of having no self. On the contrary, being secure in one's self-knowledge can be a necessary precondition for making passing a positive and effective learning experience.

For example, I am a Protestant Christian professor, but my very Christianity allows me, even encourages me, to pass myself off in the classroom in a variety of guises—as skeptic, Buddhist, Catholic, liberal, and conservative. I do not do this to fool the students. I have small, intimate classes, so I could not get away with deceiving them about myself even if I wanted to. I do this in part because it is the nature of my profession. Religion teachers must pass as something all the time, appearing as near native speakers of other traditions, and they must pass as outsiders to religion when they teach the reductive theories of Freud, Marx, and Nietzsche. More importantly, I can do this because my identity comes to me from without, as an external gift of God, and not from within, as some inner core that can never change or evolve. I can be open to other religions not because I am anxiously seeking my salvation from multiple sources of revelation, but because the work of Jesus Christ has made me secure in God's acceptance of what little faith I have. In response to God's grace, I have developed the skills of passing as a Christian, and thus I can use those same skills to show my students what it might look like to pass as a member of another faith community.

The point is that I can pass as a Buddhist when I teach Buddhism precisely because my students know that I am not really a Buddhist. I am not pretending to be a Buddhist, which would be an insult to that religion. Such pretension would send the pedagogical message to my students that religious convictions are fluid and fleeting, hardly worthy of serious study. Instead, I am publicly performing some aspect of Buddhism, which honors the power of another faith by showing students that understanding religion involves one's whole being. Moreover, the very fact that my performance of some aspect of another faith is partial, incomplete, and not very convincing demonstrates to my students the real difficulties of working one's way into the heart of another religion. Becoming religious is a matter not just of passing one's self off as religious, but also of being called. In a way, then, when we teach religion, we are inviting our students to become near native speakers of a foreign language and thus to see what it would be like to pass as a religious believer. We are also warning them that becoming religious is more than just an act.

This is why Denys Arcand's film, *Jesus of Montreal,* which I often teach, is so important. It follows a troupe of actors who stage the passion narrative of the gospels and soon become indistinguishable from the characters they play. The film blurs the line between performing and becoming a new identity, thus making a statement simultaneously about theater and religion. It shows that when one starts imagining the religious life, putting oneself into that drama, it becomes difficult to separate oneself from the religious character one is only pretending to be. There is no theoretical way to resolve the question of when passing becomes transformation, when one identity is left behind for another. In the film, for example, when the actor who plays Jesus dies, it is not clear whether he is sacrificing himself for the integrity of his art or his faith. He finds his artistic voice only when he starts to act like Jesus, but at what point does the act become religious? That point is impossible to establish because it is impossible to know when the line has been crossed between "objective" academic discussion and "subjective" spiritual formation when religion teachers ask their students to try out a religious belief.

Just as Generation X is characterized by an immersion in cyberspace where virtual reality games blur the line between playing and the real thing, the religious studies classroom invites students to reflect on faith in ways that cannot always be distinguished from the actual practices of religious traditions. The study of religion, then, can be *virtually religious*. Playing "make believe" can actually make someone change his or her beliefs.

And just as being religious involves not only belief but also action—a performance of ritual and morality—so studying religion must have a performative dimension. Becoming religious is a matter of impersonation, a matter of learning to pass as a member of a new group. Studying religion is a matter of trying on religious beliefs to see how they fit, playing with religious ideas to test their power and limitations, and revealing one's faith or skepticism to find out how others respond. When a teacher gives a student a passing grade, it is a declaration that the student has entered into the religious world sufficiently to get around in it, even if a slip of the tongue or a passing remark subsequently demonstrates that the student is not really a native speaker. Religion teachers do not necessarily want students to become converts to the religion under discussion, even though that happens. Some, fearing this possibility, want their students to acquire only a genial appreciation of religious faith—that is, to appreciate any expression of religion from an appropriate distance. Other teachers want their students to show enough familiarity with religious faith that the students can pass as insiders.

What it means to be a spiritual or religious person, or a member of a specific religious tradition, are contested notions in our society. Even the most committed believers are entering new terrain when they explore their faith in the religion classroom. For example, in many classrooms, identifying oneself as a Christian is made untenable by the insistence of most academics that Christianity is a privileged position. Christians are urged to divest themselves of their identity to enable them to relate to oppressed groups. They are asked to pass as something academically more acceptable. Yet the rhetorical situation on our campuses is complex. Christianity can have a lot of power in university towns and in extracurricular groups students attend even while being rendered quite powerless in the classroom by secular prejudices.

Arguably, it is easier for white students to pass themselves off as black, or straight students to pass as gay, for the purpose of countering social wrongs or entering a new world that demands comprehension than it is for the seeking student to pass as a believer. Consequently, passing as a Christian often is done in ways that merely reject and dismiss the liberal politics of secular education, so the strongest Christian voices, unfortunately, are often the most reactionary. Christianity becomes the one rhetorical vehicle in which students feel sufficiently propelled by forces outside of education to resist publicly the rigid procedures of secularization and radicalization. For such students, it can be hard to know whether they are Christians passing as conservatives or conservatives passing as Christians. Either way, they demonstrate the power of passing in the study of religion.

Teaching Religion Religiously Defined

There are legitimate ways to teach a wide range of topics that do not directly and immediately raise theological issues. Nonetheless, the best way to approach religion will include, or at least be open to, theological issues. Because pedagogy of religion is essentially theological, I call my model a theo-pedagogy, in which teaching religion ultimately is indistinguishable from attending to the mystery of God. Theo-pedagogy is, first and foremost, a matter of hospitality and sharing. The teacher welcomes the students with an invitation based on mutual trust and respect. In Christian terms, such teaching resembles that moment in the liturgy when the faithful bring their gifts to the table—even though the classroom table is a long way from the communion table where the offering of Christ's sacrifice is remembered.

More fully defined, theo-pedagogy is the art of endowing students with a religious imagination so they may have some sense of what is at stake in the spiritual life, enabling them to place their own religious commitments in a wider and richer context. That definition divides into three parts worth briefly elaborat-

93

ing to make clear what I mean by teaching religion religiously. First, thinking about religion is fundamentally an imaginative activity. Religion is best evoked in the stories, histories, customs, doctrines, practices, rituals, and art of religious traditions. This means that the stories students tell about themselves can become the curriculum of the classroom, a primary means of exploring the density of religious worlds.

Second, students should experience the gravity of religious faith and understand why virtually all cultures have been religious and why religion always provokes such passion and enthusiasm. They should know that the stakes of religion transcend the intellectual classroom and that we cannot master the religious quest or fully understand it or replace it with our own mental gymnastics. Nothing we say or do can account completely for the hold religion has on most people. Religion is a wager, and students should have some appreciation for its palpable excitement and existential risk.

Third, students should be invited to delve deeper into their own religious journeys by finding concrete connections between what they believe and what the great theologians and saints have believed, hoped for, and loved in the past. If we allow them to place their own experiences in those broad contexts, by providing them with the widest possible historical horizon, then their imaginations can grow, rather than shrink, when confronted with the intimidating mass of religious information. This does not mean students should be forced to reveal themselves. When studying religion, students sometimes need to be silent, because much religious growth takes place in the individual's solitude. That silence should be honored not as a stubborn rejection of the teacher's leadership of the class but as a lingering time and expansive space that, while daunting, is necessary for the hard task of religious reflection. Indeed, letting silence work for the students is one of the best ways a teacher can honor the voice of religious faith in the secular classroom.

THREE

THE THEOLOGY OF TEACHING AND THE TEACHING OF THEOLOGY

In the rush to reform our schools, many voices are converging on the realization that education is a process of formation that cannot be completely separated from religious values and concerns. Of course, there are still polarized debates about vouchers, prayer, evolution, and the constitutional separation of church and state. Nevertheless, a surprising consensus is emerging in the recognition that education is more than just the technique of transferring information. Education, when it is effective, inevitably reaches out toward the broadest questions of meaning just as it reaches deep into the hearts of students, drawing on their passions to convert them to the world of learning. It is almost as if a revival is sweeping through our nation, but the schools, not the churches, are convulsing with the desire for dramatic change.

Various factions in this revival chant diverse but related mantras summing up their hopes for education: the transmission of culture, the formation of character, the development of civic responsibility, and the cultivation of various kinds of intelligence. These formulae have in common the sense that education is a sacred endeavor involving transcendent values and

95

moral commitment. What remains to be seen is whether a common ground can be found for the relationship of religion and education. To do that, we must, as a nation, determine not only the purpose of education but also the nature of religion.

Indeed, it is remarkable how the language of education overlaps with and is, at times, indistinguishable from the language of religion. We want our classrooms to be a community of learners, not just a random and transient collection of expressionless faces. We want to teach the whole student, not just the mind but the heart and spirit as well. We want to restore a sense of transcendent purpose and moral gravity to education, so students not only will respect their teachers but, more important, will be grateful for the opportunity to participate in this long, life-changing process. We want to decentralize the classroom so teachers can learn to grow by listening to students, and students can learn to value their own voices. To do this, we must begin to respect the stories students bring to the classroom, and we must make room for their commitments. We also want to reaffirm the Western heritage and its traditions, even as we want students to be more aware of the plurality of traditions in their backyard as well as the diversity of cultures throughout the world. All of these goals for education are hardly separable from religious issues and values.

I have made the claim that all teaching of religion is theological. But is all teaching—teaching of anything—religious? Can we name education with the language of religion? Is education an essentially religious enterprise? Can the two converge? A case can be made for these claims. Religious language comes naturally to the description of teaching. After all, teaching has ancient roots in the passing down of myths, rituals, and doctrines. Anyone who teaches feels the burden of being responsible for young people, and that responsibility, like parenting, has a sacred dimension. Education is of utmost importance for the survival of individuals and societies, but it transcends the bare requirements of survival, allowing us to rise above our environments and the world of animals. Only language chock-full of unconditioned absolutes seems appropriate to it.

In a way, it would make debates about religion and education much easier if it could be argued that education is an essentially religious enterprise. But are there dangers and limitations to this endeavor? What aspects of religion must be sacrificed for it to support the entire edifice of education? Do we need a theology *of* education, or do we simply need more theology *in* education? I am skeptical that a religious interpretation of teaching will have much hold in our culture. I will begin this chapter by examining the views of Parker Palmer, who is one of our nation's most popular writers about teaching. His views are, in many ways, close to mine. He conceives of education as a spiritual quest for wholeness. In this chapter, I will suggest some limitations to this quest and thus clarify my own position. Then I will discuss two writers who connect education to a spiritual search for freedom: Peter Hodgson, a theologian who is an established scholar specializing in the German philosopher Hegel, and bell hooks[1], an African-American who has written many books about feminism and race. I will argue that this definition of education limits the role of religion in the classroom. Concluding this chapter with a more concrete theological interpretation of teaching, I will suggest that, while there is no general view of the spiritual dimension of teaching that is acceptable to everyone, nevertheless, people of particular religious faiths must try to come to terms with education through their own religious vocabularies.

Parker Palmer and the Quest for Integrity in the Classroom

Basing his insights on the Quaker theology of inwardness and self-examination, Parker Palmer emphasizes the spiritual integrity of the teacher as the secret to the art of teaching. Technique can never be an adequate substitute for the character of the teacher, the power of the teacher's classroom persona to inspire and provoke. For Palmer, teaching is not a kind of performance, akin to theater and the arts. Instead, teaching is a search for wholeness and healing. "We can speak to the teacher within our students only when we are on speaking terms with the teacher within ourselves."[2] Only when the teacher is able to enter fully into the classroom, joining self and subject matter into one seamless whole, can teaching work. The magic of teaching, then, is in doing it so well that it does not seem like magic at all. There are no tricks to be performed, only a self to be revealed.

While I agree with much that Palmer has to say about teaching, and I have learned much from him, I have some reservations about his approach to pedagogy. It seems at times that teaching, for Palmer, is a means of self-discovery for the teacher rather than of learning for the student. If true teaching can only come from that place where the self knows itself most fully, then the best preparation for a teacher is to look inward rather than outward. The danger here is that teaching will be viewed as a means of self-development, and all teachers know that if self-fulfillment is the criterion, teaching can be a frustrating business.

Perhaps the real problem is that Palmer holds unrealistic hopes for self-integration in the classroom. Teaching is a matter of playing many roles simultaneously, because the classroom consists of multiple audiences, all of whom must be reached in some way. The teacher who wants to experience a transcendent sense of personal unity in the classroom—a spiritual bonding with the students through the material of the curriculum—most likely will spend most of the time being discouraged and disillusioned. Teaching is not about the discovery of self but about openness to the other. Such openness means that teaching, when it works, will be a mystery of grace, just as acts of hospitality come as surprises that we hardly deserve. To expect the teacher to enter the classroom as a complete person is to risk suggesting that teaching never takes place at all.

True, I have argued that all religion teachers should reach back into the past to discern their own relationship to faith, so they may understand why and how they teach. But ultimately, a teacher's relationship to God must be mediated by the appropriate religious institutions, symbols, and stories, not by students. A teacher cannot find salvation in the classroom—indeed, the teacher who tries is more likely to find damnation instead.

Students cannot save us; only God can do that. The religion teacher almost always is a divided self, struggling to meet the demands of reason while listening to the rhythms of faith. As Palmer wisely writes, "When I forget my own inner multiplicity and my own long and continuing journey toward selfhood, my expectations of students become excessive and unreal. If I can remember the inner pluralism of my own soul and the slow pace of my own self-emergence, I will be better able to serve the pluralism among my students at the pace of their young lives."[3] Therefore, it is best not to stake one's spiritual life on the success of one's teaching.

But Palmer is right that academic culture distrusts the personal, and this is especially true of religion classes. Religion teachers know that personal experience is used by students to take intellectual shortcuts around difficult material or to cut off debates about controversial topics. Yet the personal cannot be avoided if students are to learn in ways that deeply affect them. When I encourage students to use the word "I" in their papers, they often are surprised and tell me they are penalized for that in other classes. They go to great lengths of stylistic awkwardness, constructing sentences in the passive voice ("It is believed . . .") and with indirect references ("Some people might argue . . ."), to avoid the obvious and obfuscate their honesty. In college and graduate school, I was sufficiently alienated from my past that I was drawn to teachers who lectured, who so filled the classroom with themselves that I would not be asked to reveal myself. But now I wish I had been asked to say more about who I was so I could have begun the process of finding my own voice earlier. Asking students to say "I" is one way of teaching them that they learn the most when something personal is at stake.

Nevertheless, teaching religion is not just a matter of letting people display their personalities in the classroom. It is also, and more fundamentally, about opening up a space where the personal can be called into question. I began to realize this when teaching the works of Flannery O'Connor to my students. It is impossible to teach her stories without asking whether she is writing about us, her readers, when she so severely judges modern

99

liberals. She seems to be indicting our blindness, arrogance, and shallowness when she argues that God can intervene only violently in the lives of good-hearted and well-intentioned liberals. My students always point out that surely she must be exaggerating, which leads us into good conversations about whether some instances of hyperbole can be true. The point of many of O'Connor's stories is that those who try to order their lives through reason often end up losing sight of themselves. By trying so hard to understand everything and do the right thing, they shut out reality, which can break in only with a vengeful force. Reading O'Connor, I feel judged, but it is not the kind of judgment that contemporary culture bemoans when it opposes every kind of judgment with a permissive tolerance. Instead, it is a judgment that liberates. God is surprising, and one of the ways God surprises us is by freeing us from illusions through the painful discovery that we do not know who we are, and yet we can know ourselves as we are known by God, whose knowing is not separated from love.

Peter Hodgson and the Quest for Freedom

Palmer focuses on the spirituality of the teacher as the religious substance of education. In *God's Wisdom: Toward a Theology of Education,* Peter Hodgson argues that the goal of education is essentially religious.[4] His work is an excellent example of a philosophically ambitious attempt to envision education in religious terms. His primary goal is not to defend the role of religion in the classroom, although that might be a byproduct of his position. Rather, he is trying to understand the educational process as a whole from a religious perspective. If something like his position is possible, it might provide a common vocabulary for the factions trying to revitalize education. But if there are problems with his position, as I will argue, we might be forced to rethink current educational reforms to discover another way to match education and religion.

Hodgson's book is deceptively brief and simple. He is best known as an important scholar of Hegel, and Hegel's thought, shorn of its complexity, guides this work. Hegel is the great thinker of the "both/and," seeking syntheses where others find only contradictions. Following Hegel, Hodgson sees no opposition between Christian education and Greek *paideia* (the nurturing or upbringing of a child, *pais*). *Paideia* was the central ideal of Greek culture, and the term was used in the epistle to the Ephesians to characterize the proper raising of children (Eph. 6:4). Indeed, all cultures develop institutions and ideals to educate children, and Hodgson argues that such processes are inherently religious. Education is one of the great mysteries of life, a process that creates by destroying, bringing renewal to a society by marking the passage from youth to adulthood. Education involves trust, hope, and faith, and it is guided by a search for wisdom that entails values that can only be called religious.

Of course, not all cultures understand education in the same way. Christianity, for example, has not always been so positive about the dignity and value of teaching. When Christianity parted ways from Judaism, it left behind the title of teacher (rabbi) for Jesus, which not only denigrated Christianity's dependence upon Judaism but also devalued pedagogy in general. In Christian history, Jesus has been considered many things but rarely has been honored as a teacher. As Gabriel Moran, a professor of religious education, points out, for Judaism and Islam, "Nothing greater can be said of a religious leader than 'teacher'."[5] While this demotion of the status of teaching in Christian history is regrettable, the lesson behind it is important. For Christianity, Jesus is first and foremost the living Word of God and only secondarily the speaker of words that can be used for instruction and edification. Christianity does not merely offer words of advice to its followers, but God's Word of salvation.

Nonetheless, Hodgson suggests that although the Greeks, Hebrews, and early Christians all said different things about education, they all sought the same wisdom that God grants through the nurturing of his spirit. Like Hegel, Hodgson looks for similarities rather than differences, and he draws together different strands of educational theory into one vast vision of how God works through history as the Spirit that uplifts and guides human thought. God, Hodgson writes, teaches all people

101

through "the 'educing,' or leading forth, of the human spirit into the widest range of possibilities."[6] The aspect of God that enables human education is the divine wisdom *(sophia)* that seeks to persuade us to pursue our intrinsic capabilities to their fullest. To say that God is our teacher, then, is to indicate that "there is something primordial, mysterious, and overwhelming about the experience of teaching and the event of education."[7] Only God's wisdom can provide the foundation for the human quest for wisdom that is education.

The instructional power of God thus enables education to reach its most radical potential. Hodgson divides education into three elements: critical thinking, heightened imagination, and liberating practice. God's wisdom radically deepens and strengthens these elements, but they are there regardless of whether or not God's presence is acknowledged. Talking about education in religious terms, then, does not alter or challenge educational goals. Instead, it lends an aura of ultimacy and sacredness to education.

Hodgson sees education as essentially religious, which forces him to define religion in sufficiently broad terms to do justice to the diversity of educational practices. Thus, he argues that one spirit constitutes the educational dynamic, pulling individuals toward the broadest horizon of their potential. But this spirit can be named in many ways. In fact, it does not have to be named or known at all to affect the way it works. The name of Jesus Christ, for example, is but one way of naming the power of education that is at work in all of us. Indeed, Hodgson writes, "God's Wisdom becomes 'incarnate' not only in Jesus Christ but in every human being who is open and receptive to it."[8] The human spirit, with the aid of the divine Spirit, seeks after a wisdom that is universal and constant throughout human history.

The goal of education, for Hodgson, is not to know the glory of God but to experience the liberation of freedom. Like Hegel, Hodgson can hear the march toward freedom throughout human history, and he thinks it is an inherent dynamic in human education. Education liberates students "from bondage to immediacy, parochialism, and ignorance."[9] Education as a journey is more than a metaphor. Education frees students from their "particular time, place, ethos, family, culture."[10] By traveling through the world of ideas, students can leave their own, smaller worlds behind. By becoming radically open to new ideas, they can "resist established social forms rather than adapt to them."[11] In education, the self learns to leave behind the particular and espouse the universal truth in history, which is the ever-resounding march of liberation.

Freedom is such an uncontroversial ideal for North Americans that it is hard to pick an argument with Hodgson. Nevertheless, there are alternative goals for education. The emphasis on freedom points education in the direction of a politicized critique of the status quo and an affirmation of diversity, both important components of critical thinking. Nonetheless, in an age when critical thinking often degenerates into a cynical dismissal of everything traditional as well as a superficial celebration of everything non-Western, the emphasis on freedom can lead to a permissive nihilism, in which everyone is free to do his or her own thing. If education were to be conceived more in terms of the formation of character, the resulting instruction in the virtues would have to take place in the context of a stronger appreciation for community and tradition.

The problem is that Hodgson assumes students are free. They already have the spirit of freedom within them; they merely need some nurturing for its liberation. In this scenario, institutional religion is a barrier to their expressive individualism, although their journey toward freedom is essentially spiritual. If one assumes instead, with the Christian tradition, that students are mired in sin, then they need transformation, not liberation. They need to be immersed in a tradition that can empower them to become something other than what they are. Freedom, in other words, is something that must be learned, and it is learned through the discipline of setting one's desires within a larger set of demands and expectations.

Hodgson talks about education in moving and insightful ways that will appeal to all educators. Perhaps that is the problem. In trying to reach the broadest audience, Hodgson ends up trimming Christianity to fit it into his general theory of pedagogy.

Not only is it hard to find anything objectionable in Hodgson's book, it is also hard to find anything specifically religious in it. Christianity makes no difference to education here because Christianity is no different from any other religion. This seems a heavy price to pay for a theological interpretation of pedagogy. The alternative would be to think about education as an event in which students confront ideas previously unknown to them. Christianity could thus be presented in all of its depth and uniqueness as a challenge that demands to be considered on its own terms. Rather than baptizing education in religious sentiment, the aim of theologians should be to carve out a space in the classroom for Christian voices in all of their particularity and singularity. By contrast, developing a theological account of education in general seems like a more ambitious but less transformational option.

bell hooks and the Radical Classroom

Another writer who affirms freedom as the primary goal of education is bell hooks. She is also explicit about the religious dimension to her teaching. "To educate as the practice of freedom is a way of teaching that anyone can learn. That learning process comes easiest to those of us who teach who also believe that there is an aspect of our vocation that is sacred; who believe that our work is not merely to share information but to share in the intellectual and spiritual growth of our students. To teach in a manner that respects and cares for the souls of our students is essential if we are to provide the necessary conditions where learning can most deeply and intimately begin."[12] Like Hodgson, hooks's ultimate concern is liberation, and she uses the classroom as a space to share her own journey of freedom to inspire a similar quest in her students. Education has been, for her, a difficult but ultimately liberating process of self-actualization, and like all teachers, she wants to reproduce in her students what has meant so much to her.

In an interesting admission, she acknowledges that "the students I encounter seem far more uncertain about the project of self-actualization than my peers and I were twenty years ago."[13]

She comes close to saying that students today need more traditional ethical guidelines rather than more sermons about liberation and freedom. Nevertheless, she is on a mission to liberate students from social conventions and prejudices.

That mission can only be understood in the context of her growth as a teacher and writer. One of her most significant confessions is that she is nostalgic for the segregated schools of her youth, where teachers were filled with a "messianic zeal to transform our minds."[14] Teachers at black schools had a purpose that was born of their desire to prove that, with limited resources, they could produce students every bit as good as those of white schools. If integrated schools took some of the enthusiasm away from this mission, hooks found a pedagogical substitute in the excitement of the feminist movement in the 1970s. The feminist classroom captured some of the moral gravity and reforming fervor of the all-black schools. To her disappointment, the feminist classroom, in its early years, did not challenge racism, but it did "provide the one space where students could raise critical questions about pedagogical process."[15] Questioning pedagogy sounds much less radical and transformational than interrogating racism, but for hooks, this critical space allowed her to develop as a teacher and thinker. She needed to be permitted to criticize pedagogy precisely because her blackness kept her from conforming to the typical patterns of academic success and professional development. All of the discussions of gender left her, as a black woman, out of the picture, but because feminism was trying to decentralize the classroom and permit new voices to be heard, she was able to begin the process of finding her voice.

She laments that today's teaching of feminism has adopted most of the priorities and standards of the traditional classroom, so abstract and rigorous theorizing are more important than listening new voices into being. She attributes this to the nervousness of women in the academy concerning their status in a profession still dominated by men. She has a utopian vision of education, and she wonders where one can find a liberating classroom today. She talks about the civic value of liberating

105

student voices, but her political references are more revolu-tionary than democratic.

Indeed, her high expectations for the classroom can be seen as a consolation for the failure of the social movements she has joined, so the classroom becomes the place to fulfill her other-wise defeated dreams. Her goal, following the influential work of Paulo Freire—whose book, *Pedagogy of the Oppressed,* first connected literacy and political emancipation—is helping stu-dents become conscious of the social factors that shape their lives, thus aiding them in criticizing their environment and finding freedom from it.[16] "The call for a recognition of cultural diversity, a rethinking of the ways of knowing, a deconstruc-tion of old epistemologies, and the concomitant demand that there be a transformation in our classrooms, in how we teach and what we teach, has been a necessary revolution—one that seeks to restore life to a corrupt and dying academy."[17] The classroom is the last place where radicals can exercise real power in our society, so they are forced to argue that real change can only begin there. She wants to convert her students to an essentially religious understanding of the sacredness of radi-cal equality and convince them of the need for radical change to achieve that equality. Marginalized students become the new oppressed class who can carry the idealistic hope for economic uniformity in place of the exhausted industrial proletariat. This hope is so countercultural that leftist professors cannot appeal to their students' experiences, but must instead encourage them to mimic the rhetoric of political radicalism.

The Hidden Question of Religious Studies and Economic Class

Reading her story, I could not keep from thinking about my many religious students, some of whom have an evangelical faith that is marginalized by secular education today in ways that are not nearly as painful as race and gender were thirty years ago, but that are significant nonetheless. What would it mean for these students to be able to find their voices by being given a space to tell and develop their own stories? Could they do that in a classroom that teaches religion, just as women were encouraged to find themselves in feminist classrooms in the '70s or blacks were encouraged by the rise of African-American studies in the '80s? Or are religion teachers, even if devout believers, too worried about what their colleagues will think if they "lower their standards" by allowing students of faith to speak out?

With courage and insight, hooks talks helpfully about the hidden dynamic of economic class in education, a topic we too often do not want to acknowledge. A fascinating collection of personal accounts of education from a working-class perspective, *Strangers in Paradise,* demonstrates a tremendous amount of anger, alienation, and guilt from working-class professors, summed up by Jane Ellen Wilson's comment: "The whole process of becoming highly educated was for me a process of losing faith."[18] People lose faith in themselves when asked to act like something that they are not in order to succeed. By learning to pass as someone who is not economically disadvantaged, a poor student learns not to trust the things she once believed.

There is also a class dimension to the study of religion. To the extent that religion classes reflect and mirror church experiences because teachers and students carry with them the mindset and social customs learned in church, religion classes look a lot more like an Episcopalian or Presbyterian religious experience, orderly and circumspect, than anything in an evangelical tradition. These differences among the denominations, as sociologists of religion tell us, often are a matter of economic class, although we should not be too quick to overly identify religious conservatism with the more disadvantaged classes. Evangelicalism has spread throughout all sectors of society. Yet class distinctions and religious affiliation often remain correlated, so moving up to a higher class, which education facilitates, often means one must learn how to change religious behavior.

One of the chief marks of the educated elite who run our cultural institutions is the ability not to take religion too seriously. The religion classroom that is modeled on mainline denominations tries to promote civil values that educate the working classes in the social skills of how to frame and diminish religious enthusiasm. As bell hooks explains, "I have found that students from upper- and middle-class backgrounds are disturbed if heated exchange takes place in the classroom. Many of them equate loud talk or interruptions with rude and threatening behavior. Yet those of us from working-class backgrounds may feel that discussion is deeper and richer if it arouses intense responses."[19] Decorum is used in every society as a means of keeping social control, and it works in the classroom as well. The resulting study of religion is thus more like a high-church experience of a calm recollection of God's grace than a low-church experience of the tumultuous and tortured ways in which God redeems the lowly.

Indeed, evangelicalism is the one segment of religion everybody is free to stereotype and condemn, and from the choice of texts and topics in the typical religion class, you would never know that evangelical Christianity was a significant phenomenon in the world, more popular today than the mainline churches. Censoring low-church values surely takes place in very subtle ways in the academic study of religion, but such subtlety is only a mark of how effective the censoring is. Class mobility depends at least in part on learning when, how, and to what extent it is appropriate to bring up the topic of religion in public conversation. As bell hooks writes, "To avoid feelings of estrangement, students from working-class backgrounds could assimilate into the mainstream, change speech patterns, points of reference, drop any habit that might reveal them to be from a nonmaterially privileged background."[20] Evangelical faith speaks a provincial dialect that must be assimilated into the proper English of religious modesty and self-control. It is no wonder that many religion departments have few students in their courses while campus Bible studies and student-run religious groups are overflowing.

An Alternative to bell hooks

Like many professors, bell books wants a revolutionary classroom where the status quo is interrogated and marginalized voices are liberated. To a certain extent, I have been influenced by her pedagogical model in thinking about the liberation of religious voices in the classroom. Nonetheless, there are serious differences between us. Her classroom models a utopian society in which equality is imposed by her own dynamic and charismatic example. She identifies traditional forms of thought, such as religion, with the oppressive barriers that need to be overthrown for true liberation. A truly democratic classroom, I would argue, would allow even those voices that seem reactionary to have their say, because they too are born in alienation and oppression. Giving students the freedom to speak means not asking them to give up what they value most highly in order to affirm a highly politicized vision of equality.

Indeed, when religion teachers talk about moving their students from dogmatic and narrow positions to critical openmindedness, they treat them as victims of their religious backgrounds, and student passivity in the classroom is the inevitable result. Students lose faith in themselves when their beliefs are not taken seriously by their teachers. It takes courage for a student to resist the idea that religious development is a progressive achievement of moving from emotionalism to ever more refined forms of rationality. We are taught that we must give up something to move ahead, and religion often is portrayed as the baggage that we must leave behind to advance in the modern world. The result is either psychic turmoil or compartmentalization. Either way, students learn not to take too seriously what their professors say.

Many teachers of religion entered the field as a way of exorcising their own religious pasts. Such teachers, and I am one, tried to master their ambiguous relationship to religion by passing as sophisticated experts with nothing personal at stake in their chosen career. At some point, however, we start feeling like frauds. A past that is neglected can catch up with you and take you by surprise. Those of us with evangelical backgrounds in the academy often stay in the closet, passing as good old liberals. But life has a way of making you pay for such deceptions.

If religious students could be allowed to challenge the liberal views most religion classrooms convey, then they would be able

109

to develop intellectual confidence, and the religion classroom would become a place of intense pedagogical engagement. Unfortunately, many religion teachers are afraid of religious passion and excitement. One reason: The perspectives of blacks, gays, women, and other marginalized groups have only recently been introduced into the classroom, making the management of information increasingly challenging, so opening up the classroom to religious passions might, many teachers fear, tip the classroom scales from a minimal orderliness to chaos. Another reason is that teachers often view the expression of contrary religious views as a challenge to their authority. Too often teachers think they can remain well-liked by students only if they avoid conflict. A class that ends with disagreement and even anger might, teachers fear, leave students with a bad feeling about the teacher.

I must have been very nervous about the faith of several evangelical students who took the first college classes I taught. I was operating under the model of teaching I had learned indirectly in graduate school. My graduate school, like most others, did not deign to talk about teaching directly. I was presenting students with theories of religion and asking them to analyze disinterestedly their strengths and weaknesses. In my zeal to move my students toward enlightenment, I was trying to make them appreciate religious diversity by asking them to give up (or at least drastically revise) any religious claims that might exclude the beliefs of members of other faiths.

My conservative students were so much like an earlier version of me that I wanted to impress them most of all with the mental gymnastics made possible by daily training in the theories of religious pluralism. Because I had moved onto a higher religious plane, or so I thought, I could not understand their resistance. Without being able to theorize the contributions such resistance can make to the teaching and learning about religious diversity, I grew increasingly impatient with these students.

The breakthrough came when some Hindu and Muslim students from India began questioning whether the religious theories we were studying included them. It dawned on me that my attempt to proclaim a broad religious space in the classroom actually did not speak to any of my students; the more inclusive I was, the more I excluded everyone. My ideal of religious dialogue was actually an attempt to convert my students to a monologue of Enlightenment liberalism, so that pluralism was just as exclusive as any form of traditional faith. I also knew I was excluding myself, because the theories I was preaching sounded false and boring on my lips. I knew I had to reconfigure the classroom to let the students be themselves, and the first thing I needed to do was be more myself. Just as writers often do not know what they will write until they start writing, I did not really know what I believed about some of these issues until I started to teach them. The students, by listening with patience and responding with their own beliefs, helped me find my way as a religious teacher of religion. I could only expect as much from them as I was willing to give of myself; otherwise, my eagerness for their stories would have appeared coercive and intrusive.

At first, revealing bits and pieces of my faith in the classroom struck me as a dangerous and manipulative act. But the revelations were rarely gratuitous. I found that the more I let on about my beliefs, the more my students felt empowered to reveal themselves. I also learned that the way in which I framed my experiences was more important than being overly scrupulous about the details. Teaching is a matter of improvisation, a kind of performance that invites participation from others, and I learned to present my religious explorations in ways that would best allow student engagement rather than sticking strictly to the facts. The point was not to talk about me, but to talk about issues in a personal way in order to motivate students to think through their lives and join in the discussion.

Sometimes, just the act of listening to the students is all a teacher needs to do. I once tried to get my students to talk about pluralism among world religions when they kept returning to the differences that were most important to them: those between Protestants and Roman Catholics. Suddenly a memory came back to me, and I told the students that my first expe-

111

rience of religious pluralism came when I found out the family of a neighbor friend had beer in the refrigerator. When I told my dad, who never allowed alcohol in our house, he smiled, shook his head, and said, "That's to be expected. They're Catholic." I told this story to reveal more about Protestant prejudices than Catholic practices. I then asked the students when they first realized they were Protestant, Catholic, or whatever, and we got into a good discussion about religious attitudes toward alcohol. When I asked if Catholics grow up with a different attitude about drinking, I had to step out of the way for a conversation that unfolded to the end of the hour and spilled out into the hallway. My students taught me that day to begin with concrete religious experiences and let the questions go from there. Rather than imposing a sense of homogeneity on them, I had to let them sort out their differences, and only then could we try to struggle for mutual understanding.

There is an alternative, then, to the pedagogy of freedom that is preached by Hodgson and hooks. In many ways, freedom seems like an obvious and unarguable ideal, but it is a deceptive theme. To emphasize freedom in the classroom is to give education over to relativism and individualism. Freedom as the theme of education also tempts teachers to politicize the classroom, with the result that critique of the status quo and suspicion of tradition and history are the rule. Many philosophers have argued that absolute freedom is not freedom at all. It leads to a capricious willfulness that collapses the exercise of freedom into the pursuit of fleeting desires. For freedom to be integrated into one's life, people need to have a context for their free decisions. They need to be able to say who they are, where they have come from, and where they are going. Otherwise, freedom becomes a mask for the capitalistic consumerism that is so rampant today.

Christianity is a religion about freedom, but it is a freedom from sin and for God, not a fundamental freedom of the self to do what it wills. A theological interpretation of education cannot rest, then, with the theme of freedom. To teach students in the context of their spiritual development, limits must be recognized as well as possibilities. Indeed, there is a tragic dimension to life that fits well with Christianity but not with American optimism and cheerfulness. Education is about learning to live with—and within—limits. We need to be taught how to age and die in order to learn how to live. Most secular and liberal theories of education assume unlimited possibilities and unrestricted growth of knowledge. Nothing is forbidden, and nothing is impossible. Educating students in religion, for example, means teaching them to experience the variety of religious faiths and imagine that variety as springing from a singular root accessible to all with little specialized training or effort. However, people must make choices if they are to learn to live with the consequences of their actions. Virtues are learned only through choices that limit our possibilities, and virtues become habits only through ritualized and institutional support. Developing moral character means saying no to a variety of options as much as it means saying yes to what kind of person one wants to become. Only if you think human nature is inherently malleable and human history is inevitably progressive can you teach all religions as expressions of a common moral message that is easily learned and practiced.

Rethinking Sacrifice and Love in the Classroom

Rather than holding up freedom, an essentially secular concept, as the goal of education, and then diluting religious traditions in order to make them fit that goal, it would be more honest to acknowledge that there is no single religious view of education precisely because there is no single religion. Instead, there are many conflicting religions that cannot be sorted out and boiled down to one essence. This does not mean, however, that religious people should not think about education in religious terms. It simply means that any religious interpretation of education must be grounded in the specifics of a particular tradition, rather than in the general ideals of modern, secular culture. For Christianity, for example, an interpretation of pedagogy should begin and end not with freedom but with the values taught by, practiced by, and embodied in Jesus Christ. Foremost among those values will be love, especially the form of love

113

that is self-sacrificial. Freedom, for Christianity, is found in service, obedience, and community—not in the individual pursuit of fleeting desires.

Drawing on her interest in Buddhism, hooks argues that teachers need to integrate their own spiritual journey into the classroom to create a holistic space of learning. A pedagogy that begins with talk about the care of a teacher's soul will sound appealing to all teachers who struggle to keep the attention of their students, a demoralizing activity at best. It is hard to preach a pedagogical theology of self-sacrifice to teachers who believe that, given the isolation of their profession and the relative lack of monetary reward, they are sacrificing too much already. Indeed, a sacrificial ideology has been imposed on most teachers whether they like it or not; they are expected to do everything that is good for the school and the students, with little thought about what is good for themselves. The rhetoric of self-sacrifice can sound a lot like the traditional division in Western philosophy between the mind and the body. Teachers should sacrifice their bodies on the altar of the classroom to enhance the minds of their students!

The Enlightenment, with its Cartesian emphasis on the mental over the physical, is responsible for the dualism that tells us to leave our bodies at the door when we enter the classroom. Christianity, with its story of the incarnation of God in the person of Jesus Christ, has a different understanding of the relationship of mind and body. Unfortunately, many people today simply equate religion with a denial of the body, so it is important to distinguish between Enlightenment dualism and a Christian ethic of self-sacrifice. What goes on in the classroom is one of the best topics for trying to come to terms with a specifically theological understanding of sacrifice.

There is much talk these days of the teacher's integrity and of the search for holism and unity. Parker Palmer, for example, talks about finding the teacher within. Such language, which assumes an inner unity in need of outer expression, can sound vaguely spiritual, but it does not sit well with classical Christianity. Christianity does not have a unitary understanding of the self or of ultimate reality. We are no more solitary individuals than is God. Christianity teaches that God exists as a community, not as an isolated, solitary, and timeless individual. This doctrine has radical implications for pedagogy. The concept of the Trinity portrays God not as a divine monarch who is master of all and demands our obedience but as a society of mutually enriching relationships, a network of bonds that, ever changing, is constantly overreaching itself. In the Trinity, truth is relational, a process that always involves more than one. God exists in community, just as we find ourselves by acknowledging our dependence on others. This does not mean, however, that we should submerge ourselves in others, losing our identity for the sake of the whole. The Trinity is God's life; we will partake of it fully only in the afterlife. In this life we must learn to live with a great deal of divisiveness and disintegration. Nevertheless, we know that our future lies in participation with, and not separation from, others.

I am convinced that a reflection on the Trinity in the context of pedagogy can be a profound way of putting Christianity into practice. Christians talk about love all the time but are embarrassed to talk about love in connection with the classroom. All teachers want their classrooms to be a bit of paradise, but they also realize that this is an elusive dream. In fact, love in the classroom is held in suspicion because teachers are expected to be committed to all their students, not just a special few. This suspicion, however, thinks of love as a personal and private passion that is unable to extend beyond a closed relationship, as with the couple who shuts out everyone else. What the Trinity teaches us is that love can form a community of three and more. In God, love is creative; each person of the Trinity is equal in dignity and responsibility. Moreover, God's love spills out of the godhead to create beings who are capable of responding in kind. Through the Holy Spirit, God works not toward radical freedom, as in Hodgson's Hegelian metaphysics, but a community of givers—people whose very dependence on each other is not experienced as a limitation but as the source of their courage to love.

Love must be active in the classroom in a twofold sense. The idea of the course, the very words of the text, must be loved as more than a means to some extrinsic end. Ideas must be lived with to be taught well; words must be dwelled among to become effective parts of a conversation. Books, as English professor Wayne Booth has insisted, must be loved as best friends.[21] But what about the students? Must teachers love all of them? The answer to this question is difficult. Teaching involves an act of self-giving, and we usually give ourselves only to those we love. Surely teachers do not always love all of their students enough to warrant that kind of self-sacrifice. Yet there are various kinds of giving, just as there are various kinds of love. Christians believe that, with the aid of grace, one can give oneself even to those whom one does not love. That will be a comforting thought to many frustrated teachers! Yet, to teach effectively is to treat the classroom as the site of a gift exchange, in which something mutual and extravagant happens. Even where there is no love as a precondition for mutual giving, the giving itself creates, if not love, then mutual respect and solidarity.

The classroom becomes a trinitarian community, in which all give to all; the teacher is not primarily the giver and the students the receivers. To teach is to ask for the gifts of the students, to make oneself, in some ways, the chief receiver, the one most in need of what the other has to give. To teach is to beg, to open one's hands and, with that gesture of emptiness, to expect nothing less than everything the student has to give. Teaching is thus eucharistic, in the original sense of that word, which means thanksgiving. In the religion classroom, teachers and students alike are thankful for the invitation to come to the academic table, bringing their gifts as they attend to the mystery of God. This give-and-take can be called love, though, like all rituals, it is real while it is happening but does not necessarily remain in the same form after the class ends. The class is the sacred space that creates, for the moment, a society of givers; when class is over, profane time returns, and, while people are changed and relationships continue, the ritual is suspended until the next class meeting.

The Christian sense of sacrifice, then, differs radically from the Cartesian notion of self-denial, by which the body is subordinated to the mind. Cartesian philosophy was a noble but misguided attempt to guarantee intellectual objectivity by minimizing the body's interference with the mind. Christian self-sacrifice can point toward a different kind of objectivity, one that is embodied but still open to the reality of others. Indeed, Christianity defends its own kind of empiricism, a radical commitment to the concrete reality of the world, as a result of the doctrine of the Trinity. That doctrine teaches that the fecundity of grace is incarnate, foremost in the individual life and teaching of Jesus Christ but also in the history of the church and even in the cosmos. Truth is embodied, and the body of truth has a life, a history of its own. Self-sacrifice is thus not just an ethic but an epistemology, a way of knowing the world as well as the primary precondition for community and mutuality.

The way in which Christian love operates in the classroom can be analyzed more carefully in three trinitarian moments. First, the teacher speaks the creative word, an apparent plenitude of meaning, but it is a word that only takes life in the myriad words of the participants. Students often want teachers to have the final say with some lasting word, but the teacher can never say what they think they want. The students must say that for themselves. The word must be spoken, broken, and multiplied for it to be effective.

Second, the participants reveal themselves in response to these words, but they must discover themselves by sacrificing their immediate needs and desires, placing them in the patterns and rhythms of the text, the ideas, and the teacher's directions. Knowledge is not abstract but instead is made incarnate in the very stuff of the curriculum. When students become a part of this body of material, they risk becoming something different from what they thought they were.

Third, although the search for truth seems to be the elusive goal empowering the performance, the participants frequently find that the performance itself expresses the power they sought. A discussion in which everyone is having a good time and reinforcing each other's prejudices is not a good example of theopedagogy. Instead, a discussion that draws a group together by reaching outward is not only animated by a spirit of relatedness but also leaves everyone realizing how much more still needs to be said. It is this element of something more that both energizes

117

and frustrates the discussion, bringing students together but also leading them beyond the limits of the classroom.

In sum, teaching is christological in that it involves a moment when teachers must sacrifice their privileges to attend to others. Teachers must let go of their knowledge and thus repel the presumption, which students often bring to the classroom, that they can answer all questions. Teachers have to relinquish the wishful thinking of clarity, concision, and control—the fantasy of reproducing themselves in their students without any alteration. By giving up on the tricks of staging their own mastery of the material, teachers can allow their students to confront what they want from them and to see that the problems and issues being discussed have no easy solutions. This broadens the students' frames of reference to include the spiritual as well as the intellectual, the church as well as the classroom, faith as well as knowledge. The teacher can show students that what the teacher knows is neither what they are seeking nor what they need. As teachers resist their own desires, they can best enable students to reach for something different from what they have—something else that might even be something more.

I know the teacher is not an ideal believer, the classroom is not a substitute church, and knowledge is not faith. The classroom, after all, is situated in and of the world, and students must, in the end, be judged (graded). Teaching occurs in a state of sin, so the classroom can never be a sphere of absolute equality and pure mutuality. At its best, teaching a religion class can be only an anticipation of the norms and goals that are made more explicit in the church, where a mutuality of giving is sustained through ritual and prayer. I do not want my students to become just like me, but I am left to hope that some will decide that what I have taught them can be learned best in church after all.

FOUR

CLASSROOM CONFESSIONS

REDEEMING A THEOLOGICAL TROPE
FOR PEDAGOGY

Clearly, theology will be afforded a place in the secular classroom only to the extent that education is seen as a personal experience. In theological terms, the personal classroom will make room for religious confessions. The idea that teaching is an act of confession and that students should be encouraged to confess their personal positions in the classroom is hardly remarkable. Feminists, for example, have succeeded for some time in drawing attention to pedagogical strategies that personalize the classroom. Nonetheless, those who teach religion are often suspicious not only of the practice of confessing in the classroom but also of using confessional language to describe the art of pedagogy. Confessionalism, after all, has a specific history in Christianity. It smacks of sectarianism, fanaticism, and subjectivism. Indeed, what is a good Disciple of Christ (if I may be permitted to get confessional for a moment) doing talking about the value of confession, when we Disciples believe in no creed but Christ?[1] Surely *confession* is a term too overtly theological to name what goes on in the classroom. Or is it?

Confessionalists are often stereotyped as those who do not want to articulate a public theology and join in with mainstream

119

opinions and conversations. Confessionalists stubbornly pit Christ against culture, as opposed to those who see Christianity as transforming, complementing, or just supporting Western culture. But is this the full story? Confessional theology is arguably the opposite of foundational theology (which accepts only those religious beliefs that can meet specific rational criteria). But just as all foundationalism is not logical positivism, all confessionalism is not fideism (an obscurantist rejection of all standards of rationality).

Confessionalism is not just an attempt to inoculate religion against the virus of secularity. If confessional approaches to religion make religious beliefs incorrigible, that is, not subject to revision or reformulation, then confessionalism has no place in the academic classroom. I will argue, however, that confessional theology creates an open, not a closed, circle of religious reflection. By trying to bring all events into an interpretive framework that is grounded in a personal response to divine revelation, confessionalism will engage a wide range of alternative paradigms as it sharpens and expands its criteria for appropriating new knowledge in order to deepen religious commitment.[2]

When confessional modes of pedagogy do not work in the classroom, it is due to secular rather than theological versions of confessionalism. Taking a personal approach to religion by saying, "That is just my opinion," can be a way of ending rather than beginning fruitful conversations. A theologically informed confessional pedagogy, by contrast, will reconnect confession to the questions of responsibility (ethics) and truth (the reality of God). Theology thus can contribute a critique of current trends in pedagogy by presenting a full portrait of religious confession.

Secular vs. Theological Confessions

By confession in theological circles we can mean two things—the confession of sins and the confession of faith. The two are interrelated. While Christians ordinarily confess their most personal sins in private, to a priest or directly to God, they confess their faith in public, with others in church. Yet it is arguable whether a Christian can do one without the other. In Augustine's *Confessions,* for example, confessing one's story is equated with confessing faith in God. Indeed, to know oneself is to know God. Every confession, even the most personal examination of one's private faults and vices, entails a drive to know God, the author and guide of all life. To examine the conflicting desires that drive us is to demonstrate our longing for wholeness and healing. Self-interrogation enables a purging that makes possible a purity of the heart.

This double structure of confessional acts is broken apart in modern culture. We are no longer confident that there is a true self amid all of our conflicting desires and that the self is encompassed by a true end that transcends those desires. Perhaps that is why we endlessly talk about ourselves, in the hope that we will stumble upon who we really are. Ironically, today the public confession of faith has been privatized, while the confession of sin has been increasingly publicized. Indeed, we live in a hyperconfessional culture; everybody wants to divulge private things, but nobody has anything really interesting to say. A public expression of faith can lower one's social status, but talking about one's flawed past can do just the opposite. Especially for the economically disadvantaged, confession is a way of saying, "Here I am; notice me, please!" For those with nothing left to lose, confession can be an empowering way to draw attention and reclaim dignity. Consequently, confessions are likely to be about negotiating power more than expressing the truth.

It is not exactly sin, however, that is confessed, but having been sinned against. People are anxious to divulge their most personal stories because the language of victimization is used so easily to justify any deed. Nobody takes responsibility for sin, because somebody else is always to blame. People are so certain they can find somebody to blame that they agree to tell it all on television talk shows. Indeed, somehow the very act of confessing on television seems to have an absolving effect. Jerry Springer, for example, ends each of his television shows with a moral minute apparently meant to justify the carnival atmosphere he hypes. He trades on the peculiar phenomenon that

121

people are willing to admit to anything to get on TV. True confessions are the most basic building blocks of the entertainment industry.

Given this climate, to let anything go in the classroom—to encourage students to bring forth their opinions without subjecting them to critical examination—can be as much a form of disrespect as disallowing personal opinions altogether. The move toward personal confessions in the classroom has to be more than merely a way of duplicating and reinforcing questionable societal trends. It is probably true that many teachers first learned their trade by watching Phil Donahue and later imitating his ability to be so concerned with the opinions of his audience, but do we want our classrooms to sound like a TV talk show? Unfortunately, our postmodern rejection of meta-narratives and universal truths leaves us with the pedagogical criterion of trying to please the student, who is treated, in the absence of other ideologies, like a consumer driven by capitalist expectations. The content of a course does not matter, as long as the student's voice is heard and affirmed. Pedagogy has become, in many cases, the pleasure in prompting, hearing, and making confessions. The classroom is the confessional, and every confession is true.

A conservative reacting to these pedagogical trends no doubt would lament the loss of hierarchical authority, emphasize the need for personal responsibility, proclaim the deleterious consequences of abandoning an account of truth as objective, and grieve over the decline of modesty and reticence inside and outside the classroom. While I share these concerns, most of my sympathy lies with the students who resist the more overtly performative aspects of much teaching today. The secularization of confession results in an experiential expressivism, to use postliberal theologian George Lindbeck's loaded phrase, that privileges the subject as the beginning and end of all truth claims.[3] Students know that when their feelings are made the substance of a course, they are missing the opportunity to feel their lives anew by learning something they did not already know.

The Christian trope of confession, then, cannot be applied simply to the classroom, because confession is an activity that has been appropriated and distorted by secular culture. Given the widespread skepticism about every external constraint and demand on individual freedom, the classroom has deritualized confession and made it routine. Narcissistic chatter is all that remains of the Christian emphasis on the responsibility of every person for self-examination and a public commitment of faith. Confession needs to be redeemed—returned to its theological roots—before it can become an essential element in religious pedagogy. Is there a theological notion of confession that can save us from a culture that loves to talk about itself, even when there is so little to talk about?

Foucault and the Genealogy of Confessions

More than anyone, Michel Foucault, the controversial French philosopher, has emphasized Christian confessional practices as the origin of modern views of selfhood. He focuses on sexuality, but his real interest is in the ways in which we learn to construct ourselves through divulging something interior and secretive. Christianity gave Western culture the idea of confession as a form of private piety that is virtually synonymous with self-examination. For Foucault, however, confession is not the expression of some prior state of being. Instead, it is a way of constructing who we are, indeed, of constructing new ways of being altogether. Confession is about the invention of the self, not deliberation over what the self should do or a disclosure of what the self believes. The confessional, then, only superficially resembles the judicial inquest as the model for getting at the truth. According to Foucault, acts of confession teach us that truth lies not in the painful facts that cannot be avoided but with the fictive stories we enjoy telling about ourselves.

To demonstrate the pivotal role of confession in the West, Foucault tells a story about its rise as a ritual and its proliferation as a way of life. As one of the seven sacraments of the Catholic church, confession is a channel of grace. Through confession, the church asks every believer, in Foucault's words, to "transform your desire, your every desire, into discourse."[4] Early Christian tradition practiced the communal confession

123

of general sin during worship as a sign of spiritual need and transformation, but the church also recognized the need for a personal account of sin that would lead to concrete signs of God's forgiveness.[5] During the patristic period, penance was a public ritual of ecclesiastical reconciliation reserved for those Christians who had lapsed from the faith or who had committed grave sins. Introduced from Ireland and influenced by the custom of monks serving as spiritual directors, private confessions were institutionalized in the Roman Catholic Church during the Middle Ages. After the Fourth Lateran Council in 1215 required a yearly confession from all Christians who committed serious sins, confession became the primary means for enforcing social morality.[6] The legal rhetoric of penance—absolution as a judicial act and penance as a means of making satisfaction for sin—was strengthened in the Catholic Reformation by the Council of Trent (1551).

At their best, confessors are educators, teaching people how to reform their lives. The confessor serves to remind us that mercy does not come without justice. Protestants, however, were suspicious of the power of confessors, with the priest functioning as an *alter Christus,* exercising the authority to judge and forgive. From the Protestant perspective, the penitential system smacked of blackmail and calculative exchange, which could only be rooted out by interiorizing the act of repentance. Nonetheless, the Protestant Reformation did not do away with confession itself. Arguably, by "liberating" confession from the penitential structure, Protestantism made confession more ubiquitous. At its most daring, the idea of the priesthood of all believers transforms confession into something we share with each other (James 5:16), without the mediation of an authority figure who imposes upon us a specific remedy for our sin.

The Protestant reformers tried to retain the essence of confession without the support of church or divine law, but the result was that the actual practice of confession soon fell into disuse. Confession continued in the Catholic church, but after the Second Vatican Council, many Catholics found the legalistic framework of confession unhelpful in a time of great moral complexity and confusion, so this ritual was administered only infrequently, if at all.

If the Christian churches no longer provide a framework for confession, secular culture has filled the vacuum with a vengeance. Shorn of its ritualized forms, confession has multiplied and spread to the point where it is hard to find cultural forms that are not confessional. In fact, Foucault argues that Western culture is characterized by an insatiable need for confession that has outstripped its religious context. "The confession has spread its effects far and wide. It plays a part in justice, medicine, education, family relationships, and love relations, in the most ordinary affairs of everyday life, and in the most solemn rites; one confesses one's crimes, one's sins, one's thoughts and desires, one's illnesses and troubles; one goes about telling, with the greatest precision, whatever is most difficult to tell."[7] Confession becomes a trope for truth, indeed, a trope for human nature itself. "Western man has become a confessing animal," Foucault writes.[8] We determine who we are by deciding what we need to reveal about ourselves. Scrupulosity becomes a virtue. Confession is naturalized, so that we no longer see the obligation to confess as a power that is imposed upon us.

The diffusion of confession, Foucault argues, begins the Western world's slide into subjectivism. Selfhood comes to be seen as an internal world that requires articulation, rather than a public world of relationships that are formed through initiation and imitation. Foucault contrasts the confession of sexuality as it develops in the West with the *ars erotica* tradition more prevalent in the East, in which truth "is drawn from pleasure itself, understood as a practice and accumulated as experience."[9] This tradition also regulates sexuality, but it places sexuality in the context of a practice that requires expertise, and thus a community and a tradition. The master transmits an esoteric knowledge that both disciplines and heightens the disciple's practice of pleasure. The science of sexuality that results from confession, by contrast, makes sexuality an interior secret whose very avowal constitutes the self in its most private relationship with itself.

125

Contrary to Foucault, we could say that the traditions of confession and *ars erotica* have met and joined hands in our secular culture. Sex has become an object of scientific scrutiny that nevertheless still titillates the imagination, a topic that incites a discursive explosion. We love to hear serious discussions of sexuality, precisely because they draw from a personal world that is ordinarily hidden from view. Of course, secular discourses gradually have come to take the place of theology, so that the unity that self-scrutiny can lead to is posited by the ideologies of psychology and other social and political sciences, rather than religion. As a result, there is little hope for any unity or healing in the interrogation of the self, and yet the fascination with confession continues unabated. We are transfixed by those who bare their souls only to show us that the modern soul is, at best, a fiction, a story without any ending. We are voyeurs of other people's confessions, an obligation we anxiously attend to with the foreboding that we are running out of things to say.

There has been a gradual realignment, then, from the connection of confession to a cosmology of order and purpose to a confessionalism that is purely and merely anthropocentric. Contrition was once an integral aspect of confession, but the deritualization of confession makes it more of an act of self-exaltation than repentance. Confession originally was a ritual in which the speaker and the object of the discourse coincided for the purposes of purification and, ultimately, salvation. In traditional Catholic teaching, confession is connected to penance, so that words were intimately related to deeds (that is, one was held responsible for the confessed acts). To confess was not to negotiate a contentious narrative about who did what to whom; instead, confession was meant to put an end to such endlessly vindictive plays of power.

Now the practice of confessing is a performance art, so that moral norms seem inappropriate and intrusive. Perhaps confession is inflated in our culture because there is no sense of what constitutes absolution. Without forgiveness, confessing becomes another form of rationalizing. We turn our failures into a coherent whole by dramatizing them through a plausible plot.

We have aestheticized confession, so watching a confession is like watching a play—and the more melodrama the better. Everything must be confessed, because nothing can be hidden from public inspection. Confessions are public, but only in the sense of blurring the boundary between what is public and what is private, making all of us into voyeurs. Confessions are not public in the sense of forming a community of those who seek the truth.

The strange and the bizarre have thus been normalized and even trivialized, so the possibility of linking confession with penance nearly has been erased from our culture. One cannot confess something if everybody confesses everything. Confession is everywhere in our culture, but it follows a peculiarly scripted form, allowing people to delve into their private lives with narcissistic abandon. (Notice how television viewers do not seem to mind that many of Jerry Springer's shows evidently follow a precise script written by the producers, by which guests seem encouraged to lie or exaggerate in the interest of dramatic effect.) Curiously, in an age that prizes individuality and confession as the means to therapeutic healing, everybody sounds alike, and nobody feels any better for it.[10]

The Challenge of Confessing

As teachers of religion who deal with some of the most personal aspects of our students' lives, we need to model in our classrooms a rhetoric of confession that can challenge and transform these longstanding and seemingly intractable social pathologies. The proper practice of confession in the classroom can go a long way toward restoring confession to its theological context. Christian theologians need to recontextualize confession by reinstating its traditional boundaries. To confess is to believe, and it is to open oneself to judgment. In a discussion of confession, evangelical theologian Miroslav Volf emphasizes the connection of confession and commitment: "As a speech act, confession is essentially commissive; I commit myself to something by making this confession."[11] Confessions point outward, not inward, by making claims about the truth that demand

127

some kind of verification. Broadly construed, confession can take nonverbal forms, as when a believer professes faith in Christ through works of righteousness. Conversely, as Volf points out, a false life can deny Christ as much as or more than the confession of false doctrine. Confessions, then, do not simply unveil and illuminate the dark corridors of the inner life. Instead, confessions point to the future by suggesting where the past has gone wrong and where one hopes to be.

The important biblical point about confession is that it is a public act occurring between persons. Every confession also is an invitation, an interpersonal gesture of inclusion made possible by and reinforcing a sense of community. Because of this social dimension, the confession of faith often is done according to established formulae. However, Volf insists that "Every genuinely Christian speech act is, at least formally and implicitly, an act of confession."[12] Confession of faith is what Christians do; indeed, it is what the church is, in the sense that one person confessing the faith leads to another and finally constitutes the church. Volf pushes the importance of confession to defend a Free Church ecclesiology, an argument that is beyond the scope of this book. For my purposes, it is interesting to ask to what extent confession can constitute the classroom, and to make that inquiry in the context of theological reflection on the fundamental role of confession in the life of the church.

The practice of confession should link notions of human flourishing with the recognition that freedom can be found only in community. To confess oneself is to acknowledge that one is accountable to others. Nevertheless, confession alone will not magically create community. Confession must be grounded in a community, reflecting its moral consensus and ultimate truth, if it is not to lead to moral subjectivism. When practices of confession become thoughtless and routine, they can reinforce the sense that confession is about the self in its autonomy and isolation. The penitent looks inward rather than outward for the truth.

Confronting the absence of such vital communities today, Foucault wants to retrieve pre-Christian notions of subjectivity in order to redefine the role of the body in modern identity.

128

Foucault would replace confession with the arts of imitation and initiation, what he calls technologies of the self, relying on the pleasures of the body to guide human conduct. There is no deep self, Foucault and many other postmodernists insist; indeed, the notion of a deep self is a Christian invention, a result of the practice of confession. Instead, there are only bodies in motion and various ways of regulating, managing, and enhancing our embodied pursuits. For Foucault, the self is opaque until it invents itself. Rhetoric thus replaces subjectivity as the essence of selfhood.

This pagan restoration, with its antinomian ethos, is not open to the Christian theologian. Individuals have infinite value and thus infinite depth because God is both creator and redeemer. It is true that Christian theology too often has spoken in almost gnostic terms about the soul and a ghostly afterlife. Theology too frequently has treated the soul as an abstract entity essentially unrelated to anything but God. The incarnation and the resurrection, however, affirm the utterly material nature of the human body, and prophetic images of a new world acknowledge human dependence upon nature as a whole. The practice of confession should lead us to a greater sensitivity to the various relationships that sustain human life. Confessionalism does not need to be attached to an ideology of subjectivity, especially if it is reconceived in terms of its original theological roots.

Richard Miller's Critique of Confessionalism

So how do we deal with personal confessions in a classroom where religion is being taught? This is one of those questions that stirs a host of pressing pedagogical issues. Confessions, after all, are particular, so they raise the question of how we move from the personal to the public and how we rationally scrutinize the personal without discouraging confessions altogether. Confessions need some type of supervision, which can make everybody nervous. How do we decide what is appropriate in our classrooms? Moreover, all classes take place in a larger context: an academic institution with its own values and priorities. Thus, no confession is neutral and void of conse-

129

quences. Every confession is in part a statement about what should or should not be said in the institution as a whole. So there is a politics of confession. Who has the privilege of making confessions, what kinds of things are confessable, and who gets to decide these issues? For these reasons, the role of confession in any classroom is a controversial issue that goes to the heart of what teaching—as well as religion— is all about.

One of the most useful discussions of the role of theology in a religious studies program can be found in Richard B. Miller's *Casuistry and Modern Ethics*. Miller, who teaches religious ethics at a state university, actually sets out to defend theology. Drawing on philosopher Ludwig Wittgenstein and anthropologist Clifford Geertz, he argues that the field of religious studies has no essence and therefore cannot be kept pure from scholarly discourses that might pollute it. Miller takes a poetic or inductive approach to scholarship and wants to celebrate the many different discourses that constitute religious studies. The only criteria for what should count as legitimate in the study of religion concerns the skills that are being developed and practiced. Nevertheless, he is interested in establishing some boundaries for the study of religion. He appropriates some terminology from philosopher Stephen Toulmin to suggest that, although religious studies is not a "compact" discipline, capable of being judged at every stage by established canons and procedures, it is a "diffuse" discipline, which can conform loosely to the rigid requirements of scientific progress.

Even a diffuse discipline needs to distinguish between proper and inappropriate questions, issues, and methodologies to make its researches productive. Thus, for all of his poetic pluralism, Miller insists that one of the duties and obligations of the religion teacher is to discipline the study of religion by establishing its boundaries. The price of admitting theology into religious studies is that some form of theology has to be excluded. Miller accepts that every theological school is, to some extent, apologetical, but what he does not accept is confessional theology. "Confessional theology is creedal, seeking to articulate the meaning and implications of an ostensive religion's beliefs. Typically, confessional theologians care little about whether they make sense to a wider public. But apologetical discourse is different: It attempts to defend religion according to wider canons of experience and rationality. [. . .] Insofar as confessionalists seek only to develop their truth claims from within the practices and beliefs of a particular religion, religionists have it right: Confessionalists seem to disavow canons of inquiry that might be shared by the nonbeliever, and so develop claims that are wholly 'from the inside.' "[13] Miller equates confessionalism with relativism; even though those on his list of confessional theologians—George Lindbeck, John Howard Yoder, William C. Placher, and John Milbank—would hardly accept that label.

Although he begins with a trenchant critique of essentialism, Miller ends up policing the field of religion to keep it free of confessionalism. Rather than making an argument against confessionalism, he begs the question by assuming that confessionalists reject the mode of public inquiry so essential to academic discourse. Ironically, many of the theologians he cites make use of his own authorities, Wittgenstein and Geertz, by trying to synthesize them with Karl Barth. Nonetheless, he does not argue with confessionalists about what constitutes public inquiry and rational debate. Indeed, he tends to equate theological confessionalism with the narcissistic chatter that so often passes for confession in our secular culture. The confessionalists he identifies make strong arguments about the role of religion in society and the ways in which religion best can be understood, but these arguments go unanalyzed in Miller's sweeping dismissal.

In a footnote, he does make the condescending concession that confessionalists can be tolerated to some extent, which "parallels tolerating the intolerant in liberal political philosophy."[14] But he also can sound the following warning: "Theologians who prefer a Religious Studies department to a seminary, divinity school, or theology department as a more desirable location for carrying out research and teaching elect that option at some risk."[15] The risk, evidently, is that someday they might be told they really do not belong. Miller says all this while admitting that very little theology in public education is intended for a parochial audience. The study of religion,

131

in other words, already has succeeded in keeping itself pure by forcing theology into a rationalistic mode, even though there are noticeable exceptions.

Miller wants a distinction between acceptable and unacceptable versions of theology, so that religious studies cannot be infected with the wrong kind of theology, which would be dangerous and unhealthy. Indeed, there is no better way to define theology than to try to define religious studies, because theology is always taken to be the other that remains when one is finished drawing a border around the proper study of religion. An anthropologist might be tempted to say that confessionalists are made scapegoats by religionists to ensure cohesion in a field that otherwise is very diffuse indeed. The only thing many religion scholars hold in common is their distrust of theology.

The problem with Miller's argument is that he essentializes confessionalism to avoid essentializing religious studies. He regards confessionalism as having a distinctly circumscribed agenda and set of presuppositions. I suggest it is questionable to think about confessionalism as a separate theological school rather than as an inherent element within every religion—especially a religion like Christianity, which is so dependent upon trustworthy testimonies and witnesses. Even when confessionalism is thought of as a specific school of theology, its arguments must be considered plausible and worthy of a critical response. A confessionalist like Stanley Hauerwas tries to base ethics upon a recovery of narrative and community in ethics, but others have come to a kind of confessionalism in theology from a feminist perspective, or even a postmodern critique of objectivity.

Confessionalists make strongly public arguments about the limitations of certain kinds of rational discourse and scientific approaches to religion. They might argue, for example, that religious discourse is best understood by the practitioners of that discourse, an argument not dissimilar to some things women say about women's studies or blacks say about black studies. Confessionalism also validates and defends the personal experience of the investigator of religion, so we are all

132

confessionalists in the sense of admitting and clarifying the intersection of autobiography and research. After all, if the Heisenberg uncertainty principle teaches us that when we apply physics, the position of the investigator determines how one isolates and measures an atom, how can we suppose that the subjectivity of the researcher of religion will be any less important?

In sum, confessionalism is a tendency that runs throughout the academy, not just across the religions. Confessionalists are those who draw certain inferences from the confessional nature of all knowledge. They make the argument (publicly and rigorously) that there are no universal audiences or neutral observers, so who you are writing for and what you believe shapes what you have to say. To that extent, I would say that confessionalism is a dimension to all theology that is downplayed or minimized by some theological schools for epistemological reasons that are now largely outdated and unwarranted. In the postmodern academy, confessionalism in theology should become more accepted and popular just as it has become more standard in almost all other humanistic disciplines. Miller singles out confessionalism in theology as a type of thinking that could pollute religious studies by endangering civil discourse only because of his own confessional position, a liberal Roman Catholicism that, following a limited appropriation of St. Thomas Aquinas, illuminates universal aspects of the human condition without accepting any role for special revelation or divine law.

Indeed, the field of ethics can be conceived as a tool for teaching religion in public education without being confessional. Most programs in ethics remain rooted in Christianity (courses in cross-cultural ethics are rare), but the fact that ethical issues, not doctrinal issues, are being examined gives these courses the allure of objectivity and universality. Even though courses in ethics teach Christian theologians, ethicists can insist that they are keeping theology in the background while accentuating the search for a reasonable and widely shared position on topics of universal concern. When Miller, for example, talks about the ways in which Augustine's *Confessions* can be taught

133

in religious studies, he talks about Augustine's parallels with Freud, his role in intellectual history, and his hermeneutics of the self. What he does not mention is the question of God that Augustine's text relentlessly pursues.

Hauerwas has noted how the field of biomedical ethics has given theology new life in public education. Life-and-death issues naturally raise religious concerns and invite theological explorations. Hauerwas is skeptical, however, about ethical models that emphasize abstract principles. What if ethics is tied to what one believes? And what if one's beliefs are tied to a particular community and its tradition? And what if the ethicist took as a mission the formation of ethical belief and conduct in students? If so, one would end up with a noticeably different course in religious ethics. Unfortunately, the field of ethics is one of the last strongholds of liberal Protestantism in the academy, an attempt to be in the realm of Christian influence while speaking to a wide audience on the basis of the broadest principles and premises. It is a hybrid discipline that teaches religion indirectly by focusing on common ethical problems. Maybe someday we will all be forced to admit that we speak out of particular situations and from personal commitments, which is what feminists have been arguing all along. Ethicists, after all, work out of particular traditions and raise questions of ultimacy and meaning that transcend the canons of materialism, naturalism, and secularism.

Confessional Practices

Should religion departments try to police religious belief among their faculty to foster higher levels of objectivity than is presumed possible by the rest of secular education? Who is more in tune with postmodern epistemology, confessionalists or social scientific reductionists? Can religion be taught as a live option (to use William James' terminology), a phenomenon that has the potential to change lives, just as art historians, I presume, teach art as an aspect of human creativity that can make life more worthwhile, that can entertain, challenge, demand, and even transform?

Some recent essays on pedagogy and religion give one cause to hope that confessionalism is not a dead issue. In a candid essay in the *Journal of the American Academy of Religion,* Miriam Peskowitz wrestles with the issue of bringing religious ritual into her classroom and revealing her faith to students. She raises the question of how professors establish their identity in the classroom when they are teaching students that religious identification is such a complex issue. What do professors ultimately identify with in the religion classroom? Peskowitz suggests that their identification with their academic training might actually hinder rather than promote good teaching. Professors are, as she wonderfully puts it, "accidental teachers."[16] Graduate schools and professional guilds define professors as producers of knowledge, which distinguishes them from primary and secondary school teachers, who merely distribute knowledge. Beginning with this premise of the privilege of professors over "mere" teachers, the classroom will be seen as a problematic space that, in itself, cannot contribute to the construction of knowledge.

Peskowitz discusses her various attempts to bridge the gap between research and teaching. She notes that her students are analytical and imaginative when they discuss things that matter to them, such as romantic situations or sports, but they do not carry those same skills into their academic studies. She can try to enable them to personalize their studies, she acknowledges, yet how can she ask something of them that she does not require of herself? Her attempt to make learning a reciprocal process led to a climax when some students, after reading an assigned text about feminist Passovers, wanted to organize a Seder as a class project. She offered her apartment for the ritual, further blurring classroom boundaries. The students, including Jews and Christians, created the ritual and wrote about it for their final project. During the course of the evening, stories were shared, and Peskowitz talked about herself. Such self-disclosures, she argues, are more than appropriate. "They must ask themselves whether I am the kind of human being they want to be influenced by."[17] Learning and trusting— which includes learning whom not to trust—go hand in hand.

135

Assessment of the teacher is precisely one of the skills we need to be teaching our students.

Peskowitz suggests that her classroom Passover was a transgression not only of Enlightenment models of pedagogy but also of the dominance of Christianity in religious studies. She argues that the ideal of universal reason as it is practiced in religious studies really reflects the specific religious tradition of Christianity. The scholarly subdisciplines of religion (Bible, religious history, ethics, and theology) and even the attempt to define an essence to the various phenomena of religion are inherited from Christian theology. She thus protests our well-meaning culture "in which a white Protestant ethos is still hegemonic and Christianity's others cannot feel welcome, despite additions and changes to curriculum, if the ethos does not change."[18] Personalizing the classroom means, to her, de-Christianizing it.

Her political reading of the contemporary academy can be challenged. It is interesting, for example, that it would be much easier to hold a Passover Seder as part of a course than any Christian ritual. I know religion professors who require their students to practice meditation when studying Buddhism but who would be alarmed at the idea of inviting students to perform any Christian practice of meditation or prayer. Somehow, Christianity represents a danger to academic freedom, while the beliefs and practices of other religions are exciting and liberating. The problem is that academics wrongly perceive Christianity to be dominant within the academy because they read about its alleged dominance in the wider culture. In reality, Christianity is struggling to maintain its standing in American culture, and more to the point, Christian voices often are muffled among teachers and students alike. If Peskowitz conveys to students her distrust of Christian hegemony—which she surely does, given her attempts to bring her views into the classroom—how can she encourage her Christian students to develop their voices, rooted in their traditions?

What Peskowitz is trying to uncover is not the dominance of Christian theology but a pervasive attitude of cultural liberalism that is as hard on traditional Christian faith as it is on other forms of religious expression. For lack of a better label, we can call this attitude a kind of liberal Protestantism, although its manifestations no longer are directly connected to the denominations that gave it birth. Ironically, much of the anticonfessional rhetoric in religious studies reflects the values and taste of mainstream Protestantism. Unlike sectarian Protestant movements and unlike Roman Catholicism, mainline Protestantism always has been rather cool toward the importance of acts of confession.[19] Ecumenical Protestants were allowed to establish the civil religion of North America in the twentieth century only because they treated religion as a rational enterprise stripped of overtly ritualized and evangelical elements. As a result, as John Murray Cuddihy argues, civil religion today is a religion of civility: don't ask about religion and don't tell.[20] It is okay to go to church, but don't talk about it too much. In religion departments, many of which are still dominated by faculty with some (perhaps tenuous) connection to the mainline Protestant churches, professors perform religion through the tradition of exegesis, intellectually reflecting on texts. But professors do not tell others how they became religious or what religion means to them.

Peskowitz thus exaggerates the Protestant hegemony over America's civil religion, which has taken liberal Protestant assumptions in New Age directions. Indeed, religious studies programs provide the theoretical foundation for this civil religion by treating all religions as diverse manifestations of one common experience. What I am suggesting is that we do not need more civil religion in the classroom, but more space for the articulation of distinctive religious voices, since all religions—even the most inclusive and civil religion—is particular, emerging from specific traditions and communities rather than reflecting universal features of human nature.

One possible outcome of letting religious voices into our classrooms is illustrated in a splendid essay by Kimberley C. Patton, " 'Stumbling Along between the Immensities': Reflections on Teaching in the Study of Religion." Patton rejects many of the typical characterizations of religious studies and argues instead that the study of religion is a religious enterprise. Students try to synthesize what they discover about the religious traditions we teach them, and we have an obligation to help

137

them in that quest. Indeed, the teacher of religion is a role model for students in their pilgrimage into religious studies. She quotes a lament from biblical and Jewish studies scholar Jon Levenson: "It is sad that within universities, the principal echo of the venerable, multicultural institution of mastership and discipleship should today be heard in the context of race and gender, as if these things determined our deepest identities and only minorities and women had need for the ancient pedagogical relationship."[21] When it comes to politics, teachers are eager to serve as mentors and guides to students, but such relationships are thought to be improper in the study of religion.

Pilgrimage is a powerful metaphor for the study of religion. I wonder, however, if the price of allowing religion into public education is the assumption that all religions must receive equal appreciation. If we allow confessions into the classroom, are we forced to become comparativists, seeking the good in every religion and finding common threads that tie all religions together? Where does pilgrimage end and tourism begin? In some religious studies programs, every course has to discuss at least two traditions, so no religious tradition is examined on its own terms. Does not such an approach risk reducing the study of religion to an aesthetic of appreciation, in which every religion is seen as a beautiful manifestation of broader themes and patterns? The problem is that this leaves little room for evaluation and judgment. It would help matters if comparativists admitted that they function as theologians by making constructive judgments about religious norms. Indeed, theologians are increasingly relying on comparativists, because Christianity is such a plural phenomenon. As a result, theology and comparative religious studies are growing closer and closer together.

Where comparativists and theologians meet is in the need to take a more personal or confessional approach to the study of religion. We need to let students tell us their stories and thereby teach us about how they learn. And we need to tell them our stories so they can learn to evaluate what they are being taught. We need to confess that we do not have all the answers and that the answers we do have emerge from our own commitments. Religion departments often are designed to hide religious passion and faith by introducing students to an exasperating multiplicity of traditions and methodologies. The study of religion is patched together from parts of other disciplines and seems to lack a center, like Frankenstein's monster without a soul. Students are pressured to cover so much ground that there is little time left for personal reflection and spiritual growth. Comparativists can remind theologians that such diversity simply is a fact of life in today's shrinking world. Theologians can remind comparativists that comparing religions is a spiritual practice that begins with personal belief and ends with making and defending truth claims. Even the most agile comparativist stands in a particular tradition, supported by the insights of others. To confess any religious belief is to be a part of a body of believers with whom one confesses, just as to confess is to say what one wants to become, as much as what one already is.

The Return of Confession to Theology

The theological dimension of confession cannot be directly translated into the classroom experience, of course, because the classroom is not the church. The goal of teaching is to create a body not of believers but of knowers, but knowing can include knowing what one believes. It is appropriate not only to integrate personal confession into the classroom through the use of journals and storytelling but also to make confession a more explicit aspect of the study of religion. Students should be encouraged not just to tell their stories but to tell those stories to each other, thus holding each other accountable to the class and its texts. In other words, students (and teachers) should be encouraged to think about the ways in which personal confessions are rooted in tradition and shaped by communities to the point of not being all that personal. Confessions can serve to bridge the gap between the production and the distribution of knowledge that Peskowitz worries about by demonstrating the personal character of all knowledge as well as the public character of personal opinions.

Indeed, confessions are so pedagogically useful because the performative acts of students cannot escape the history of religious beliefs and practices. Every confession is as much about the critical questions of religion as it is about the penitent's personal history. If students can recreate rituals in the classroom, they can create their own confessional statements. Especially in a course on theology, they could read, discuss, and compare a sample of ecclesial confessions and talk about the role of confession in our culture. Then they could try to write a confessional statement for the entire class as a group project. Wouldn't that be an impossible task? How could all of the students agree on everything? What issues would be raised?

Of course, the classroom is not the church, so the confession would not be written in the context of an ecclesial community and tradition, but that would be the point that needs to be made. Religious confessions can be made only from a specific context, in the course of worship, and to have students struggle with the act of public confession and the extent to which they can agree about ultimate values would be a good way of teaching them what a confession is and what it is not. The traditional task of a confession of faith is to publicize the personal in a communal context. To what extent that is possible today in public education would be a topic worth thinking about in any religion class.

A Note on Kierkegaard

Søren Kierkegaard represents for many people the zenith of nineteenth century subjectivism. The trends that Foucault outlines come to culmination in his work. He defines the truth as subjective. He would agree with Nietzsche's confession about the autobiographical nature of all thought: "It has gradually become clear to me what every great philosophy has hitherto been: a confession on the part of its author."[22] Indeed, even Kierkegaard's most theological works can be read as commentaries on and distortions of his autobiography, especially regarding his broken engagement with Regina.

Nevertheless, Kierkegaard did not have a romantic notion of individuality. As theologian David Wisdo points out, he rejected recollection as a romantic mode of self-understanding. Memory is not the sufficient stuff of selfhood. The person who artfully tries to craft episodic moments that transcend time in an effort to ensure the consistency of the self risks losing the self's identity altogether. Such aesthetic moments do not carry temporal weight, so to speak, with the result that the self is disconnected from the very activities that tie people to the world and each other. Kierkegaard's entire critique of the aesthetic realm, then, is a rejection of inwardness as a criterion of authenticity. As Wisdo makes clear, for Kierkegaard, subjectivity is only possible if self-understanding is possible, and that is only possible for the self that stands before God. To confess before God is not to tell God something that God does not know, because God is omniscient. Instead, it is to acknowledge that God already knows us, a knowledge that enables us to know ourselves. As Kierkegaard writes, "To come to oneself is self-knowledge, *and before God.* For if self-knowledge does not lead to knowing oneself before God, then indeed there is something in what the merely human view says, that it leads to a certain emptiness which produces dizziness. Only by being before God can a man entirely come to himself in the transparency of sobriety."[23] To confess, then, is to repent by acknowledging God's knowledge of us. God has chosen us; we do not choose ourselves. Kierkegaard's existentialism thus ends up with a traditional theological argument about prevenient grace.

Kierkegaard does not commit the error of exalting the self in its subjectivity. The truth does not come from within. It comes from our transparency to the divine that is outside us. This is made clear in the *Philosophical Fragments,* that great book about teaching.[24] Kierkegaard criticizes the Socratic theory of learning because it assumes the student already knows the truth and merely must be reminded of it. The teacher does not do anything other than set the stage and get out of the way. The Socratic teacher is the midwife, who helps the student give birth to her true self. Truth is constant, universal, and inward, easily appropriated if the student is given the opportunity.

In Christian pedagogy, Kierkegaard argues, the learner is in untruth. The teacher again gives nothing, but this nothing is not the occasion of appropriation. It is the confrontation of an

141

impossibility. The teacher prompts an acknowledgment of the absence, not the fullness, of truth. Religious truth, writes Kierkegaard, is external to the personal, something that is disrupting and transforming, rather than appealing and confirming. What the student needs is the condition for understanding the truth, something that can't be generated by the student. This condition can be given, Kierkegaard insists, not by just any kind of teacher but by a god, or a savior, someone who saves the student from a state of impossibility (or sin).

Christian teachers, then, need to remember that we cannot give the students what they ultimately need. Kierkegaard makes it clear that the truth is up to God. The theologian as teacher should not try to be a savior figure, just as students should not be disciples, no matter how tempting that can be. To save the student from sin, the teacher would have to presume to have the authority to replace the student's knowledge with something else. This would be a deception—the opposite deception of the Socratic teacher, who presumes that the student already knows the truth, but a deception nonetheless. What the Christian teacher can do is to make room for a kind of truth that is neither the teacher's nor the student's. Kierkegaard defines the search for truth as the paradox of wanting "to discover something that thought itself cannot think."[25] This is what the theo-pedagogical classroom does. It tries to say what cannot be said, in the hope that a voice that does not speak can be heard. The theologian must listen to what is not said and *how* it is not said and speak in such a way that what is said does not pretend to say it all.

True confession, then, cannot be reduced to an act of mutual sharing, no matter how positively that act is portrayed. Another being must be present when students share their most personal responses to religion. Confession creates authentic selfhood when it is done with others and before God. Otherwise, we are left with a postmodern fiction that begins anywhere and leads nowhere. The most significant task for the Christian teacher, then, is to make room in the classroom for God, to remind students that God is more than an object of discussion, and to prepare students to think about themselves in terms of their relationship to their creator and sustainer. Teachers need to be ready to ask their students: What understanding of God does that opinion or argument entail? How would you make that point in a religious community? Would you say that differently if you were putting it in the form of a prayer? And teachers can be ready to ask themselves to what ends they are teaching and to whom they ultimately are talking when they walk into a classroom with the privilege of reflecting on religion. How teachers place classroom confessions in a context that attends to God as the ultimate audience is the most important challenge for Christian pedagogy. The failure of teachers to take up that challenge—indeed, the inevitable failure of every classroom, no matter how pious, to be pleasing to God—should be the point at which the personal confessions of teachers begin.

FIVE

RELIGION AMID THE RUINS OF THE POSTMODERN UNIVERSITY

Higher education ain't what it used to be. Whether that is cause for concern or celebration is a matter of mixed opinion, but there is a consensus that the standards and values that provided the foundation for higher education in the past have run their course. The idea of fixed rules for everything from grammar to the canon is being called into question, and the consequences are ambiguous. The source of pedagogical authority is no longer certain, which means students can get away with more than they used to, but there is also an opening for new voices in public education. These voices have their own rules and codes. When the norms of rationality are up for grabs, the results can lead to a healthy and creative multiculturalism or a repressive and restrictive political correctness. In the midst of the new freedom to challenge educational standards and traditions, there is a search for new forms of authority to manage the ensuing chaos.

Fundamentally, the standards of objectivity I criticized in the previous chapters have been called into question by postmodernism, a loosely organized philosophical movement that means nearly anything to anybody. Can postmodernism, by attacking traditional notions of objectivity and neutrality in the classroom, lead to a reconsideration of faith-based learning? Could it even lead to a renaissance of religion in general, giving people of faith more confidence in themselves?

Postmodernism can be interpreted in two ways. First, it can be seen as a superliberalism, attacking metanarratives and metaphysics alike to maximize personal freedom. In this case, postmodernism actually brings nothing new to the table, and its emphasis on individualism and subjectivity merely reinforces trends that sequester religion in the realm of private decision and personal fantasy. Second, postmodernism can be seen as a new romanticism, a rebellion against modernism that parallels the Romantic critique of the Enlightenment. As a form of romanticism, postmodernism permits the return of premodern traditions, but it welcomes them only ironically, as ways of life that cannot be inhabited fully in the modern world. Thus, even when postmodernism is at its best with regard to religious traditions, it transforms them into eclectic and consumeristic lifestyle decisions. In sum, the fashionable reign of deconstructive difference, where everything that is not mainstream is prized and privileged, can lead to either ethical nihilism or a frenzy of New Age religious inventiveness, but not an embrace of religious traditions for their own sake.

Some theologians have connected their wagon to the long train of postmodern proposals in the hope that, in the midst of the confusion, they might be overlooked and thus allowed to stay for the ride. After all, postmodernism rejects the totalizing forms of modernism (like Marxism and Freudianism) that were so critical of religious faith, and, as the old saying goes, an enemy of my enemy is my friend, or at least my ally. If deconstruction, the most successful and visible philosophical representative of postmodernism, rejects modernism, then perhaps there is an opportunity to retrieve premodern traditions that did not survive the onslaught of hegemonic definitions of rationality. The problem is whether this strange marriage of deconstruction and theology will produce anything that is viable for the life of faith. When theology attempts the infiltration of deconstruction to use it to make room for Christianity in secular education, theology likely will end up being mastered by the discourse it sought to employ.

But there is another side of the story. Postmodernity has put pressure on the academy to acknowledge that there is no longer a center to higher education. Without metanarratives, the point of a liberal arts education no longer is clear. The old rules, then, about the purpose of education—what should be taught and how we should teach ethical and religious values—are up for grabs. It might be true that deconstruction is good for the practice of theology only in small doses, but it also might be true that the influence of deconstruction on the academy as a whole might open up new spaces for the practice of theology within the classroom. Trying to be religious while using the language of deconstruction stretches faith in unrecognizable directions. But recognizing that the academy has entered a postmodern era might give new life to the role of Christian theology on America's campuses.

The Crisis of the Academy's Perpetual Crisis

That the university is in a state of crisis has become one of the defining features of North American culture. The lack of a consensus about educational issues is the driving force behind many academic debates. We academicians profit from such anxiety by keeping a conversation going about who we are and what we do, but it is not clear how long these self-centered conversations can hold the rest of the world's attention—or even our own. The university accounts for an incredible expenditure of energy, but for what purpose? Where is this inward turn of hypercritical rationality going?

As we approached the end of one millennium and the beginning of another, talk about apocalypses and eschatons became more common, so it should not have been surprising that there was talk about the end of the university. In *The University in Ruins,* the most important postmodernist reading of academic culture, Bill Readings argues, persuasively and brilliantly, that

147

the crisis of the university has become habitual and permanent.[1] The reason is that there is no national culture to which it corresponds and, more important, no ideal student who can be the beneficiary of this culture. The university has had its day, and now we live among the ruins of books, ideas, and arguments that no longer seem to make a difference outside of the halls of the academe.

Those who teach religion are used to thinking about ruins, and those who are religious are used to living in what is left of religious traditions after the shattering impact of their collision with the secular modernity of the Enlightenment. If the university is entering a kind of twilight, with the dimming of the Enlightenment and the passing of anything like a high culture, where does religion fit into this gloomy picture? The house of learning has fragmented and is in decay, haunted, perhaps, by even more ancient ruins and memories. The university, built over the ruins of religion as the secular pursuit of knowledge replaced the centrality of the church and theology in Western culture, is breaking apart, and the question is if there is now a glimpse of some previous foundation on which to rebuild. Or are there just many different ruins through which we have become adept at wandering, a purposeless meandering that we now call education?

The Enlightenment philosophers boldly proposed replacing the church with the schoolroom, but the results have not been as successful as they hoped. Indeed, Gabriel Moran has suggested that education is in trouble precisely due to the decline of religious authority. "When modern European writers rebelled against Christianity, they also fled from teaching. Eighteenth- and nineteenth-century writers did not eliminate the term, but they narrowed its meaning to a rationalistic core devoid of religious meaning. Teaching remained a part of the necessary burden that a child carried until the child could overthrow the oppressive power of adults."[2] If education is only about maximizing student freedom, then there is little room for authority in the classroom. Only if our society can reevaluate the ways in which education, like religion, is about entering into submissive relationships that liberate rather than oppress can teaching regain its central role in Western society.

148

Readings, who died in the crash of American Eagle flight 4184 in 1994 while he was making the final revisions of his book, provided more than just another jeremiad about the declining fortunes of liberal education. Indeed, if there is a weakness in his book, it is his narrowly materialistic explanation for the disconnection of the university from its traditional cultural mission. Readings' entire project rests on the popular argument that the nation-state is no longer the primary site for the reproduction of capital. Transnational corporations transgress national boundaries with impunity, and where capital goes, Readings insists, culture follows. Now that the Cold War has been won, the university is not needed to defend our nation's honor by propagating its cultural interests. If economic power is not confined by national ideologies, culture is not needed to legitimate and defend national boundaries.

It is a common observation that we live in a world where corporations feel no geographical obligations because capital crosses borders so easily. The nation-state used to need workers who embodied the distinctive characteristics of that nation as a way of justifying national restrictions on the mobility of capital. Now that the nation is a bureaucracy in the service of transnational capital, such representative citizens no longer are needed. The university also, of course, produced rebels who heroically protested national culture, but that is not needed, either, because there is no ideological national culture to resist. Conservatives have won the culture wars in the sense that the logic of the market is our controlling metaphor, but that market is global and is challenging the very mission that once comprised higher education.

Consequently, culture, like capital, is free to go global; consumerism and culture converge. Soda pop, basketball, and movies are the international currency of cultural exchange. The university, stripped of any ideological function, is pressured to treat students like customers, sell them marketable skills and evaluate constantly their satisfaction with the institution's performance. Universities become brand names supplying the same product differentiated by sports teams, star professors, and the availability of overseas programs. How students are expected to be loyal postgraduate contributors to such institutions is a nagging question.

Indeed, the real problem is that education no longer is an adventure, because the progress of the student no longer tells a coherent story. The university no longer incarnates an idea of what it means to be a subject within a specific time and place, which means students no longer go to college to find themselves. What student can imagine being a hero, journeying from ignorance to knowledge, perhaps even achieving the bliss of becoming a professor? In our posthistorical moment, Readings argues, culture no longer has redemptive power when everything is culture (there remains no distinction between high and low culture, a collapse exploited and magnified by cultural studies).

Rather than telling the grand narrative and fulfilling the national mission of culture, today's university speaks the empty rhetoric of excellence. In the ancient world, the idea of excellence was underwritten by a particular narrative about the virtues, which was appropriated by Christianity. Today, however, excellence is the language of bureaucratic and autonomous institutions that promote productivity but maintain no external standard of value. Excellence is the perfect term for an organization void of referential capacity because it does not mean anything. A lecture, a ball game, a play, dorm food, a freshly watered lawn, all can be excellent in their own way without raising awkward questions about how they relate to each other or what they mean. Excellence almost has come to mean, "Yes, well and good, but so what?" In other words, in the contentious climate of the university, the term is useful precisely because it is meaningless. There is no irony in the fact that the pressures of assessment are increasing just as the university is less and less certain about what purpose it serves. Indeed, the university is so anxious to prove itself (to compete for consumers) that more and more of its energies are going to administration, not teaching or research. If Readings' book does nothing else, we can only hope it will make administrators have second thoughts about the pervasive use of this term in evaluating academic programs.

Readings traces the origin of the modern university to Immanuel Kant, who organized learning on the basis of a single idea, the concept of reason, the overseeing of which is the responsibility of philosophy.[3] For Kant, theology is a practical discipline that has nothing to do with the pursuit of truth; like medicine and law, it should train a specific profession, rather than contribute to the basic questions that hold the university together. The businessmen (as Kant calls them) of these three faculties deal with basic needs: how to be happy after death, how to enjoy physical health, and how to protect one's posses-sions. Unfortunately, Kant argues, the drive to meet needs is not a sufficient basis for the intellectual pursuit of truth. Phi-losophy, unlike theology, medicine, and law, does not meet indi-vidual needs but instead pursues universal ideals.

The German idealists expanded Kant's narrow conception of reason by substituting culture for it. As a result, Readings argues, "reason must replace belief; the state must replace the church."[4] Once the university becomes responsible for national culture, it competes with religion to articulate and legitimate a nation's deepest values.

British and American universities replaced philosophy with literature instead of a general sense of culture, because national literature was thought to be the primary expression of national identity, reconciling the ethnic with the demands of reflection and rationality. The study of literature produced "the cultivated gentleman whose knowledge has no mechanical or direct util-ity."[5] English departments became the centerpieces of the lib-eral arts. In North America, the canon serves the function of a tradition of national literature, because the canon represents, allegedly, a free and collective decision, an expression of the will of the people. Therefore, it best formulates the character of a people who are not bound together by an ethnic identity. American culture, then, is structured more by a promise than by content, and the open and rational conversations of the uni-versity are meant to model how that promise can be kept.

The medieval university could make a constructive distinc-tion between the active and contemplative life, because people then believed in something worth contemplating. Today, the contemplative is equated with frivolous leisure and play, so the university must be efficient and productive to be taken seri-

151

ously. Indeed, the university produces a student who is capable and adaptable but not bound by any cultural content that would impede that proficiency. Because the political realm no longer controls the economic, and nations manage capital without imposing an ideology on economic affairs, nations need not cultured individuals but adept managers who have no commitments to specific traditions. Instead, these managers incarnate the skills of flexibility and openness to change. The university must produce someone who can process information quickly and make decisions unhindered by local loyalties or sentimental preferences.

Indeed, the university can privilege the virtues of diversity and tolerance precisely because specific religious and philosophical traditions have lost their ideological power. Cultural meaning resides in the economic sphere, not the political, so consumer choice becomes the highest expression of human freedom and creativity, while changes in style and fashion are the nearest things we have to revolution and conversion. (Can you imagine an Augustinian journey today, on which someone's life is changed totally on the basis of something that was *read?*) In a world where all traditions are evaluated by the pragmatic criterion of consumer satisfaction, diversity becomes important precisely because it is meaningless. Consumerism is transnational because consumers seek satisfaction on the basis of a cost-benefit analysis that inevitably commodifies even the most ancient and durable traditions.

Consumerism affects learning at all levels, but perhaps most disastrously in the act of reading. Philosopher of religion Paul Griffiths argues that religious traditions perpetuate themselves through a particular practice of reading.[6] Religious reading presupposes authority, hierarchy, community, and tradition, concepts that are all in trouble in public education today. Religious reading is a skill that involves recitation and memorization, and it can be developed only in communities that support a moral relationship with sacred texts. University-trained scholars use books to promote their arguments and to establish their cleverness and sophistication. Professors use books as springboards for creative speculations, writing essays that encapsulate their ideas while merely mentioning or footnoting the work of others. Religious readers, on the contrary, submit themselves to texts that they know are greater than anything they can write in response. Thus, commentary—the careful attention to what sacred texts say—is the most common genre of religious reading.

Griffiths laments that religious reading is all but extinct today, in part because religious institutions no longer treat religion as a skill that requires years of practice. He holds out some hope that universities, with their emphasis on the dedication required for close reading and the passion needed for a commitment to ancient texts, can make room for reading practices once prized by nearly every culture. Can the universities turn the corner on consumerism by offering students something worth sacrificing for, a way of life that requires daily discipline and moral submission? We ask students to pay for their education, but to what do we ask them to pay attention?

The Obligation of Pedagogy

Readings' solutions to the problems he raises actually are ways of prolonging the crisis by permanently holding certain questions to be unanswerable. He argues that the university cannot be an ideal community by modeling the norms of procedural rationality because too many groups are vying for communication and are too suspicious of each other to agree to any ground rules for communicating. Instead, the university should be a place where people come together to question whether it is even possible to come together in the first place.

Most important, he argues that teaching and learning should be structured around the question of obligation rather than the truth.[7] Teaching, for Readings, is an ethical practice in which paying attention to the other constitutes the recognition that consensus is out of the question. The goal of the classroom is not to produce autonomous, independent students but to practice the rhetorical negotiations of complex situations in which obligations are never mastered and debts are never paid. "Doing justice to Thought, listening to our interlocutors, means trying to hear that which cannot be said but that which tries to make itself heard."[8] Globalization makes the Enlightenment goal of creating subjects who bring culture to a self-conscious transparency impossible, so we are faced with an intellectual task that cannot be integrated by a single idea or purpose. Thinking cannot pull together the scattered loose ends of our culture, but it can try to do justice to this cultural complexity by criticizing our need to create unity in the first place.

Readings seems to be saying that otherness has ruined the universality of culture, but dwelling among others is what gives rise to a thinking capable of making those ruins bearable. Of course, there is always the temptation, which he warns us against, to romanticize the ruins of the university. The romantics read ruins as emblematic of a lost organicism, and they were content to dwell nostalgically among the ruins. For Readings, ruins are neither aesthetically pleasing nor capable of being rebuilt. The ruins of national cultures leave us with fragmented traditions that make us pause and think, and time spent at the university is the time of that thinking, a time that is unproductive and inefficient. Thinking is a wasteful activity that in itself should threaten the strictures of capitalism. In the place of its lost cultural mission, the university has a social responsibility to carry out the patient task of slow and costly reflection that capitalism cannot afford.

The Return of Religion

Religion, too, is a means of organizing time that does not appear to contribute directly to economic growth. Readings raises the question of what new space is opened up for religion in a university that abandons its redemptive claims for culture and reason. Perhaps a university that no longer competes with religion to save souls can allow religion again to be the primary signifier of transcendent meaning. Yet it is wishful thinking to suggest that religion can exist in the university without serving some function or providing some benefit.

Where does religion fit in during the postcultural age of the university? Readings does not deal directly with the role of reli-

154

gion in universities, but his analysis seems especially useful for thinking about religious studies. Religious studies departments that emphasize non-Western religions and a scientific, neutral pedagogy doubtlessly are preparing students for a world in which workers frequently change jobs and corporations rapidly reinvent themselves to meet the fickle demands of customers. Given these social conditions, the idea of being passionately loyal to an abiding tradition must appear to be increasingly sentimental and quaint. The question is whether universities should be supporting the social dynamics initiated by transnational capital or fighting against them.

Religious studies departments that celebrate the history of any and all religions, to the point of diminishing the significance of the monotheistic faiths for Western history, can be accused of producing subjects who are mobile, disconnected, and free of restraining traditions—the perfect subjects for a global, transnational consumeristic culture. Surely teaching students that all religions are equal and interchangeable and that, because of this, individuals may migrate from one religion to another only plays into the hands of a global capitalist mentality that is afraid of local commitments and particular attachments, values and traditions that are not exportable and expendable. Is religion nothing more than the capital of the spirit, a means of making a profit from the circulation of hopes and longings that defy traditional boundaries—hopes that are traded by target groups who most express those particular needs? Readings' thesis can only leave the reader suspicious of the ways in which religious studies departments have been used to spread the good news of multiculturalism.

The alternative, however, cannot be a simple revival of religion courses as lessons in traditional values and civic virtues. Religious studies departments that want to privilege Western religion as the source of everything that makes Western history unique can be accused, in Readings' terms, of mourning for a lost connection between education and national purpose. It is no longer clear that what is good for the church is good for America. Recovering religious tradition does not guarantee national unity. Such acts of recovery, in fact, might fragment

155

our national character as Christians learn to distinguish between biblical revelation and national self-interest. Furthermore, the move to reconstruct a lost cultural authenticity will be compromised by those who want to use religion to battle against liberal political ideas. This will hardly do justice to religious faith, which transcends and critiques both the left and the right.

To the extent that departments of religious studies (even the title reflects the values of transnationalism) hover between these two models, it is hard to know which is better or if both are equally disappointing. Certainly we cannot pretend that Christianity is the national religion of America, but is the alternative a kind of diversity that treats all religions like corporations that meet spiritual needs in a competitive religious market?

Readings insists that teaching is an ethical activity that cultivates an attentiveness to otherness. If a liberal arts education no longer can represent some ideological core, the alternative is not to teach contentless skills. Instead, we need to motivate students to create for themselves intellectual identities that allow them to salvage from our fragmented world a sense of place and time. The university no longer is a world in itself, the place where students can feel at home, so we need to pay more attention to the worlds the students bring to our classes. They are just passing through our institutional homes, and the best we can do is to make sure that they do not leave behind everything they brought with them. Indeed, it is too easy to see our students' religious traditions as weighty baggage, a load we are trying to lighten through our intellectual labor. We should not try to ruin their traditions when we have none of our own.

An ethical pedagogy that lets the students teach the teachers would go a long way toward leading students further into and not out of the richness and power of their own religious traditions. It is too easy to be enamored by every variety of otherness except the very otherness of the students sitting in front of us. Ironically, it is imperative in a global age to keep in mind that the other closest to us, so close that we may not even see it, frequently is the most provocative and challenging other of all. If we truly want to promote diversity, a renewed emphasis on the ways in which religious traditions resist modernity would give our students an opportunity to retrieve something from the ruins of the university. At their best, religious traditions embody a memory without nostalgia that allows the past to function in critical and utopian ways in the present. Studying religion amid the ruins should teach us that the first lesson of learning is to discover what we have forgotten, along with the reason our culture is so invested in teaching us to forget.

Religions have resisted not only one-dimensional definitions of rationality but also pressures to flatten the cultural landscape, so studying religion can be a way to question the expansive void of consumerism. Religions, of course, also have been shaped by economic and political forces, which makes religions more, not less, important in the posthistorical academy. Recognizing that the traditions of both reason and religion are in ruin should keep us from idealizing the ruins of other cultures (as if ruins are always elsewhere, an appealing deception in a culture priding itself on a fast pace of change that is constantly demolishing the outdated). This recognition also should keep us from thinking that we can manage our own ruins, as if we can turn our technological prowess toward rehabilitating and restoring our past, making it suitable for tourism, if not permanent inhabitation. We need to be constantly reminded that the university cannot redeem the ruins of religion, as if religion itself were in need of redemption. The point of the study of religion is to allow students to find within their own traditions a place that allows them to scrutinize and withstand the pervasive thoughtlessness of modern culture. Judaism and Christianity, especially, have been so close and yet so alien to the Western project of fusing culture and reason that they should serve as particularly striking test cases for any potential limits to consumeristic homogeneity.

Moreover, every religion tries to reveal a final kind of otherness that is the horizon of human origins and hopes and is variously named the divine, salvation, the ultimate, or simply God. To think about religion without allowing the topic of God to be raised—that is, to think about religion without theology—is

157

certainly to limit the questions religion asks us. Theologians are people who have multiple and inconsistent commitments, thus serving as ideal examples of how diversity must be confronted in the future. Theologians remind their colleagues that we all speak from a particular place and that these particular places need to be cared for and maintained if they are not to be lost in the cultural miasma of basketball shoes, fast food, and talk shows. Theology is one of the ruins of the university, a crumbling wall that has been allowed to stand as a monument to a forgotten past, but even the most debilitated structures can provide shelter to those who are desperate and can secure no other home. Theology is the interminable, patient response to the question of God, a protracted conversation that tries to say what it might mean to listen to something that scarcely can be heard anymore. To be questioned by religion is a call to be quiet enough to hear if the ruins still speak.

The End of Politicized Education

If the essence of the academy is its capacity to call on its citizens to diverge from their set ways of thinking, this mandate can be made only on the basis of an understanding of something greater, something "other" than that which goes without thinking. If the academy loses this capacity to challenge thoughtlessness from a higher vantage point, it forfeits the right to make any demands at all. The university then becomes a multiversity, which might be acceptable for large, impersonal, incoherent state institutions but would be disastrous for liberal arts colleges. Questions of transcendence and ultimacy must be staked if the academy is to do more than merely initiate students into specialized fields of knowledge, with their attendant jargons and methodologies.

The great medieval universities were held together by theology, the early modern universities by philosophy, and the modern universities by the natural sciences, but the postmodern universities are not held together by anything. Conversely, with its limited imagination, the postmodern period looks to politics—under the guise of that catch-all word "diversity"—to provide the unifying vision for all cultural and educational endeavors. Readings, then, underestimates the need of many educators to rely on a political ideology to give shape to their profession. However, Readings is right that in our consumeristic age, no political vision can provide the unity that the academy seeks. Without some common understanding of our history, without a deeper vocabulary of values, and without shared methodological assumptions, the political can only fragment, not unite. In this day and age, the attempt to frame all intellectual debate in political terms is a manifestation of the narcissistic desire not to think, or to think only in one's own terms.

Under the pressures of a bureaucracy that seeks to manage rather than challenge student needs, the politics of diversity quickly degenerates into a pernicious relativism that subordinates the question of truth to the rhetorical strategies of special interest groups. Nobody believes in Kant's pure reason alone, only in a pragmatic psychology that fits academic pursuits with social and individual functions. The university supplies various commodities for student self-fulfillment and gratification, and the center no longer holds. Everything is available, but without a plan, a common goal, diversity threatens to render everything indifferent. Among the students one can sense an emerging dissatisfaction with the precarious epoch of the politics of diversity. The other epochs—theology, philosophy, and science—lasted for centuries, but we live in a culture in which change for its own sake is becoming a primary goal, and rapidity is the way in which we perceive time.

One response is to go backward, to rebel against the politicizing of secular education by trying to retrieve one of the paradigms that has been left behind. This seems impossible and undesirable. Religion in the academy is under increasing attack by the accelerating secularization to which the academy, in reaction against the growth of religion in the wider culture, tragically seeks to align itself. To the extent that secularization is taken as the norm, the academy will continue to lose significance and relevance to the wider public. Philosophy no longer is the search for the metaphysical worldview that provides the foundation for all cultural activities. In its analytical mode, it treats reason as an instrumental tool, and thus is subordinated to science. In its continental mode, it critiques all metaphysical systems and so displaces the desire for foundations altogether. The sciences seem to be losing prestige in our culture. Scientific language cannot provide a universal basis for the search for knowledge because it is so highly specialized. Moreover, the interface of science with the wider culture in technology is the site of increasing ambiguity and trouble.

This leaves us with the predictable battle lines of politics, but the deep divisions within the political sphere mean that it cannot provide a common basis for education. The other option, then, is to go forward, but the future is always unknown. If the political realm is not to be merely a power struggle, pitting, for example, professors against students, liberals against conservatives, religionists against secularists, the political battlefield must be transcended, but by what? Perhaps now we can begin to listen to Heidegger's final cry, that only a god can save us. Even so, there are too many gods on the horizon, and many of them are menacing. Whose god, what god? The only way out, I would suggest, is not to transcend the politics of diversity but to accelerate and intensify it—to accept anarchy, the lack of an ultimate, unifying principle (arché), and to permit that embrace of confusion to give birth to new modes of thought, new forms of freedom and conversation. Anarchy is, after all, antitheitical to all things political. The purpose of the liberal arts education would be not to encapsulate a set of vague and inclusive values but to enable students to create their own intellectual identities. Perhaps by having the tools to ask questions the academy no longer knows how to answer, the students can begin the task of rebuilding the ruins of modern education.

THE MYSTERY OF THE DISAPPEARING CHAPLAIN

A CASE STUDY OF WABASH COLLEGE

When religion teachers think about their teaching, they need to look not only inward to find their truest religious selves but outward at their institutional contexts. Frequently, when I talk about teaching to friends who teach at other universities, we end up talking most about our institutions, their ethos, expectations, and history. So much of a teacher's classroom experience is determined by the institutional setting that it is important to consider the entire college as a kind of classroom, a large audience we seldom address as a whole but that nonetheless overhears what we are saying to our students. The institution affects one's teaching in ways that are pervasive but frequently hard to discern.

My institution, Wabash College, can provide a test case for many of the topics I have been discussing. It is a small, private, all-male, liberal arts college. We celebrate the Presbyterian ministers who dreamed of a college on the frontier, and the chapel is our most prominent building, looming over the mall as our most vivid symbol and appearing in all of our publications. Yet we are proudly independent of church and governmental intrusions. Wabash has deep religious roots but is independent of any official affiliation with a religious denomination. Historically, it has tried to meet the religious needs of its students without supporting or being supported by any particular Christian church. Thus, it occupies a rare position in North American higher education.

Can a college that is independent of church and state maintain some kind of religious heritage? There are no constitutional pressures at Wabash to make us conform to the practices of state institutions, with their secular presuppositions, but there is also no official church connection to remind us of our obligations to our religious roots. There is, however, a lot of freedom to define the college as a place where religion is more than just accepted, even if not exactly promoted. While many church-related colleges follow a pattern of becoming increasingly removed from their religious roots, and many secular universities are struggling to make more room for religious viewpoints on their campuses, Wabash College could serve as a good test case for giving religious teachers and students the freedom to express themselves and integrate their theological convictions into their academic work.

Respecting religion while remaining independent has been a tricky balancing act for the college. How can a school acknowledge the power of faith without becoming unnecessarily entangled in religious debates or favoring one form of faith over another? The story of religion at Wabash is not simply one of increasing secularization, although there is a lot of that. It is the story of how religious faith changes its institutional shape in response to national pressures for less connection between the churches and higher education. And it is a story of a religion department that has kept the focus of the study of religion on the question of what it means to be religious.

A Religious History?

Follow the history of most colleges and universities in North America back far enough and you find a religious origin. One does not have to be nostalgic for the near unity of church and culture in the early nineteenth century to wonder why religion no longer shapes higher education in any significant way. In most cases, even in church-related colleges, religion has had to change its form to keep up with the progressive pace of higher education. The story of education most frequently told is that religious commitments hindered the access of colleges to the broadest possible student body and stifled the freedom of thought that is a prerequisite to scholarly development. This seems like a natural story to tell, but it is actually much more complex and ambiguous than that. Educational histories that trumpet the triumph of secularism over religion are usually written by secularists themselves. History is full of contingent events that could have been otherwise, so the secularization of education was not the product of inevitable or necessary forces, just as the return of religion to the classroom is not an impossible or utopian goal. But there are many hurdles to face for those interested in reviving the role of religion in education, and Wabash College provides a good lesson in how high those hurdles can be.[1]

One of the great stories Wabash people like to tell about ourselves is how the founders, most of whom were Presbyterian ministers, knelt in the snow in what was then Indiana wilderness to dedicate the college. It was an act of faith, made possible only by their determination to train clergy and teachers for the frontier. As an alumnus and a faculty member, I have heard the story many times, but not once have I heard what these men were kneeling for. The story is usually told in such a way as to imply that they were kneeling in reverence for the college itself, but the college was only an idea in 1832. The fact is that, as good Calvinists, they certainly were not kneeling in tribute to an institution but were dedicating "the grounds to the Father, Son, and the Holy Ghost for a Christian College."[2]

163

When I first looked up this story in a history of the college, I was startled to find these words in a firsthand account of the event. Every retelling I have heard or read censors the fact that the Trinity played a major motivating role in the founding of the college. True, the churches today hardly know what to do with the Trinity, so I guess it should come as no surprise that an independent college would revise its history to overcome this awkward bit of theological dogma. Nevertheless, something is lost when institutions develop amnesia about the historical forces that led to their birth and prosperity.

The independence of the college actually was more of a historical accident than the result of planning. Those who founded the college wanted it to have a Presbyterian charter, but the townspeople thought the Presbyterians already had too much power in Crawfordsville. They were worried that only Presbyterian students would be admitted, so the college became nonsectarian, but it is important to note that nonsectarian in those days meant neutrality in regard to denominations, not in regard to religion. Thus, the college would not favor Presbyterian students in its admissions policies. The college certainly did, however, promote the Christian faith on which it was founded. Indeed, donations from churches in New England kept Wabash afloat during its difficult early years.[3]

The inaugural address of Rev. Elihu Baldwin, the first president of the college (1834–40), is a good example of how the school understood itself as both religious and independent. Baldwin, like most educators of his day, could not conceive of education as an enterprise separate from religious nurture and moral conviction. "The study of mental and moral philosophy and the Christian system, as presented in the sacred oracle, is doubtless indispensable to the highest cultivation of the heart."[4] Ignorance of the Bible and Christianity would not only make liberal education incomplete, it would also hinder the development of good character that is the primary goal of education. But Baldwin did not stop there. He also insisted that historical instruction must include the writings of Greeks and Romans. He argued against those who were concerned that the classics would only instill pagan notions in the minds of the students.

Pagan religion provides an instructive contrast to the historical origin of Christianity, and students should be able to see for themselves what pre-Christian life was like. Baldwin had great trust in the ability of the students to think for themselves, but he also saw world history in a narrative form that climaxed with the Christian revelation.

Caleb Mills, the first professor at Wabash, also was motivated by a love of God. He was a Presbyterian minister and one of the founders of public education in Indiana, and those two things fit together perfectly in his mind. Wabash was an open college, but that openness was not unbounded and indiscriminate. The receptivity of the college to all students and all ideas was firmly based on Mills's confidence in the work of God through history and the special promise of God for the expanding American nation. Mills could promote a nonsectarian curriculum just as he could defend the rights of all young people to an education because he thought scholarship, morality, and piety were all interlocking pieces of the educational puzzle. Although Mills hoped the first graduates of Wabash would become preachers and teachers, he thought the best way to achieve this goal was to give them an education as broad and diverse as possible. Because the founders of the college treated education as one branch of the missionary work of the church, they could develop an independent college that nonetheless had a cohesive sense of its moral purpose and educational plan. Byron K. Trippet, longtime dean and president of the college, asked in a chapel talk in 1953, "With what, if anything, have we replaced Caleb Mills's love of God as a motivating force to which we can all subscribe?"[5] The question seems impossible to answer in today's multiversity, with its factions and competing ideologies.

The college maintained its identity as an independent institution with a religious mission by requiring courses in religion during the junior and senior years in addition to core courses in the classics and sciences. There were also communal meditations on the higher purposes of education. The first students at Wabash were required to attend morning and evening prayer in the chapel and a Bible recitation on Sunday mornings as well as a religious lecture by the president on Sunday afternoons. The Sunday morning services lasted for thirty-two years, at which point students were required to attend a church (chosen by their parents) on Sunday, but the Sunday afternoon sermon by the president continued as a foundation for the community's commitment to the spiritual aims of education. Evening prayers were omitted beginning in 1868, but morning worship continued as the way in which the college gathered itself to begin the day's work.

By the end of the nineteenth century, courses on the evidence of Christianity began to disappear from the college catalog, reflecting the decline in the popularity of rationalistic apologetics. In the colonial period, the unity of all knowledge had been presupposed, so education had been construed as essentially a religious process, and theology was integrated into the curriculum. By the latter half of the nineteenth century, however, the ideal of a religious education was increasingly achieved by a course in moral philosophy, frequently taught by the president, who often was a clergyman. Such courses were the culmination of the students' education, and the president was the central figure in the college precisely because he was the one who could provide a unifying account of the higher purposes of education.[6] Wabash was following national trends when it assumed that the office of the presidency should provide moral instruction for students and that the instruction had to be rooted in the study of religious tradition. It was not until 1926 that Wabash had a president who was not an ordained Presbyterian minister (although he was a Presbyterian).

During the first decades of the twentieth century, the college continued to emphasize its Christian roots, but it did this more in extracurricular ways than in the classroom. Indeed, having the president teach religion no doubt made it an ambiguous experience, giving the study of religion a certain prestige but also identifying it as an extracurricular activity imposed from above. Religious atmosphere rather than instruction became the college's emphasis, allowing administrators to avoid confronting many of the intellectual issues that were raging between modernists and fundamentalists. This arrangement of a core of secular courses surrounded by an environment of moral inspiration and religious expectations enabled the college to assume that pious moral values were a natural complement to the most rigorous course of study. Thus, the college could be both independent and committed to the aims of the church. As the catalog of 1889 bluntly said, "The college, while not sectarian, is distinctly Christian." One of the chief means the college used to foster this religious atmosphere was official support of a chapter of the Young Men's Christian Association.

Much of the work of maintaining a religious atmosphere at the college was done through required chapel services, but by the 1920s, chapel was required only twice a week, and the tone of the services was becoming less religious. The skeptical attitude about required chapel at Wabash reflected a growing national trend to make chapel attendance voluntary and secular. When asked his opinion about required chapel, Charles E. Gilkey, dean of the chapel at the University of Chicago, shared with Wabash in a 1934 letter a stanza from the Princeton faculty song:

> Here's to all the Trustee Board,
> Who took away the student Ford
> They built the Chapel, where we cough,
> And make us pray while they play golf.

After World War II, chapel gatherings were diminished to two required secular meetings and one voluntary religious meeting. Secular chapel survived for many years as a quasireligious expression of the college's identity. However, with the absence of a religious mission for the required chapel services, many students and faculty alike no longer could find a reason for them, and compulsory chapel was eliminated by the faculty in 1971.

The college thus passed through several stages of religious development. For its first sixty years, religious courses were required, as was attendance in chapel and church on Sunday mornings. By the end of the nineteenth century, however, religion no longer was a required course of study. Nevertheless, the presidents of the college continued to provide a religious justification for the mission of the college as a whole, and students continued to attend religious chapels. By the 1920s, the president of the college no longer taught religion, and the chapel services became more diverse and less religious. Consequently, throughout the 1920s and subsequent decades, the role of religion at the college was increasingly focused on the actual teaching of religion, which evolved from being the task of the president to being the responsibility of an official department of religion. The story of this evolution at Wabash is a fascinating tale of unrealistic hopes, precarious compromises, and unresolved questions, all brought about by the persistence of one man, Edgar H. Evans.

The Evans Controversy

The study of religion at Wabash became an academic specialty only gradually and with many false starts and heated debates.[7] Although the Bible and Christian theology were taught at Wabash from the beginning, the Department of Biblical Literature was not established until 1903 with the appointment of George Lewes Macintosh, an alumnus who was a Presbyterian pastor in Indianapolis and a trustee of the college. He came to the college two or three times a week to teach English Bible (Greek Bible was taught in the classics department), and in 1905 he was made a professor of philosophy and biblical literature. Although this was the official beginning of a separate department of religion, the tradition of having ministers, in addition to the president, teach religion continued. None of Macintosh's courses were required for graduation. He became acting president in 1906 and president in 1907, but he continued to teach moral philosophy to the seniors in the classroom adjoining his office. He also began the plans for the building of the chapel as a symbol of the consensus that Protestant religion, vaguely defined, was the foundation for all liberal education. Ironically, the chapel was completed, in 1929, at about the time that religious chapels and the assumption that religion was the

168

foundation of education were becoming increasingly hard to defend.

Macintosh was hired by the college to restore religion to its central place, but his later promotion to president and his success as a fundraiser meant that he became too busy to continue teaching the Bible. His administration thus initiated the process of severing the ties between religious and administrative leadership. At first, his classes were taught by a local minister, C. W. Wharton, and finally, in 1922, the first truly academic appointment in religion was made with the arrival of Ralph Case as professor of Bible. Although Case was not an ordained minister, it was understood that the post of professor of Bible included the duties of religious instruction. This was made clear in 1929 when Obed Johnson was hired as chaplain and head of the Department of Religious Education (he served in that capacity until 1944). He was the only professor at Wabash who had firsthand experience in China (his Ph.D. dissertation was on Chinese alchemy), and he could teach Chinese history and language (setting a precedent for the religion department's longtime emphasis on Chinese studies).

What is interesting is the story of how the duties of "chaplain" were separated from the duties of "professor of religion," a change that occurred more by accident than design. In the 1930s, during the administration of Louis B. Hopkins, who succeeded Macintosh, alumnus Edgar H. Evans offered Wabash $100,000 to endow a professorship in religion. The condition was that the college would agree to require all students to take a course in Christian religion and the Bible. The faculty rigorously resisted, seeing the proposal as an infringement on faculty and student freedom. Later, under the presidency of Frank H. Sparks, the college accepted Evans's offer on condition that the religion requirement last for only ten years and that Jewish and Catholic students be exempted if they wished. Thus the Evans Professor of Religion chair was born, and early descriptions of this position clearly include the duties of a chaplain, even though that official title is omitted. That the religious duties of this position were made unofficial rather than official is part of the ambiguous heritage of religion at Wabash and the complex role the religion department plays in that heritage.

When I heard stories about Edgar Evans, he was portrayed as a stern and puritanical bigot who had tried to use his wealth to control the college and impose his narrow view of religion. Although he certainly did try to influence the college, he was hardly a narrow-minded zealot. In his memoirs about Wabash, Byron K. Trippet acknowledged the prejudices of the faculty against Evans, but also offered a more nuanced portrait of him: "Edgar Evans was a classical puritan with all of the strengths and shortcomings of that way of looking at life. He was a mild-mannered, soft-spoken, even gentle person. But he was tough-minded about what he believed in and remarkably tenacious and resolute. Hard work, honesty, self-discipline, frugality, avoidance of even the minor vices of the flesh, faith in the will of God, prayer, repentance of sins—all of these were as important to him as life itself. They were, as he saw it, important also to the fabric of American society, and he took seriously his sense of obligation to do what he could to restore these virtues to their proper place in the minds of people. Education, he decided, was the best instrument to accomplish this end."[8] Evans, then, was following in the footsteps of the college founders by assuming that education and religion were inseparable. But while the founders could rely on a consensus about the value of religion, Evans was living in a different era, so he had to push hard to get his views heard, and he inevitably came off as disgruntled and stubborn.

Evans was a remarkable visionary who understood that the expansion of higher education, which in the 1920s was moving out of the clutches of the upper classes and into the hands of the growing middle classes, would make colleges and universities the center of American culture.[9] He concluded that if Christianity were to be taken seriously in that culture, it was important for religion to be taught as a living faith, not as a dead object. That his actions, at first resisted by the faculty but finally successful, actually led to the diminishment of religious life on campus is one of the great ironies of his life work and a perplexing inheritance that still plagues the college.

170

What prompted Evans's crusade was his discovery in 1929 that only three students out of four hundred were enrolled in the Bible course. As a man who essentially belonged to the nineteenth century, Evans could neither understand nor tolerate this dismal situation. Interestingly, what Evans found at Wabash reflected national trends, because many of the "scientific" religion programs established at the beginning of the twentieth century were in serious decline by the 1930s. This reflected the impact of neo-orthodox theology, the Depression, and the increasing importance of the natural sciences.[10] The study of religion as an academic specialty within the humanities did not find its voice in higher education until after World War II, but Evans began pushing for a full-fledged religion department at Wabash in the early 1930s.

Evans had been much influenced during his senior year by a course titled "Evidences of Christianity" taught by President Joseph Tuttle. It was a vigorous defense of the rationality of religion that was old-fashioned even when Evans took it. He knew religion was under attack in the modern world, but he also thought religious people had an obligation to respond in kind. His passage through Wabash College had taught him that religious expression and a rigorous, all-male education could be combined into one consistent outlook on the world. Religion should be forceful, aggressive, masculine, and confident. It had worked in his life, enabling him to become a successful businessman and civic leader, so why wouldn't it work for others? If religion was about building character, even in those who are recalcitrant, there should be no problem with requiring all students to study it, Evans argued. Religion was something that was good for you whether you liked it or not, and it was good for you especially if you did not like it, which merely demonstrated how much you needed it.

The goal of requiring the study of religion at Wabash became Evans's lifelong passion, indeed his obsession, as evidenced by the volumes of letters he exchanged with educational leaders, the pamphlets he wrote, and the minutes of the hundreds of meetings he chaired on the topic. In 1936 he organized the Indiana Council on Religion in Higher Education, which conducted a national survey on religion and education (one of the first such surveys) and sponsored an annual conference on the topic. Papers at the conferences had titles like, "Church and State in Higher Education," "Democracy and Religion," "The Church College in American Life," and "What College Graduates Should Know About Religion." Some of the most articulate debates about religion and education in the 1930s were taking place in Indiana as a direct result of Evans's attempt to require religion for graduation at Wabash College.

Evans solicited opinions about required religion courses from the presidents and leaders of many universities and colleges. Most responses were negative. A letter from John J. Coss of Columbia University was typical. Coss argued first that, because religion is chiefly a matter of personal attitude, compulsory courses would be a hindrance in religion's advancement. Second, an institution best advances religion through the whole temper of its approach to students. Religion has to do with the quality and commitments of a college, not with what it teaches. Third, religion would be served best with a voluntary course on the Bible, perhaps taught in the English department. A faculty committee agreed with these considerations and in 1936 rejected Evans's plan. In 1942 the matter came to the full faculty, which voted twenty to two, with four abstentions, against accepting Evans's money.

Perhaps the faculty resisted Evans's offer in part because there was already an unofficial religious environment at the college, and a more direct promotion of religion could be seen as a threat to their freedom. Certainly, however, the days were gone when faculty were held up to stringent moral standards, exemplified by the expulsion in 1908 of Wabash's most illustrious professor, Ezra Pound. He had the misfortune of offering his assistance to a young woman from a burlesque show who had been stranded by a blizzard. She slept in his bed while he slept on the floor of his study. When the lady from whom he rented his bachelor apartment went to make his bed, she found his guest, a situation that was not deemed acceptable in a small Midwestern town at that time. She informed the president, and the rest is poetic history.

If Wabash remained a Christian college prior to the Second World War, that had more to do with a social milieu of main-line Protestantism than any specific moral or religious standards. Reflecting national trends, the Wabash faculty of the 1920s and '30s were emerging as an increasingly liberal group, suspicious of religious authority. Education was becoming a kind of secular religion in America, a community substitute for the church, with its own demands of unconditional devotion and promises of social transformation. But while faculty at the leading institutions were expected to be utterly committed to the pursuit of pure knowledge, many teachers at Wabash remained old-fashioned in their emphasis on wisdom and character, with the expectation that only the education of the whole student could make the world a better place. Having a Christian heritage meant that Wabash could resist some of the pressures to move toward specialization and professionalization that were beginning to separate the elite schools from those that were second best.

In his comprehensive history of religion and education, *The Soul of the American University,* George Marsden portrays this period as a crucial phase for religious education. The 1920s and '30s were a period when the threat of totalitarianism abroad led to a greater emphasis on academic freedom at home. It was also a time, on the domestic front, of the great fundamentalist menace, when faculty everywhere were beginning to define their academic freedom in opposition to what they perceived to be religious intolerance. Populist fundamentalism tended to move liberal Protestants and agnostics closer together, so that the distinctiveness of a liberal Christian approach to education was lost altogether to a broader vision of religionless education. Fundamentalists defended a view of education as a lesson in obedience to external authorities and a matter of disciplining the will to develop moral character. Modernists, on the other hand, with their optimistic view of human nature, equated education with the expansion of the scientific method into all areas of study. As liberal Protestants fought with their fundamentalist cousins, they increasingly enlisted modernists as allies. As the price for their aid, mod-

173

ernists demanded that the study of religion be turned over to the methodologies of the social sciences.

Marsden also notes another reason religious colleges began turning their backs on more explicit statements of religious identity during the 1930s. This has to do with economic class and the growth of Roman Catholicism. Simply put, in a time of great social change and emerging ethnic groups, the ruling classes wanted to maintain their unity as well as their control over the power of higher education, and they could little afford divisive theological debates. Ethnic groups stood out due to their striking religious customs, while liberal Protestants were trying to blend Christianity into the civil religion of the nation as a whole. The Enlightenment in North America took a religious form, because Protestants successfully argued that their beliefs were the necessary foundation for progress, freedom, and equality. Liberal Protestant educational leaders, therefore, did not want to call too much attention to the particularities of their religious beliefs for fear that they, too, would look like outsiders to the power elite. Protestants were allowed to control higher education as long as they taught all of the positive and sentimental aspects of Christianity without bringing in too much theological baggage.[11] The result was the establishment of a civil discourse of religion that had little to do with historic Christianity. William F. Buckley Jr., called attention to the dire situation of religion on college campuses with the publication of *God and Man at Yale* in 1951, but Edgar Evans had anticipated and reacted to these problems twenty years earlier.

By the 1920s, then, evangelical Protestantism had reached the end of its influence on the leading colleges of America. Although evangelical Protestants played a leading role in establishing and supporting a great number of American schools, liberal Protestants effectively took over that control by the 1930s. While conservative churches defected from the emerging consensus about higher education and established their own schools, liberal churches encouraged secularizing trends. Indeed, this internal battle in Protestantism would become decisive for higher education, because liberal Protestants, like the Presbyterians who led Wabash, had a more universal understanding of the mission of education. They wanted their schools to be open to all students and all ideas. "Liberal Protestants could and usually did view the establishment of the new university—nondenominational, devoted to scientific research, and exerting its influence at many points in modern industrial society—as evidence of the progress of civilization and the coming of the Kingdom of God on earth."[12] Educational objectives and ecumenical Protestant theology merged because mainline Protestants promoted the ideal of scientific objectivity as a way to win the battle against fundamentalism. An emphasis on character was equated with lower standards of education, so liberal Protestants promoted the trend toward a value-neutral pedagogy as an expression of optimism that their self-critical and democratic principles could transform society and enable America to fulfill its dream of becoming a promised land.

Some liberal Protestants, like the ones who led Wabash, still saw education as an essentially religious process, but they did not want to root education in any particular religious tradition. They defined religion in sufficiently broad ways to accommodate nearly everything that was happening on America's campuses. Consequently, religion provided the spirit for the expansion of American education, but it was not a demanding religion, nor was it a religion with a specific identity. The result is what Marsden calls a "liberal Protestantism without Protestantism." This meant in practical terms that Protestants could retain effective control over institutions of higher learning because nearly everyone could subscribe to their religious claims. Nobody could foresee the dire consequences for Christian colleges that tried to emphasize character development and spiritual formation as opposed to specialized training. Moreover, once the unspoken hegemony of liberal Protestantism began to crumble, there remained no clarity about what provided the foundation for a moral education that would speak to the whole student, not just the student's career objectives.

One promising effort to stem the tide of secularism was the movement to establish schools of religion within universities and colleges. The National Council on Religion and Higher Education, the parent organization to the Indiana Council that

175

Evans chartered, was established to pursue this policy in 1922. By the 1930s, many institutions were offering courses in religion that resulted in what Marsden calls "a hybrid field that typically had Christian form and implicitly Christian direction, but in which specific Christian purposes were subdued."[13] Given that the majority of private colleges, nearly all church-related colleges, and even many state universities had religion departments by 1940, Wabash's resistance to a religion program might seem odd. But the Wabash faculty taught at a school in a small Midwestern town where most of the students were Christian and the churches had more influence over the town than did the college. Thus, even though Wabash had a religious heritage, it was harder, paradoxically, to get religion on its feet at Wabash than elsewhere. If it wanted to emerge as a strong liberal arts institution, Wabash College could not afford to be too closely identified with religion and consequently be branded as an outsider to the world of elite education.

The trend toward the professionalization of religion was underway across America in the 1940s and 1950s, and in many ways this trend provided a solution to Wabash's complex relationship with its religious heritage. Professionalizing the study of religion was convenient for liberal Protestants because it gave religion prestige in the academy and extracted it from the passionate and divisive debates of the day. At Wabash, before Evans endowed the chair that still bears his name, religion was handled as an extracurricular activity that should have everyone's participation. It was promoted most forcefully through a chapel program. In terms of academics, the study of religion was not on par with other scholastic programs. Wabash had a religion department in the 1930s, with one professor aided by the local Presbyterian minister. The department offered six elective courses, but they did not count toward distribution requirements and were poorly attended. A two-semester course on the Bible was taught in the English department, but religion proliferated most at Wabash in the daily chapel. Moreover, students in the '30s still were being encouraged, though not required, to attend church on Sundays.

Evans's opponents argued that requiring religion would make it a boring chore for students, but Evans noted this argument did not seem to change opinions about the need for math, science, and English requirements. Most were of the opinion that religion was a private matter, and requiring it would only lead to indoctrination. In response, Evans argued that the Bible was too essential to Western history to be classified as an optional area of study. I think Evans could sense that graduation requirements in science, English, and history were reflecting a broader cultural shift away from the importance and value of religion for the life of the mind. It infuriated him that people could think of themselves as well-educated while knowing nothing about the Bible or church history. But he also believed religion primarily functioned to build character. In his own mind, the study of religion and the development of moral character could not be separated. As a result, he pushed for a required religion course at Wabash without fully understanding how such courses and the religion department would evolve as they were integrated into the specialized, professionalized ethos of the academy.

Evans was a relentless campaigner, and he finally found an ally when Frank H. Sparks was appointed president in 1941. Sparks had been a successful businessman before returning to college and going on for a Ph.D., all with the goal of becoming a college president. He had great plans for Wabash and needed Evans's money, but he also had a deep and abiding faith in the importance of religious education. He was able to broker a deal between the trustees and the faculty by emphasizing the prestige of a chair in religion and downplaying the temporary experiment in required religion courses. Evans settled for a chair in religion and a prescribed time period for the religion requirement because he believed a chair would make the most permanent impact on the college. Because religion was being taught alongside other disciplines, the forces who wanted more religious presence at Wabash were appeased. The faculty liked the idea of a chair because that elevated the religion professorship from the orbit of part-time ministers and chaplains into the higher reaches of academic respectability. And everyone liked the idea of a large donation to the college endowment fund.

As a result of the Evans chair, the religion department became a scholarly unit just like any other department. It was expected to have the highest academic standards, indeed to have higher standards than other departments to prove its appropriateness to the college. In the mind of the faculty, religion was boosted into a full-fledged department, which meant the more informal religious programs for students could be allowed to diminish and eventually disappear. Evans thus unintentionally helped shift religion's role away from character formation and toward becoming yet another scholarly field.

Sparks recruited Professor D. Elton Trueblood, a much-respected Quaker theologian and church leader, to help plan a religion program at Wabash. Trueblood was convinced that a required course in religion at Wabash would be a revolutionary experiment of great significance to the place of religion in higher education. He, along with Sparks and Evans, wanted Wabash to be a pioneer and example for the rest of the nation's colleges. Trueblood almost took the job himself, after announcing his departure from Stanford University, but instead chose to go to Earlham College in Richmond, Indiana. However, he was dedicated to finding a worthy person to guide the new program, and he chose Fred West, an ordained Disciples of Christ scholar who was chair of the religion program at Texas Christian University.

The difficulties of establishing the program were tremendous. In his letter asking West to accept the job, Sparks wrote, "No letter I have written since I accepted the responsibilities of this high office has involved more than this one." Sparks and Evans were idealistic, even utopian, in their fervor for this religious experiment. They thought they could encourage students to become interested in religion without proselytizing or offending them. Students at first expected the required courses to be dogmatic and sectarian. West, however, was a product of the creedless Disciples of Christ, which perhaps made him, in some respects, an ideal person for the job. He was convinced that a nonsectarian but Christian-focused course could be developed at nonchurch colleges. He wanted an ecumenical program, and he even insisted that he wanted any atheists in his classes to become better informed atheists, not converted Christians. He was aware of student hostility to the idea of required religion courses, but he argued that freedom of conviction did not mean freedom of ignorance.

West's official duties were not limited to the classroom. One of his most important responsibilities was to connect students to the churches in town, which was not too difficult because denominational preferences of new students were known from student surveys. West also was to organize a religious emphasis week (which might have been tolerated by the faculty because, during this week, all nonessential committee meetings were canceled) along with a religious life program and Sunday evening vespers. Chapel speakers were to include Roman Catholic, Jewish, and Protestant leaders.

For the first few years of required classwork, the Bible was taught in the first semester and theological anthropology (a popular topic at the time) in the second semester. During the second year of the program students could choose to study comparative religions instead of the Bible. For a time, an Episcopalian rector was hired to help with the required religion courses, because it was impossible for one person to handle the enrollments.

At first, a kind of compromise or tension was built into the chair, because religion faculty members were expected to act as unofficial chaplains of the college. When Hans Frei was hired to replace Fred West in 1950, his title was assistant professor and director of religious activities. Thomas J. J. Altizer, who later became famous as a death-of-God theologian, replaced Frei. And then came Eric Dean, who guided the department for many years and was one of my role models. Gradually, the title of director of religious activities was dropped, but the department's members continued to function unofficially as religious counselors, and the department was charged with organizing the religious baccalaureate service, leading parts of the annual Christmas service, and conducting periodic, voluntary religious services for the students.

Without official recognition that the religion department was also a chaplaincy, there could be confusions and resentments about the role of the department on campus. Nevertheless, an unofficial chaplaincy was perhaps the best and only way to preserve the college's religious heritage and meet the religious needs of the students while the college was struggling to equate itself with the best, and therefore most secular, national institutions.

An Unofficial Chaplaincy

The history of religion at Wabash is so mixed that it is simplistic at best and misleading at worst to say that the college is independent. The very word "independent" is ambiguous. Being independent of something is only a first step in a relationship; independence from the church means that an attitude toward religion can be freely chosen. So, what is that attitude? The fact is that the college often is forced to describe itself in cumbersome circumlocutions, such as, "An independent liberal arts college with historically Presbyterian roots." There is no easy formula to capture the complex ways in which the college tries to make use of its past. Historically, Wabash, like our national government, walked the thin line of being independent but not secular, an institution that favored the expression of religious faith but did not want to be officially identified with a particular religious tradition. In the pursuit of national standards of excellence, the college failed to maintain that precarious balance, but the loss of its religious heritage paradoxically made the teaching of religion at Wabash even more important. The religion classroom was the one place where students could find an affirmation of their faith.

George Marsden has developed an influential thesis about the secularization of America's colleges and universities. According to his narrative, the demise of religion in higher education is not the result of some sinister plot by radical secularists. On the contrary, liberal Protestants themselves are to blame. In their rush to articulate universal values such as tolerance and in their zeal to establish uniform educational standards for research and specialization, liberal Protestants prepared the way for their own irrelevance. I have drawn from Marsden's theoretical model to explain much of what has happened concerning religion at Wabash, but his thesis could not have explained the Wabash religion department. Indeed, in his

180

most recent book, he holds out the hope that religious faith again can shape academic research in significant ways, but this faith is not the self-critical faith of academically trained theologians.[14] If liberals got us into this mess in the first place, he implies, then only evangelicals and conservatives can get us out of it. Marsden wants all disciplines to be open to reasonable and well-researched contributions from traditional Christian perspectives. Christians should be permitted to express and defend their faith to the extent that those commitments inform their research and teaching in significant and constructive ways.

Marsden's views on the role of Christianity across the disciplines are imminently reasonable and persuasive. Unfortunately, however, Marsden downplays the overwhelming forces of specialization that keep all professors from integrating their beliefs into their highly refined methodologies. Moreover, Marsden does not take into account the fact that the battle for religion in higher education will continue to take place precisely where religion is researched and taught, that is, in religion departments. Marsden is not confident that the teaching of religion can serve the religious needs of students at secular institutions. Given the state of most religion programs in public education today, perhaps he merely is being realistic when he hopes for more integration of Christian views into other disciplines than into the teaching of religion. What the Wabash example can teach the academy, however, is that a religion department can define itself as a religious department without sacrificing either the faithfulness that Marsden wants to foster or the professional standards that are crucial for academic respectability.

The settlement that resulted from the Evans affair left a religion department on par with other academic fields but also with the increasingly vague and ill-defined expectation that it function as a chaplaincy. In many ways, this has been a blessing for the religion department at Wabash. When colleges have chaplains, religion departments sometimes go overboard in teaching non-Western traditions and in claiming to be religiously objective and neutral, in order to distance themselves from what a chaplain does. Likewise, when the chaplain is not a part of

181

the academic community, the chaplain ends up offering religious services that are not integrated into the theological task of intellectual reflection on faith. The competition between the religion department and the chaplaincy for the attention of religious-minded students often leads both into extreme positions. The chaplaincy is defined as anti-intellectual and the religion department is defined as anti-religious.

One key to the success of the Wabash religion department, then, is that it has taken on many of the functions of a chaplain, which keeps it in touch with students and shows them that religion is a living tradition, not just a dead object of study. The religion department runs the annual baccalaureate service during commencement, a weekly worship service, and a Christmas service. Religion professors counsel students, help those who are interested think about the ministry, and support student-initiated programs in religion. It is a traditional department demonstrating that the highest levels of scholarship are not incompatible with the articulation of religious faith. Unfortunately, this is increasingly rare in the world of religious studies.

Of course, there are still worries among the faculty that the department is too religious, and these worries seem rooted in concerns about the college's image to outsiders as well as the perennial problem of potential Christian hegemony and intolerance. Some colleagues fear that permitting religious voices will open the floodgates to some sort of religious control, but these fears are so obviously exaggerated that they are hard to take seriously. The best way to deal with Christian nostalgia for a lost cultural unity and Christian claims for infallibility and superiority is not to bypass the power of religion on campus but to raise these issues to the surface. When theology is taken seriously in the classroom, students have an opportunity to talk about the relationship between Christianity and other religions. Christian students, for example, need to know about their roots in Judaism and the orthodox theological position on the eternal covenant God sustains with the people of Israel.

People sometimes are amazed to learn how many non-Christian students take religion courses—even the courses that are the most theological—at Wabash. Perhaps this is due to the respect these classes show to all religious faiths and the fact that questions of ultimacy are made the topic of discussion, not the object of repression. Inviting students to make clear their religious commitments and bring them into the light of public discussion is an essential part of both higher education and spiritual growth. Permitting religious voices and supporting religious students should be one piece of the larger puzzle of liberal arts education. Only deeply seated prejudices and ungrounded fears can suggest otherwise.

The problem with worries over a religious religion department is that Wabash College is hardly a Christian school anymore. Students receive very little religious guidance on campus. Thirty or forty years ago, when chapel was still required, there would have been legitimate concerns from non-Christian students about how religious the campus was, but those concerns hardly seem warranted today. The Wabash story is about how ill-defined religious aims allow an institution to drift toward a position of maximum civility resulting in religious neutrality. A tradition of relative independence turned into a commitment to secularity, so that religious students, if anything, are not given the kind of attention and resources that most other groups receive without a second thought.

Even if the college as a whole remains neutral with regard to religion, such neutrality, if it is authentic, should not rule out a sympathetic attitude toward religion that allows some faculty within the college to help students deal with their spiritual development. Colleges affect students' religious lives in many conflicting ways. Most disciplines take a secular look at the world that permits no religious reflection. Religious voices, then, are forced to sound defensive and aggressive as students try to articulate their deepest beliefs. If religion departments do not legitimate and support the life of faith, no academic program will give students the confidence they need to bring together faith and reason in healthy ways. Academic life will be marginalized as students turn to extracurricular groups and campus ministries to fill the void. Religion departments can serve the exciting role of mediating between church and school

183

by giving students a space to bring their full selves to the classroom. Anything short of this demonstrates that colleges and universities are not neutral but rather critical of the religious lives of students.

Historian Martin E. Marty was one of the first scholars to observe how pluralism displaced liberal Protestantism as the force that occupied the center of American culture. Before the middle of the twentieth century, mainline Protestantism gained much of its power by the assumption that it reflected the consensus values and beliefs of American culture. The evangelical witness of mainline Protestant churches, therefore, was a matter of persuading Americans to live up to principles and morals they already accepted. Liberal Protestants defended the best in Western culture, church leaders argued, and Protestant principles were necessary for democracy. Few people disagreed.

In his *Second Chance for American Protestants,* Marty argues that this kind of witness came to an end when the ground rules for public debate changed.[15] With the emergence of a truly pluralistic American culture in the 1950s and 1960s, Protestants no longer could assume that what was best for America was best for the church. They no longer could presume that they supplied the religious depth that, even if taken for granted, pervaded all aspects of American life. Protestant leaders at first reacted with suspicion and concern to pluralism but then embraced it with an optimistic assessment of Protestantism's ability to lend coherence and creativity to a culture that otherwise could become chaotic. Today that optimism seems as unwarranted and naive as the conservative nostalgia for a lost Christian America.

Marty's description of a period of pluralism tempered by Protestant leadership corresponds at Wabash to the rise of the religion department as a primarily academic program but also an increasingly vague chaplaincy. Today, the conditions of the academy have changed completely again. Higher education is increasingly fragmented and politicized. The emergence of new voices from long marginalized groups has dismantled the liberal Protestant vision of a generalized religious education open to all. Postmodernism has displaced pluralism so that even secularity is recognized increasingly as one particular voice, not the natural and inevitable philosophy of the elite. Secularism, too, is a time-bound and uncritical faith that must defend itself if it is to be taken seriously in debates about American culture. If postmodernism calls into question religious dedication, it also deconstructs every kind of founding narrative, with the result that universities no longer have a sacred purpose and a coherent agenda. The vaguely religious sense of the transcendent goals of education that liberal Protestants used to replace more evangelical notions of education are considered to be every bit as ideological and restrictive as more explicit religious goals. Without any religious foundation for education, the "higher" in higher education becomes problematic, because higher education's aspirations no longer are clear. How is higher education different from any other kind of technical training?

Such confusion should provide an opportunity for educators to reassess the role of religion in higher education. Religion is one voice among many, a voice that has contributed to Western culture in so many ways that, on the grounds of historical significance alone, it should be allowed into the conversation. Religious faith, however, also provides an alternative account of the modern world, a cosmology and anthropology that, given the corrosive effects of postmodernism on all worldviews, cannot be ruled out of court on the basis of some restrictive epistemological criterion. Religious faith needs to have a seat at the academic table, and since academia only takes seriously the intellectual side of life, religious faith must play a constructive role in religious studies departments. The Wabash religion department, then, with its mixture of academic and chaplaincy elements, can serve as a model for religion departments in the new millennium.

Reflections of a Young Hans Frei

In the end, if religion departments that promote religion are to survive in the academy, they must develop theoretical, not just practical, reasons for their pedagogical philosophy. At Wabash, a young Hans Frei, who would become one of the

185

nation's leading theologians in the religious studies department at Yale University, did just that. He had his first teaching experiences at Wabash, and he had time to think about what teaching religion means. In a fascinating report the dean asked him to write on educational reform in 1953, Frei was reacting to pressures on the department to become less theological and more comparative. Faculty suspected that a religion department sensitive to the spiritual lives of its students could not be a fully professional program, with specialized professors passing along methodological tools to initiate students into the world of higher learning. In response, Frei developed a position on religious education that seems as needed and eloquent today as it was then.[16]

The principle point of his report was to reject the bifurcation of theory and practice, faith and reasoning in the study of religion. Such distinctions are not appropriate in religion due to the nature of the object to be investigated. Religion as a field of study is determined by the nature of God, not the cultural activity of religion itself. God as a living and transcendent being unites truth, beauty, and morality. Humans ordinarily are able to analyze things by breaking them apart and bracketing personal emotions, ethical qualms, and ultimate questions. But approaching God demands a unified attitude that involves the whole of human nature.

Frei was not suggesting that human nature is unified from the beginning. On the contrary, human nature is splintered and fragmented. Indeed, it is only in the approach to God that humans can find that they reflect God's image and thus express an essential unity. "He is a welding-together of will, emotion and intelligence, and all of these together in their unitariness in man must be totally involved in this search,"[17] Frei wrote. The search for God, then, begins when people understand that they are a problem to themselves and find that the unity they seek can be discovered only in a higher power.

Indifference and neutrality in the study of religion, therefore, are impossible, and the proper field in the study of religion is theology. By this Frei did not mean theology in the technical sense. He meant the search for wisdom, an intellectual

186

search that involves every aspect of human nature. Frei admitted that this might sound narrow and dogmatic. The risk is that the teacher of religion attempts to coerce students into acquiring insights they want to avoid. The hope is that the search for a transcendent unity at the ground of all things coincides with the fullest expression, not the abridgment of human freedom.

What is clear from this report is that Frei was being pressured by the faculty to teach more comparative religion and less Christian theology. He suggested that the comparative approach is always prejudicial to some religious traditions and that it substitutes something sociological for the proper object of religion. There was also a faculty debate about retaining the requirement to study religion at Wabash, and Frei suggested that, although there were good reasons for the requirement, it might be easier to teach religion more effectively if the courses were optional. Another debate centered on the need for a religious program that would extend beyond the academic study of religion. On this point, Frei was adamant: "In this field, if in no other, there is an immediate and organic concomitance between academic study and campus community life. There can be no adequate and effective instruction in the academic study of religion where religious life or the living revolt against it are absent."[18] To study religion without the example of religious life would be like studying art without having an art gallery— that is, without having the opportunity to see art and thus fall in love with the pursuit of beauty.

Finally, Frei suggested that the only way to avoid intellectual mediocrity in the academy is to have spiritual depth. Specialization occurs not as the inevitable process of applying the principles of economic productivity to the academy but as a failure of the religious imagination. Intellectual activity that does not search for ultimate integration—which, in the end, is always a religious search—is void of wisdom and profundity.

To what extent Frei's report could be distributed today to Wabash faculty—or, indeed, any faculty—is an open question. There would have to be some changes in his language, but many of his points retain their original power. There is no record of the response to his report, and he left Wabash at the end of that school year. Perhaps he knew that teaching religion at an independent school was an uphill battle he did not want to fight, because he went on to teach at an Episcopal seminary and then at Yale University, with its proximity to Yale Divinity School. Nonetheless, his report stands as a vision of wholeness in the teaching of religion, a vision that sets religion apart as the one discipline that, if it is to flourish, cannot separate the confessional from the theoretical, the personal from the intellectual. Teaching religion religiously, not objectively, is the only way to do justice to the unique object that is religious faith.

SEVEN

TEACHING THE FREEDOM TO BELIEVE

A DIALOGUE WITH WILLIAM C. PLACHER

William C. Placher taught me religion while I was a student at Wabash College, but more important, he showed me how I could study religion while remaining faithful to my religious beliefs. His scholarly productivity, intellectual intensity, and complete trust in students' ability to find their own way combined to give me the space to work out my intellectual development with the hope that I could someday have the intellectual confidence of a theologian. It was always clear to me that Bill was a person of faith, and it was also always clear to me that he affirmed my faith, but I do not recall talking to him directly about religious faith. His influence on my faith was more indirect than direct, showing me that asking good questions could be liberating at a time when I was overwhelmed by questions I could not answer. When I returned to Wabash College to teach, Bill became my mentor, and he gave me the same freedom as a colleague that he had given me as a student.

As I have tried to develop my religious voice in the classroom, Bill and I have had many conversations about the trials and tribulations of being Christian theologians in a liberal arts college. Part of our differences are matters of style and personality, but there are serious theological and pedagogical issues at stake, too. To me, Bill represents the most serious and challenging alternative to the kind of pedagogy I am trying to develop in this book. He is a Presbyterian theologian who has clear ideas about the importance of Christianity, but he also has a deep sense of the importance of giving students their own space in the classroom, leaving them free to explore religion on their own terms. He is much more reserved than I am in the classroom because he does not want to risk manipulating students by abusing the power that comes with teaching religion. Yet our positions are compatible in our goals for education. Bill is not committed to freedom for its own sake. He gives students freedom precisely because he wants them to be free to believe (or not believe). Our differences are over the strategies of promoting that freedom while honoring the life of faith. Consequently, I have come to think of his position as not in opposition but as a counterpart to mine. Every time I write a sentence about teaching, I hear his voice raising a reservation and saying the same thing in a slightly (or sometimes significantly) different way. His position is so important to me that I could not imagine excluding it from this book, and I wanted to do more than just summarize his ideas. Teaching religion is a dialogical activity, and there is no single or proper way to pursue religious questions. In the fall of 1999 I asked him to enter into a dialogue with me by E-mail to see if we could clarify our differences and find some common ground. This is our conversation.

⚘

WEBB: Given the diversity of our students and the pressures on religion departments to be all things to all people, that is, to cover so many religious traditions, I sometimes despair of ever being able to teach religion religiously. It seems to me that religion teachers who are religious are torn between two options. First, we can try to be more religious in the classroom, but this is especially problematic for Christians, since

190

the academy is always fearful of Christian imperialism and hegemony. So I struggle with trying to make the classroom a more spiritual place without necessarily turning the classroom into a Christian place. Or, second, perhaps out of despair at accomplishing the first option, we can revert to a more objective classroom, the traditional "I am just teaching you the facts" approach, which keeps everything simple by keeping religious passions and personal convictions in check. However, I'm not sure I know anybody who really conducts an objective classroom. Besides, I do not want to reinforce our culture's notion that religious passion is a merely private matter. So I am left with some form of option one. Do you see a third way between these two alternatives?

PLACHER: I suppose my "third way" would consist of coming into the classroom, teachers and students, as the fully human beings we are, including our faith—or lack of it. I agree that the best teaching isn't just reporting facts but creating a space where people can share emotions and beliefs that really matter to us. But I get nervous about the classroom becoming a "spiritual place," except in the very general sense in which a class in literature or physics can equally be a "spiritual place" where people grow in their humanity through participating in community. I wouldn't dismiss that very general sense as trivial, but I understand you to be seeking something more. That's where I get nervous.

I suppose one of our differences is that I'm less evangelical, more high-church than you are—and therefore more inclined to think of "church" or even "spiritual place" in liturgical terms. My spiritual place is church, and a college isn't a church (and will fail if it tries to be). We may talk about our prayer life in class, but we wouldn't (I think you'd agree) begin class with a prayer, or have communion, or baptize someone. In earlier conversations, you have suspected me of a political correctness that wants to protect the college's pluralism. I'm proposing here that my real concern is to protect the integrity of faith from being watered down to a generic religiousness.

WEBB: Yes, I come from a low-church background, and we believe that church can happen anywhere, which means that

191

what we call "church" can even happen in the classroom! I wonder if we can talk about that for a moment, the influence of our church backgrounds on how we teach. I mean, you belong to a very well established, mainline denomination, Presbyterianism. Presbyterians had an inordinate influence on higher education in this country for generations. Presbyterianism is part of the American establishment. Do teachers who come from this background worry less about how to be a Christian in the classroom because they already have a sense of ownership of the educational process? My own background is evangelical, tempered by some Disciples of Christ rationalism and ecumenism. I suppose I use both sides of my background in the classroom when they are expedient, the evangelical and ecumenical. The Disciples side can be especially convenient, because it allows me to say who I am to my students while at the same time affirming their religious truths and not pushing for one particular form of Christianity, since Disciples claim to be "just Christians" and not a specific theological tradition. Nevertheless, my evangelical side wants not to convert but to persuade my students about the value of the life of faith. Moreover, I have a sense of being in a minority in the academic world that forces me to work harder to claim a space for my voice.

PLACHER: I think you are right about denominational differences. You come out of a tradition where people shared their religious experiences in church, and you want to do that in the classroom. But I never did that in church. Compared to the Disciples, my tradition makes me more conscious of coming out of a particular tradition, and therefore conscious of not wanting to presuppose or impose it. You understand, of course, that I don't believe that you're "just Christians." Adult baptism, not believing in the real presence of Christ in the Eucharist, etc.— these seem to me just as particular as their opposites. So I'd want to say that the issues ought to be as problematic for you as they are for me!

WEBB: I think there is also a class issue here. I mean, students who belong to religious traditions that are marginalized by mainstream American culture often rely more on religious experience to validate their traditions and to confirm their self-

worth. These marginalized traditions, Baptist, fundamentalist, Adventist, restorationist, whatever, are more prone to
equate religion with passionate experience, and students from
these traditions, I think, often feel like outsiders to the university environment. Academic conventions and norms leave
little room for these more experiential styles of religious worship. I worry about those students and what we are saying to
them when we tell them that studying religion is not about
sharing experiences but about behaving in certain ways or mastering rational discourse. Of course, these students are probably the ones who avoid our courses in the first place, but it
doesn't have to be like that.

PLACHER: The fundamentalist issue raises a lot of questions that we might want to explore. I'd be interested in how far
you want to go in the direction you are taking. What would be
the implications for our Bible courses, for example? If some students have been brought up discouraged from thinking about
certain kinds of issues, do we want to say to them, "You can come
out wherever you want, but we want you to look at the options"?
If the student says, "But seriously examining the options isn't
compatible with my faith's emphasis on holding fast . . ." what
do we say? (Newman said something rather like that about his
faith, so I don't mean to take it as a silly position.)

WEBB: I want to honor the student who wants to hold fast
to his or her faith. While we do not teach at a church-related
college, I do not see why the life of the mind has to be conceived
in opposition to the life of faith. Too many educators equate
strong beliefs with narrow beliefs, and they think their job is
to move students from passionate conviction to open tolerance.
This is a false view of intellectual development, of course,
because tolerant people can have very strong beliefs, and people
with very strong commitments can be very open to others. I
think students with strong religious beliefs do not get much
encouragement in public education, so where else than the religion classroom can they be taken seriously? Many colleges no
longer claim their religious roots, so that Christian students
are not even aware of the role the church played in the founding of places like Wabash College. This is why, in my history of

193

religion at Wabash, I am trying to reclaim the religious roots of the college, so that our more conservative religious students can be proud of their own heritage, how their beliefs led to the founding of Wabash in the first place, so they do not have to feel like outsiders to higher education.

PLACHER: In our particular Wabash context, it is probably true that a part of me is annoyed when you or others talk about the Christian tradition of the college. I want to say, well, actually, it was a Presbyterian tradition. Many of the students today who want to "preserve traditional Wabash" need to remember that in the past that tradition would not have included non-Christian students or even Roman Catholics.

WEBB: But our Presbyterian heritage was always mixed and complex. The college both wanted and did not want a religious tradition. This brings us back to what you said earlier about the problem with having generic religious expressions in the classroom. You are right that every religious position is particular, with its own theological commitments, no matter how general or ecumenical it tries to be. (And I would say that even your description of your nonreligious classroom—sharing common human experiences in a nonjudgmental atmosphere—is rooted in a particular theological tradition, for example, a mainline Protestant view of what it means to be religious and what it means to talk about religion in public.) The danger is that when a teacher tries to create spiritual space in the classroom, that space will be defined in generic ways, so that all particular confessions are ruled out of court. But to the extent that classrooms are public forums with a diverse student population, how can the religious classroom maintain any integrity as anything other than a generically spiritual place? I guess that I want to say that the religious classroom is neither church nor antichurch, but a kind of parallel church, where church-like transformations become possible. I don't know how to teach religion without being up front about my religiosity and encouraging students to be up front about theirs as well. I don't want some vague spirituality in my classrooms, as if we all believe variations of the same thing, but I also do

194

not want some form of objectivity that neutralizes the religious passions of my students.

PLACHER: A parallel church? But I belong to a church already; I wouldn't want another one. I think we have some promises about the Holy Spirit working through word and sacraments in the church that give us hope of what might happen there in spite of sin. But we don't have parallel promises about colleges, and therefore anyone who hopes to find a church in a college will inevitably be disappointed.

I'm not even sure about a "religious classroom." If the point is that we bring all of who we are to the classroom, then shouldn't that be true of teaching English or philosophy? If I were teaching art history and we got beyond names and dates, I wouldn't know how to explain why I respond to Rembrandt much more than to Rubens without talking about my Protestantism. And I'd hope that Catholic students might talk about how Rubens spoke to them. And we'd learn from each other. But I don't think we'd be sharing a religious experience, or functioning as a religious community.

WEBB: I agree that Christian teachers in other disciplines need to find ways to connect their faith to their fields of study, but I also think that there is something distinctive, if not unique, about teaching religion that calls forth a religious point of view. You can teach art history while only occasionally talking about religion, because you can keep the discussion on the aesthetic and historical plane. But teaching religion while bracketing the religious experiences of teacher and students alike seems to me to be impossible. If you talk about religion in nonreligious ways, then you might be talking about something very interesting, something historical, sociological, or intellectual, but you are missing the point of your topic, because religion, or more specifically, God, demands that we approach the topic with the appropriate questions and in the proper spirit.

I think your reservations about the role of religious experience in the classroom are not based on an attempt to keep religion out of the classroom. Rather, you want to maximize student freedom to explore religion, so you don't want to enforce some premature sense of what religion is. Is that fair?

195

PLACHER: I wouldn't say that I have reservations about sharing religious experience in the classroom. I agree that's a good thing. I assume we both would agree that it can't be coerced—in part, precisely for the sociological reasons you note. We would both hope to create a classroom where the student who has grown up Pentecostal would feel comfortable talking about it, but a college environment generally works against such faith, and if the student feels too threatened to divulge his faith, then we should respect that. (I would say the same about gay students: great if they feel comfortable talking about it in class, but understandable if they don't.)

So I don't think we disagree about that. But you want this sharing to be itself a religious activity (am I right about that?), and that's what I'm nervous about. Why can't it be just a human activity? As we might talk about our relations with our fathers in a psychology class?

Maybe its my Barthianism again, but (1) I don't assume that all authentic human community turns out to be, underneath, religious, and (2) I think Christians and Muslims and Hindus, at least, are members of different religious communities, and it asks them to do something inappropriate to attempt to become part of a shared religious community called "religion class." Or am I being unfair to you with that picture?

WEBB: But I wouldn't ask a Muslim (or anyone) to give up her faith, only to move into her faith more fully by sharing her experiences and by thinking through the various forms of faith, the various ways in which God teaches us. Talking about religion can create community, and the act of sharing religious experiences can take on the character of those experiences.

I'm glad you raised the name of Karl Barth. Both of us have been very influenced by him, but I continue to be puzzled by his influence on the teaching of religion in higher education. I mean, most people know Barth only as this towering intellectual giant who returned the discipline of theology to its traditional themes and wanted theologians to regain confidence in the proclamation of the gospel. Yet he was also very skeptical about any attempt to define (or practice!) religion in general. Someone isn't a Christian because she has some general religious experience but because she has been called by Christ. My problem is that this skepticism about religious experience often leads to a kind of indifference or neutrality toward religion in public places like the academic classroom. If the academic teaching of religion cannot have a religious dimension, and if religion can be understood only when it is fully engaged by the student, then religion can be understood, practiced, and even taught only in the churches, mosques, and synagogues. So what are we doing in the religion classroom? The legacy of Barth seems to make it impossible to teach religion religiously outside of the church. I agree with you that we should not try to create religious experience in the classroom, and we should not try to invent a religious outlook that would be compatible with all of our students, a kind of lowest common denominator of religious belief that we could all share. We do not have that kind of authority (or wisdom!) to do that. But why can't the grace of God be present in the classroom, and why can't I be present to my students as a Christian, just as they can be present to me and to each other as whatever religious path they are on?

PLACHER: What you say about Barth and his influence (at least on people like me) seems generally right to me. And I'm not sure I can defend my position. I will acknowledge that the "strange grace of God" can work in all kinds of ways—what is it Barth says? In a flowering shrub, a flute concerto, Russian communism, or a dead dog. Or a religious studies classroom. That certainly happened for me, when I was an undergraduate. But my instinct is strongly to leave it *ad hoc*—not to try to make it deliberate, institutionalized, systematic. I can be grateful when something that happens in the classroom becomes religiously significant for a student, but, if I start to plan for it, then I start to expect it, and students will sense that, and that imposes expectations on them that I don't have the right to impose. My sense is, by the way, that our practices in these matters aren't very different.

WEBB: I think we need to be careful about this key word, "impose." Why is it that whenever somebody brings up the topic of religion, the immediate retort is to worry about whether it will be imposed on somebody else, as if we can never talk about religion without such impositions? We need to be more religious in the classroom precisely in order to practice ways of talking about religion that do not involve imposing it on others. You talk about not imposing religion on the students, but when I hear you say that, I don't hear you coming from the position of trying to build a classroom that is neutral and objective with regard to religion in order to protect the autonomy of the student. Instead, it seems to me that you want to give students freedom precisely in order to let them enter into religion in whatever ways they are ready to do so. But you do not just give them freedom in a vacuum. And this is where our practices, as you suggest, are very close. The ways in which you present the material, the books you choose, the questions you ask, all lead the students in the direction of looking for God; that at least is how I remember your classes. So maybe we are not too far apart from each other. I agree that one cannot overtly plan or orchestrate a classroom into some kind of religious program. On the other hand, I want to retain my integrity in the classroom, and I want my students to have their integrity, so that they know that I come from a space that is essentially religious and that I want them to occupy, no matter how critically and imaginatively, a religious space when they are with me. I want them to enter into faith through what Heidegger called the piety of questioning, to take faith seriously, to see how it works, what it feels like.

But perhaps what I have just said makes you nervous a bit. I think the emphasis on the freedom of the student can be taken too far, to the point where it means that I as a teacher will not set any agendas, I will not reveal myself for fear of influencing my students, I will not push them in any specific direction, when we all know that all teachers have agendas, all teachers reveal themselves in the classroom, and all teachers push students in very specific directions, no matter how gently and carefully. Some of the teachers who are most verbal about student freedom and about having a loose, decentered classroom, came of age in the sixties and have the most visible and specific agendas in the academy. They use their so-called "open" classrooms to push their own fairly closed ideas about individualism, relativism, political liberation, and so on. The point is not to escape all agendas but to articulate them so that we allow for dissent and multiple points of entry into the space we are trying to create.

PLACHER: I think you are right that we are not really too far apart. Students should know who I am, though that doesn't preclude me from, some days, taking another position for pedagogical purposes. If they're not taking Freud's critique of the religious seriously enough, then I ought to start defending Freud for that fifty minutes.

I do get a bit nervous with the phrase "enter into faith." I'd agree that, if we're teaching the Gita, we have failed if the text just seems silly to them. And we should try to have them get what sense they can of what such a text means to a Hindu. But we shouldn't foster any illusions that they really understand it as a Hindu would. And, if they're not Christians, the same would be true for a Christian text. Perhaps what we would hope for is the attitude of Johannes Climacus, who recognizes Abraham's greatness even as he admits that he cannot understand him.

I also think students are often in religious transition, and they shouldn't be forced to define themselves more clearly than they are ready to. If some students don't feel comfortable saying that they still believe what they grew up believing, but also can't articulate what the new thing they believe is, then let them just report on what the text says and ask questions for a while. I'm assuming you would agree with that.

WEBB: Certainly. What I call a religious classroom means an openness to religion, a roominess that permits students to listen to religion, which means that we should let religious voices (the text's, mine, theirs) be heard, but they can listen to religion without saying what they finally believe, if anything. Perhaps what has come from our discussion is that the religion classroom should bring students to the brink of faith, and let God do the rest. We would never want to coerce students in anything regarding religion, but we also cannot hide the fact that we are hardly neutral scholars who have nothing at stake in the teaching of this topic. A good teacher will

199

know what each of her students is ready for, how far they need to be nudged to take an idea or text seriously, and when they need to be cautioned to slow down and ask more questions rather than jump to the answers. Probably most importantly of all, a good teacher will know when to withdraw, so that she does not take up too much space, in order to let the students come to their own conclusions.

There is one qualification I want to express to where we have come in this dialogue. I often hear religion teachers say that when they teach Buddhism, they become a Buddhist, when they teach Hinduism, they play the Hindu, and so on. While that strategy has some merit, I also think it is a bit dangerous. Students know when we are playing at being an advocate for something that we don't really believe ourselves. And there is nothing wrong with assuming such roles. Such performances can model for students how learning takes place—through the trying on of ideas in very personal ways, testing them out, teasing them to see how they fit. But I think we need to remember that they are roles, and that we are not penetrating the essence of another religion when we perform aspects of it for our students. Ultimately, I want to respect other religions by not pretending to be a member of them, which would hardly do justice to the other religion or to my own beliefs. I think that when a Buddhist teaches Christianity or a Christian teaches Hinduism, empathy is essential, but also a certain distance, to demonstrate to the students precisely how seriously you take the other religious faith, and how risky and overwhelming it would be to really enter into it, in more than just an empathetic way.

PLACHER: It would have been really boring if we had started here, because I completely agree with everything you said. It's because I agree with the last part that I'm nervous about language you used earlier in our conversation about "trying on faith."

WEBB: I guess I want to stick with saying that the religion classroom can be a religious place because I think the act of taking religion seriously, questioning it and thinking about it, is ultimately connected to our capacity to be open to God and to risk transformation, even conversion. When we invite stu-

200

dents to think about a religious text, movement, or idea, we are entering a space that is neither secular nor religious (in the strictest sense of that word), but a liminal space where all things are possible, including the grace of God. Even more strongly put, by being who we are, we are moving students toward the mystery of God, and so we have to be very aware of what we are doing and where we are going. We always model for our students strategies for talking about religion and even ways of being religious in public—and those models are based on theological traditions, whether they be, for example, a liberal or an evangelical Protestantism.

Perhaps what it comes down to, our common points and our differences, is our different understandings of the operation of grace in the classroom. We both want to be sensitive to that, and we both want to be open to the ways in which the study of religion itself can put students onto a religious path (or take them off that path). I suppose I have more of a sense of cooperating with that grace, teaching in ways that make explicit the idea that the study of religion is one way of approaching the mystery of God, so that students of religion, including teachers, need to be very attentive to how God works in the classroom. Your Calvinism leads you to be more careful about getting into situations where you can manipulate things in order to create an experience that might or might not be what God wanted. I suppose in the end that you don't want students to mistake the religion classroom, no matter how exciting and moving and edifying that classroom can become, for the church, mosque, or synagogue, where God is more directly present. I want my students to feel the relationship between the act of studying religion and the act of worshipping God, so that they can imagine an easier transition from the classroom to church than is usually made possible by the academic study of religion. After all, that is what Wabash gave me: an ability to be in both church and school, with the integrity to know their differences but also the imagination to see them as two related parts of a life that is whole.

PLACHER: I very much like the idea of the classroom as a liminal space. On the other hand, as you imagined, the idea of "cooperating with grace" chills my Calvinist soul. I think you're right; that really is a theological difference. I suppose that another difference is that you're much more comfortable thinking about "religion" than I am, and therefore you can imagine a classroom that would lead students to deepen their own commitments, whether to mosque, synagogue, or church. My suspicion of religion as a generic category leads me to worry that, trying to move them in a direction, I'd be trying to move them to Christianity in a way that I think we'd agree is inappropriate with, say, a Muslim student at Wabash. I think I know how to help students take human religiousness, in all its forms, more seriously than some secular students might, but I'm not sure what it would mean to make them "more religious" in general. If Hindu students are reading Calvin on how the human mind is a factory of idols apart from the gospel, faithfulness to their own tradition will lead them to reject that, forcefully. Conversely, with Christian students reading the Gita.

WEBB: I do have a more elastic notion of religion than you, and I think we would agree that every good religion class is trying—on some level—to figure out just what religion is. Perhaps we can agree that just as there is no one thing called "religion," there is also no one right way to teach religion! I mean that seriously in the sense that no pedagogical model can save us from these complex issues, but I also think that the topic of religion—no matter how complex and hard to define—does call forth a certain response, a certain approach, that is commensurate to it. Every topic determines its own pedagogy, so that studying religion is, in a way, a religious endeavor. The study of religion is not some thing that is totally separable from the thing that religion is, whatever that is!

I do think we agree that we are not trying to create a religious space for students that would be composed of a vague spirituality that masquerades as something acceptable to everyone when, in reality, it is believed by nobody. Instead, we are trying to create room for students to inch along their own spiritual paths and to be challenged by religious ways of being in the world that they had not previously imagined. We are not pretending that the religion classroom is this neutral space that has nothing to do with faith. We are not priests in the class-room, authorized by the church to give the students God in the sacraments of our lectures and syllabi! Yet we do bring our faith with us, and we do hope that God works through us. We do not try to answer all the questions we raise for our students, but we do hope they will find an answer for themselves.

The point is that when we ask students to think through a religious idea, argument, or event, we are urging them into a relationship to the ultimate mystery of the world, and they are doing more than memorizing names, dates, and places. It is hard to name that relationship, because it is not worship and it is not church, but it is a reverent meditation on ultimate mat-ters, matters that can move us in unpredictable ways, which makes teaching religion both exciting and dangerous.

At what point, if at all, does the religion classroom become religious? I wouldn't want to say. Only God knows that, I guess, and we must keep in mind that the religion classroom is expe-rienced differently by every participant. But the possibility that the religion classroom can transcend the academic canon of objectivity, neutrality, and passivity is the mystery of why the study of religion can be so relevant and transforming. If we can-not always name that mystery in the religion classroom, per-haps we can be forgiven for hoping that it is the same mystery that is more fully articulated in what we study, that is, the reli-gious traditions themselves.

THEOLOGY AND RELIGIOUS STUDIES

HOW EVERY RELIGION TEACHER IS A THEOLOGIAN NOW

If religion is to be taken seriously in public education, it must be taken seriously in religious studies departments. Religion can be taught in nearly any classroom, of course, but the only place it is taught in any comprehensive way is in religious studies programs. Religion departments, therefore, are the site of the real battle over how religion should be approached and valued in public education. These departments raise religion to the level of academic respectability by attending to it with a wide array of methodological and theoretical tools, but do these departments meet the social need to reintegrate religion and education? What is so religious about religious studies?

Of course, some people will wonder what the fuss is all about. After all, religion frequently exercises an authority over the lives of students that is more pervasive and powerful than educational institutions. Religion is alive and well in the world, so why should schools be pressured to give it a boost? Moreover, public schools are in such intellectual disarray that most students hardly experience an educational philosophy that is sufficiently coherent to challenge their deepest beliefs.

The problem, however, is that students are vulnerable to the secular values that schools convey. Admittedly, churches, synagogues, and mosques function like educational systems as much as high schools and colleges. The difference is that houses of worship get students when they are young, so they can lay the foundation for moral and spiritual development, while high schools and colleges get students when they are beginning to question childhood beliefs and make decisions that will determine their direction as adults. This sequence alone can give schools more moral weight than churches in our culture. The functional division between churches as suppliers of emotional consolation and universities as sites where truth is pursued at all costs exacerbates this inequality. Writing in *The University Through the Eyes of Faith,* sociologist Robert Wuthnow says, "Institutions of higher learning symbolize a sacred space—the navel of the world—where truth is closer, where the mundane concerns of business and family can be bracketed from view, where athletic prowess and physical beauty are at their peak, and where the youthfulness even of aging professors and alumni can be preserved safely."[1] If churches are defined as places of nostalgia and safety for children, colleges are portrayed as places of adventure and discovery, giving them the advantage when it comes to the adolescent need for self-questioning and reinvention.

This division of labor is not completely deleterious for religion. The academy can cultivate religious arguments that are too contentious for the churches—arguments, for example, about the role of women in religion or the morality of sexual orientation. Because the churches largely have assented to the university's monopoly on the pursuit of historical and critical research undertaken with the highest intellectual standards, the academy is, by default, the only place where thoughtful progress can be made on a wide range of religious issues. Nevertheless, such academic discussions are conducted infrequently with the best interests of the church at heart. Scholarship is about manipulation and mastery, developing ever more refined techniques and analysis to enhance human freedom and power. The emphasis is on human control over nature, texts, and ideas. This inevitably will come into conflict with the theological study of religion. While religions are in part about the manipulation of human emotion and need, religions also point to something transcendent that defies human pride and power. The churches subordinate knowledge to obedience of one sort or another, a constraint the academy can never openly allow.

Of course, the universities are hardly disinterested and independent in their pursuit of the truth. Since 1980, when Congress passed the Bayh-Dole Act in the midst of concerns about rising economic competition from Japan, universities have been able to patent the results of federally funded research. The ivory tower has become another piece of real estate for market exploitation, with private corporations buying their way into the sacred halls of academic research. Industry funding for academic research has grown dramatically since 1980, giving corporations the power to dictate the conditions and terms under which it is conducted. More and more scientists are in debt to industry grants for their work. Many also have a financial stake in the companies that fund them. Consequently, many professors and universities no longer are so open with the exchange of ideas and methods. The rush to make a profit from research also has had a disastrous effect on the humanities. Education is becoming just another commodity to be produced as cheaply and efficiently as possible. In the years ahead, it is likely that humanities professors will be united around simply the basic issue of how to survive. Worrying about whether religion teachers owe their loyalty to institutions outside of education seems like a trivial concern in the shadow of growing industry-university collaboration.

The best religion teachers often position themselves near the sectarian obligations of the religious institutions they study to better understand them, not to make a profit from their research. This is probably why the phenomenological method of religious studies is so popular, because it enables teachers to

207

demonstrate respect for the existential dimension of religion without being too specific about the contours of faith or subjecting it to harsh critique. Religion teachers who are too critical of religion or too defensive of it (the former being called reductionists and the latter being called theologians) are thought to be not playing their pedagogical roles with sufficient tact and taste. It is not that atheists and theologians are totally unwelcome in religious studies, but they tend to stick out, raising uncomfortable questions of personal belief and public truth. They upset the civility that holds religious studies together like an invisible glue.

Today, this civility is being called into question by multiculturalism, identity politics, cultural studies, and culture wars. As a result, teachers cannot hide behind the masks of Western rationalism and methodological skepticism when they deal with issues of race, gender, sexuality, or religion. Schools need new ground rules for the study of religion, but these rules will not be as firm and rigorous as the old ones. The old rules included a ban on personal confessions, theological apologetics, and religious passion. The new rules will have to do with the kind of community we want to create when all of the old laws are allowed to expire. We no longer have established criteria to judge what is permissible and what is outlawed in the religion classroom. The university is organized by pragmatic considerations, not metaphysical definitions of truth and falsity. Whoever can push intellectual conversations in new and promising directions is rewarded, regardless of where they are headed. Perhaps the only rule we have is that anything goes, as long as it is interesting and productive. For the study of religion, this should mean that all voices are encouraged, as long as we draw students (and each other) closer to the mystery, complexity, and power of that which claims such utter allegiance from so many people.

The Evolution of Religious Studies

The rationale for the study of theology has evolved along with changes in the social location of theological studies. As Clark

Gilpin, former Dean of the Divinity School at the University of Chicago, has pointed out, in the eighteenth century the study of theology was essential because church, nation, and school were united in purposes and functions. After the colonial period, however, theological scholarship changed its location from church to school. Ministers no longer were engaged in training apprentice pastors. Theological education was taken over by theological professors, and academic societies replaced professional organizations. This shift did not mean that the study of religion lost its significance. On the contrary, religion flourished under the old educational regime because it insisted on the unity of truth and the morality of knowledge. The question is, can religion return to public education under the new reigning conditions of radical pluralism and competing specializations?

The nineteenth century brought a gradual separation of church and state, and as a consequence of disestablishment, American theologians no longer could appeal to a widely shared religious heritage. As Gilpin explains, "In this pluralistic setting, no simple appeal to the belief and practice of a particular tradition could, of itself, offer a publicly persuasive reading of the American religious circumstance as a whole. At the same time, the theological impulse toward a comprehensive interpretation of reality and the social impulse toward public cohesion left religious thinkers discontent with sheer plurality of opinion."[2] A category of common religious experience was needed to fill the void of a common religious tradition. Ecumenical Protestant theologians took as their task the illumination and explication of the inner religious life, the heart of religion that, they argued, was more important (and more universal) than intellectual arguments, doctrines, and beliefs. As part of this process, they moved Christianity further away from Judaism by exaggerating the differences between law and gospel. The result was that the study of religion was not so much secularized in American education as desectarianized.

Obviously, Protestant educational leaders were not acting in a vacuum. Social forces urged them toward a more universal approach to religion. Indeed, the upswing in religious studies departments after World War II coincided with a new confidence in American colleges as they tried to distance themselves from their pasts and avoid any ecclesiastical control. Most religion departments were started with ministerial help and for explicitly religious purposes. Because one of the purposes of religion programs was to prepare students for the vocation of ministry, this type of program frequently was modeled on seminary education. As universities expanded and research institutions provided the norm toward which all colleges should strive, religion departments began to cultivate specialization and objectivity, just like most other disciplines. As historian Conrad Cherry has argued, Protestant leaders at first welcomed a more specialized approach to religion as a strategy of elevating the prestige of the clergy, combating fundamentalism, and extending Protestant influence across American culture.[3] What began, however, as a methodological secularism soon became ideological. A new rule came into practice. Religion could be taught as long as it affirmed basic values open to all, rather than confessional creeds limited to specific historical traditions.

The pressure on religion departments, then, was to develop theories and methodologies that emphasized what religions had in common, rather than their inherent differences. Religious studies professors began to look down on confessional theology as a deductive discipline, based on authoritative traditions, while promoting religious studies as an inductive discipline that revised its theories on the basis of observation and self-criticism. Confessionalism represented the way of devotion, in which knowledge is made possible by submission and obedience; religious studies embodied the way of the intellect, which pursues the goals of mastery and control.

Such stark contrasts, however, are misleading. As Eric J. Sharpe argues, the field of religious studies was born in a theological matrix. "Certainly there was a time when scholarship sought to free itself from the deductive and hence ultimately authoritarian methods of religious confessionalism, siding with historical science over against what was felt to be the dead hand of religious orthodoxy. *But this was precisely what liberal religion was doing during the same period.*"[4] Sharpe defines liberalism as "an insistent moralism and quest for human universals, coupled with a belief in the infinite educability of the human race."[5] Given this definition, it is pretty obvious that religious studies constituted not a reaction against Christian theology but another particular form of theology. Historians of religion who work in an existential or phenomenological mode continue the tradition of liberal theology's attempt to find a religious essence that underlies all of the various concrete religious traditions, an essence that is basically moral in character.

There is something to the barb, then, that "Comparative religion is an admirable recipe for making people comparatively religious."[6] Much of religious studies is a way of practicing ecumenical Protestant theology without explicitly giving it that name. As Sharpe writes in the standard history of the field, comparative religion requires a motive, which often involves "a degree of dissatisfaction with inherited religious traditions."[7] It usually presupposes, Sharpe continues, a "certain degree of detachment from a dominant religious tradition"[8] as well as an urge to seek out the religious beliefs of others. This combination of motivating elements—disillusionment with religious dogma, a feeling that Christian tradition has been discredited, a belief in universal religious structures, and a romantic notion that other religions capture those structures in more pure and powerful ways than religions closer to home—can be attributed to many factors in recent Western history, secular and religious, but surely the main one is the failure of Protestant Christianity to take its own theological heritage seriously.

Indeed, the vision of religion that was born in liberal Protestantism, with its bias against the Jewish understanding of God as a lawgiver, was brought to its fullest expression by the founders of the field of the history of religions. Under the influence of Carl Jung, scholars like Mircea Eliade and Henry Corbin downplayed the importance of law, ritual, and dogma in religion and instead emphasized myth and mysticism. In the words of Steven M. Wasserstrom, they developed a "monotheism without ethics."[9] Religions are about symbols, they argued, not beliefs, and at the heart of all religion is a gnostic acknowledgment of a *coincidentia oppositorum,* a godhead of unifying opposites. Religion thus does not bind the believer to a partic-

211

ular tradition but liberates the individual to participate in every tradition. This liberal theology provided the foundation for the history of religions for several generations, although recently it has come under attack. Much of the energy of the history of religions field has dissipated as it has spilled over into the New Age movement, and there has been a reaction against its quasi-theological elements. Nonetheless, support for a more materialistic and scientific approach to religion, which is meant to correct the religious excesses of Eliade and company, merely supplants one problematic methodology and its hidden agenda with another.

The Return to Reductionism in Religious Studies

Religious studies, when shorn of its ministerial roots, entered a period of great anxiety over its purpose and status. If the comparative religions approach still echoes the ideals of liberal Protestantism, some scholars have urged a more overtly critical study of religion. Nobody has pushed harder in this direction than Donald Wiebe. In *The Politics of Religious Studies,* he complains that the truly scientific study of religion, which emerged in the nineteenth century with a deep commitment to the empirical sciences, all but disappeared in the twentieth. Not only does he exaggerate the purely scientific motives of the early pioneers in the study of religion, he also offers a narrow definition of science that hardly anyone would accept today, calling it "the attempt only to understand and explain that activity rather than to be involved in it."[10] Although he is against the "importation of cultural, political, racial, ethnic, or other noncognitive criteria"[11] into religious studies, it is religious interests that really have him worried. Somehow, given all the dominant forces that have fragmented every academic discipline today, he blames theology for politicizing religious studies, and he imagines that religious studies detheologized would revert to a paradise of pure research, floating high above the political fray.

Wiebe portrays this fall from pure science as a failure of nerve on the part of religion scholars, especially in America where

212

the study of religion expanded dramatically after World War II. He introduces as evidence a review of thirty years of presidential addresses to the American Academy of Religion. He is dismayed that many AAR presidents have talked about their profession in terms of its significance for the life of religious faith. I would think it odd if people who devoted their life to the study of religion were not motivated by religious concerns, and certainly presidential addresses are good vehicles for trying to sum up the shape of one's career. For Wiebe, however, such talk endorses the reality, truth, and value of religion, which he thinks is the cardinal sin that ruins pure scientific research.

Behind this pollution of scholarship with religious motives lies one individual, according to Wiebe. Mircea Eliade is his main culprit, because Eliade defended the autonomy of religion and a humanistic paradigm for studying it. Eliade betrayed the discipline of the study of religion because he deceptively promoted a theological agenda in the guise of pure science. Eliade, in other words, wanted the religion scholar to be a public intellectual, speaking to contemporary religious issues and offering models for the retrieval of religious traditions in an increasingly secular age. This, according to Wiebe, amounts to partisanship, which he equates with theology.

Indeed, when Wiebe defines theology, he makes it clear that confessionalism is the real problem. "Confessional theologies presume the existence of some kind of Ultimate Transmundane Reality, whereas non-confessional theologies recognize only the cultural reality of 'the gods' (that is, some transcendental reality) and attempt to account for it rationally, but without subscribing to the supposition that the Ultimate exists."[12] By confessional theology, then, he does not necessarily mean capital-C confessionalism, which refers to theologies grounded in particular creeds and doctrines, but rather any commitment to the truth of religious claims. He would admit critical theology into religious studies, but only because it "recognizes the Ultimate as problematic; for such theology leaves open the possibility of a reductionistic account of it."[13] He thus expands the definition of confessional theology to cover all constructive religious thought. Any attempt to attend to

213

the mystery, depth, reality, or meaning of religion is a reversion to confessionalism. The religious studies teacher should be a complete outsider to the topic, not influenced by any insider commentary or assumptions.

For Wiebe, then, theology is either confessional (because it affirms the existence of God) or reductionistic (and thus it is hard to see how it is theology at all). For theology to be of a scientific nature it must be "capable of accepting the demands of intellectual honesty to the point of abandoning any absolute or ultimate commitments, and leaving itself open to radical change."[14] This definition of science, however, presupposes that honesty equals agnosticism and that scientists are never guided by ultimate commitments, an empirically false statement, given the many biographies of scientists that demonstrate their passionate and mixed motives. Wiebe's unreal account of science veers into the paranoid when he suggests that confessional theology "cannot complement the academic study of religion but can only 'infect' it."[15] He makes this hygienic analogy even though he admits that reductionistic accounts of religion have had little success in explaining their topic.[16] What he worries about most is the subordination of the academy to the church, even though few colleges and universities pay even lip service to their ecclesial heritages. Theology, then, is a disease that needs eradicating if the study of religion is to be saved. Wiebe's mixture of religious metaphors of purity and salvation with the medical jargon of infection and prevention results in an odd discourse that is itself thoroughly theological in its nostalgic longing for the mythical period of the purely scientific origins of religious studies.

Ironically, Wiebe's disappointment with religious scholarship is not directed against theology as much as against what Daniel L. Pals calls the "humanistic maneuver" in religious studies.[17] Most religion scholars see their field as closer to the study of literature, philosophy, or history than any of the social sciences. They think religion is a product of human thought, emotion, and imagination and thus cannot be subjected to strictly empirical tests. Wiebe suspects dark motives for this alignment between religion and the humanities. He suspects

214

that religion scholars choose to hang around with humanities colleagues because such arrangements are more compatible with their personal theological commitments.

Given the shoddy ways in which the humanities ordinarily treat any interest in religion, Wiebe's conspiracy theory about the hidden promotion of theology cannot be taken seriously. But there is something in what he says. A kind of liberal theology does provide the foundation for much of religious studies. The idea that religions essentially are vehicles of moral value and so can be construed as teaching the same basic beliefs did not come from nowhere. Its origin lies in liberal Protestant theology, beginning with the work of theologian and philosopher Friedrich Schleiermacher. This liberal theology and its relativistic consequences should be made the subject of more interrogation and critique than it has in the past. Although the Protestant influence on higher education is in decline, it has left a heritage that still frames the debates over the future of the study of religion.

If ecumenical Protestants no longer occupy the cultural center of American life, then our nation no longer sanctions only one way to teach religion. In place of the mainline Protestant consensus is an emerging New Age perspective that radicalizes liberal relativism but departs from the traditional Protestant ethos by injecting a heavy dose of eclectic spirituality into the study of religion.[18] It is doubtful, however, whether the New Age paradigm has the intellectual staying power to become dominant in the field, which opens the door to other positions on the organization of religious studies. There is, for example, the recent move of the Roman Catholic Bishops to establish greater ties of accountability between the Catholic church and its universities, especially theologians. For public schools, the solution to the problem of the fragmentation of the religious studies discipline is not to turn back the clock to a nineteenth-century version of scientific rigor. Not many in the academy today would subscribe to Wiebe's notion that scholarship entails the suppression of personal or emotional participation in the object under scrutiny. The solution to the problem is to ask all

215

scholars to be more open and honest about the religious or antireligious presuppositions that inform their thought.

Unfortunately, however, this is precisely what Wiebe rejects. He is terribly worried about anything that might smack of confessionalism in the academy. While scholars across the disciplines are turning to biographical studies to contextualize everything from Freud to Einstein, Wiebe would have the study of religion be a faceless and heartless discipline, void of personal spiritual interest. The problem is that no approach to religion can be purely neutral and disinterested. As postmodernists go to great lengths to point out, there are personal agendas behind all intellectual research. And there should be. Studying religion, or any topic for that matter, should not be an arid pursuit of knowledge for its own sake. Studying religion should have the potential to transform student and teacher alike in the pursuit of life's most holy mysteries.

Ironically, Wiebe's rejection of all confessions leaves him unable or unwilling to acknowledge fully his own agenda. He portrays himself as a disinterested investigator of religion who wants to rely on the empirical methods of the social sciences. However, he is obviously a partisan in the culture wars over how much power and influence people of faith should have in public institutions. His goal, in its broadest terms, is to remove anything that looks like Christian theology from public education. His agenda is to put people like me out of a job.

The same problems are apparent in the work of Wiebe's student, Russell McCutcheon.[19] McCutcheon also rejects Eliade's romantic view of primordial religions. He argues that Eliade's claim that religion is *sui generis* amounts to an apologia for religious faith. If Eliade practices theology in disguise, it is a very effective disguise and a very thin theology. McCutcheon wants to correct the wrongs of Eliade's implicit theology with a scientific materialism, but he goes too far in the opposite direction. If religion is not *sui generis,* it does not necessarily follow that religion must be treated like any other object and studied with the strictest neutrality. It could be that the study of religion involves the student in such complex and ambiguous questions that no objective perspective is possible. McCutcheon himself recognizes this when he puts a postmodern spin on Wiebe's work by arguing that the study of religion literally manufactures its subject matter. McCutcheon admits that every theory of religion is essentially an exercise in autobiography. He further suggests that every attempt to establish the autonomy of religion is a product of reactionary politics. Western scholars treat religion as an ahistorical category, he argues, because they do not want to connect religion to the larger system of political domination, capitalist exploitation, and cultural imperialism from which they benefit. McCutcheon opposes such essentialism with a political radicalism that would treat religion as nothing but the product of oppressive economic and social forces. Yet his own theory of religion—based on leftist materialism— is just as much a product of autobiography and politics as the theories he so strongly rejects.

The moral of McCutcheon's quest for a new political footing for the study of religion is that it is impossible to know where one's own prejudices end and an objective description of religion begins. My point is that we should not exclude either conservative or radical readings of religion. Instead, there should be room in public education for a wide variety of approaches to the topic, including both critical and apologetic as long as they are sensitive to student needs. I suppose that McCutcheon would accuse me of taking a reactionary approach to religious studies, since I see politics as a dimension of religion rather than religion as a subset of politics. The study of religion, in my view, is not an attempt to change students or society politically as much as it is an attempt to challenge students and society religiously. If students need to be pushed, they need to be encouraged to think more deeply about God, not about how the government is either the source of or the solution to their problems. McCutcheon, on the contrary, thinks that professors understand religion better than their students and that the language of political economy should trump theology in every description of religious activity. McCutcheon follows Wiebe in seeking to exercise a complete control over the field of religious studies, demonstrating that his own political orientation would lead him to cleanse it of any position that did not agree with his materialistic worldview.

The Difference Theology Makes in Religious Studies

No academic discipline is free from the intentions of its practitioners to promote (or, less frequently, demote) the very thing that is studied. Critics who teach literature, for example, tend to think novels and stories can go a long way toward not only helping students with their personal lives but, more important, helping all of us think through the grave issues of the day. Only in the study of religion are there teachers who wring their hands in worry that they might motivate students to enter into the world they are examining. Some scholars even have taken to calling religious studies *religion studies* to avoid the impression that teachers of religion might also be practitioners. The thing that draws students to the study of religion—the possibility that their lives might change and that they will know themselves more fully—is the very thing that many religion teachers work against as they worry about crossing the line between scholarship and advocacy.

The situation for theology in religious studies probably is not as dire as I have portrayed it, because many people who teach religion have some theological interests they are willing to share with their students, even if these interests are frequently distilled in the established genre of stories about escaping from fundamentalism into more liberal forms of faith. The fact is that theology and religious studies often work together. There is theology in religious studies just as there is religious studies in theology. Nevertheless, while working toward the theoretical convergence of theology and religious studies might be important, it is equally important to point out and preserve their practical differences so that the voice of theology is not too quickly assimilated into a liberal religious studies paradigm. Indeed, just as English professor Gerald Graff has recommended that English teachers should teach, rather than repress, the insoluble differences that plague English departments, religion teachers should let the students themselves confront the diverse ways of studying religion.[20]

Preserving these differences should not be too hard, because theology often brings to the forefront what religious studies frequently would like to repress. Theology thus functions as the guilty conscience of religious studies, reminding the field of what lurks beneath its veneer of objectivity and neutrality. And as with any guest who states what the host knows but does not want to hear, theology frequently is unwelcome in the house of the study of religion solely for its honesty and openness.

Without the pressure of theology, religious studies can theorize in the bad sense, becoming a totalizing, hegemonic attempt to dominate diversity by reducing it to one point of view. Such theorizing masks a fear of real passion, conflict, and faith. It also says that only those in the privileged position of mastering difficult theoretical material are able to name religion and thus know it. Students, many of whom have deeper and more diverse religious experiences than the teacher, consequently are rendered passive in their approach to a topic that should excite their learning skills.

At its worst, the study of religion creates a fake religion, a mirage or illusion suitable for controlling the classroom by disciplining any religious enthusiasm that would stray outside acceptable forms of public discussion. It is a manufactured discourse, an artificial syntax, replacing specific descriptions with vague and general terms. Nobody speaks about God as a social referent or salvation as a change from self- to other-orientation or Jesus Christ as a representation of our ultimate confidence in the world. Religious studies thus functions for students like a foreign language, except that foreign languages are natural to somebody else, consisting of words born out of daily usage and social need. The language of religious studies is similar to those languages, such as Esperanto, that intellectuals invented during the nineteenth century in the hope of creating a discourse which everybody would be able to speak. Such languages, of course, ended up being spoken by very few people. Likewise, nobody speaks religious studies except religious studies professors, who guard their technical terms with all of

219

the self-interest of gnostic priests, welcoming only those who are willing to be initiated into a new way of speaking about the world. Indeed, religious studies can be thought of as one long attempt to find alternative discourses to religious practices, a lexicon that would repeat religious terms but in such a way that the original passion and faith expressed in them would be evacuated.

Speaking religion differently from the way religious people speak is the goal of religious studies. Like all languages, however, this one can survive and flourish only if it is connected to social conditions that give it sense, so that religious studies anxiously reproduces itself in conferences, books, and journals, confirming itself by the like speaking to like. I am not saying that the secondary theories and critiques of religious studies have no power and truth. Their descriptive insight, however, is dependent on the ongoing reality of a religious vernacular that is spoken by people of faith. Religious studies is thus a parasitic discipline that cannot break its dependence on religious faith without destroying itself. Because the language of religious studies must use the vocabulary of faith communities, the study of religion will always be accused of being too religious. The artificial language of religious studies is in the service of the dialect of faith, to which it must always return to test itself and measure its insights. Such comparisons will always leave religious studies looking meek and inferior, because it can never fully replace that which it is trying to fathom. Consequently, the faith talk of religious communities must be given space and attention in the classroom as the living discourse that moves students to further depths of exploration and theorizing.

Theology frequently is treated as an unwelcome guest in religious studies because it is not deemed theoretical enough. Theology too closely mimics the colloquialisms of faith, which religion professors want to study from a respectful distance. Theologians have the same problem that feminists or professors of color often confront when they are told that their approach to the topic is not sufficiently critical and theoretical. This closeness, however, is nothing more than an attempt to reflect in theoretical language the naturalness of the language of faith. Theology does not try to replace religious language but rather seeks to clarify its grammar, sharpen its vocabulary, and trace its history. Theology is thus theoretical while still being true to what is really spoken. Arguably, all theories of religion are religious in this way, trying to position themselves with regard to what religious people say so that even the most critical and abstract religious theory is theological.

If the theories of religious studies are not to be moribund and elitist, they should make sense outside the classroom, to people in the pews, so to speak, which means that religious studies must be much more open to religious voices than in the past. A theory of religion that leaves students stripped of their beliefs, naked before the blinding light of critique, hardly can empower them to take control of their lives. At most, it will leave them with a disconnect between who they are and what they have been taught, causing them either to feign amnesia with regard to their religious past or compartmentalize their private faith from their public persona. Religious studies should not be a luxury affordable to only those students who have a sufficient distance from their past or private selves. It should be an invitation to all students to gather themselves more coherently and dwell in themselves more fully as they integrate their faith with a widening view of the world.

How (Almost) To Teach Religion in Public Schools

Recently, professional educators have been hearing the call to train future teachers with more sensitivity to religion. One of the best books written to meet this demand is by Robert Nash, a professor of education at the University of Vermont.[21] Nash draws from his own teaching experiences, and it is clear that he is sympathetically immersed in religion while struggling to be both a fair and critical commentator. This book comes closer than most written by professors at schools of education to taking religion seriously in its own terms. Still, Nash represents a tragic failure of the public teaching of religion to be theolog-

221

ically informed and grounded. If this is the best that public education can come up with, we still have a long way to go.

The heart of this book consists of Nash's explanation of four basic religious narratives. He presents each one in two chapters, with a positive and a critical evaluation. These narratives consist of fundamentalism, prophetic religion (liberation theology), alternative spiritualities (New Age), and what Nash calls post-theism (a postmodern agnosticism). It is daring and praiseworthy that he begins with an appreciation of fundamentalism, but that is also part of the book's problem. Nowhere is non-fundamentalist Christianity represented. By staging a debate between fundamentalism and liberation theology, Nash leaves out the great number of Christians who find themselves in neither camp.

Nash develops a fair and informed portrait of each narrative, and he uses his own teaching experience to show how to present and critique these narratives in the classroom. But he seems religiously confused, which is not necessarily a bad position to be in when teaching religion. He describes himself as a Christian realist who is agnostic and who rejects "the whole otherworldly apparatus that accompanies Christianity."[22] I have no idea what that means, unless it is a throwback to the atheists-for-Niebuhr movement with some sort of postmodern spin. Unfortunately, this religious confusion prevents Nash from taking Christian history and tradition seriously.

Nash does not encourage or even permit reflection on and expression of traditional Christian positions. His brief reading of what he calls "accommodationist" theology, represented by David Tracy, Ted Peters, and David Ray Griffin, is disdainful and inadequate. And he certainly does not have very many positive things to say about Roman Catholicism. Notice this prejudiced and uncritical comment: "Whether an ayatollah or pope, a cult leader or a Jimmy Swaggert [sic], those who feel the 'hand of God moving them within' and who see their 'crackdowns' on apostates as a 'commission from above,' are genuinely to be feared in a democracy."[23] That Christians could be both theologically orthodox and generously open to other religions and beliefs does not seem to him to be possible. Perhaps Nash does not have many traditional—as opposed to fundamentalist—Christian students in his classes. But that merely means teachers need to work even harder to present the core beliefs of Christianity as transcending the politics of the left and the right.

Nash ends up defending the post-theistic model and thus supporting a kind of religious relativism. Ultimately he is interested in a free-floating form of spirituality, not religion. Here is his advice for teachers: "A pluralistic, religious agnosticism separates out, privatizes, and secularizes those principles, values, and virtues that do not require the formal apparatus of church doctrine, revelation, or theology to support them. From a pedagogical perspective, secular educators must *respectfully* view all the rest as denominational distractions—highly significant to particular faith communities to be sure—but less central to outsiders and skeptics."[24] The result can be only a superficial and consumeristic approach toward spirituality that tries to contain and domesticate all that is significant and challenging about the Christian faith.

Nash's naive attempt to separate spirituality from theology, as if every individual can invent one's own religion in an historical vacuum, reflects his deep ambivalence toward religion. I suppose that is only inevitable: we all dramatize in our classrooms our own religious beliefs and passions. But do we have to be postmodern agnostic relativists in order to teach religion in high schools?

My sense is that if you try to force students into a multicultural mode, they will refuse, and their beliefs will go unchecked and unchallenged. If you try to help students become the best version of what they believe, they will have the confidence to be open to other traditions and views. Teaching Christianity in the classroom should help our many Christian students recover the richness and complexity of their religious heritage—and they can do that without sacrificing their need to understand non-Western traditions.

Nash admits several times that his students no longer appear to know much about Christianity, although he repeatedly insists that students are tired of the mainline traditions. How can students be tired of something they have never tried? The church is a foreign country to them, and theology is a foreign language. Why not begin Western religious education, then, with the historical specificity and the intellectual integrity of the monotheistic faiths? Nash is offering his students options on a menu when they do not even know how the standard fare tastes. Moreover, his options leave out the most important voice in Christianity, an historically informed commitment to Christian faith that is neither literalist nor leftist. The real danger with Nash's book is that he does not see the limitations of his own position—how his own agnosticism is just as exclusive as the traditional forms of faith he treats as mere distractions.

The Authority of the Religion Teacher

Nash tries to be fair to all forms of faith, but he ends up favoring a relativism that leaves little room for traditional Christianity. His problem is hardly unique to religious studies. How can you teach any subject without excluding some group or position? Inevitably, teachers do a lot of imposing on their students. In a way, that is what teaching is all about: demanding, encouraging, informing, directing, leading, testing, judging. Teachers impose their views on students on a countless range of topics, while trying to grant students the freedom to question and explore. However, there is general agreement that the worst pedagogical sin a teacher can commit is to impose religious beliefs on a student. There is something very right about this, but such worry about religion also reflects something very wrong. The fear of imposing religion can lead to an educational paralysis in which religion is avoided altogether. As a result, the classroom becomes not tolerant and open but secular and atheistic.

What is the source of authority to teach religion? On what grounds do teachers presume to tell students what religion is, how faith takes shape, and why people believe? Teaching religion is a precarious business in today's polarized climate, and rightly so. The only authority religion teachers have is their claim to give themselves, with passionate discipline, to their subject. Teachers thereby learn to listen to the many voices of faith throughout history; thus they can hear the voices of their students as the students try to come to terms with their own faith. Teachers can understand their students' stories of faith best if they know their own. Such self-understanding, according to the law of faith, begins not with narcissistic introspection but with locating oneself before the power of another. The authority to teach religion, then, is ultimately a religious authority. God is the author of the whole of life, from the intellectual to the physical world, and thus sets into play the quest for a self-understanding that is at the same time a journey in the knowledge of God.

If teaching religion is a spiritual journey, it will always be a risky venture that cannot be saved by the objective certainties of rationality. Indeed, the religion classroom should not be a place where the foremost goal is to produce authorities and experts. That merely reinforces the students' fears that they must master a body of material by gaining an ever higher and more abstract perspective on it, leaving themselves out of the picture. Instead, teachers should ask students to inquire into how their lives are authored by a myriad of forces, by seeing how their religious experiences fit into larger patterns, traditions, and histories. This kind of pedagogy is risky for the teacher, who must be open, personal, and engaging. Perhaps the biggest risk for the confessional teacher is being looked down upon by colleagues, who will wonder if sufficient material is being covered, if classrooms have degenerated into gab sessions, and if the teacher is straying across disciplinary boundaries.

The students, however, occupying the position of learner and opening themselves to judgment, take the most risk. That is why teachers must give students the confidence to bring their lives into the world of scholarship so they may see that intellectual debates are not arid and empty but pertain to real people and entail choices with consequences. The religion classroom needs to be a place of both safety and risk, a place where students can assume religious identities that will disturb, challenge, and transform them in playful, imaginative, and tentative ways. The point is not to distance them from their personal

225

experiences so they can have a wider view but to help them integrate their lives into enriching contexts.

Most important, for students of faith to inhabit their voices to the fullest effect, they must be allowed to speak in ways that annoy, and even offend, others. This principle is good for both the classroom and democracy. As Stephen Carter has argued, democracy works best when "the religions are able to act as independent moral voices interposed between the citizen and the state."[25] Teachers have the right and responsibility to signal their resistance to students who do not tolerate others and who do not promote the civility that makes classroom discussions productive. But this does not mean that some views should be ruled out of bounds before the discussion even begins. In today's postmodern classroom, all beliefs are potentially divisive as students struggle to identify themselves with one movement or another. The classroom hardly can be divided between benign beliefs that are shared by most students and dubious beliefs that cause commotion, with religion being assigned to the latter group. And religion should not be divided into progressive beliefs that promote social justice and reactionary beliefs that defend a particular cause. All kinds of beliefs cause division in the pursuit of a greater good like justice or truth, so to label certain religious beliefs as inherently divisive is to preempt the discussion that needs to take place over questions of truth, justice, and the good of society as a whole.

Every classroom needs students who push the boundary of what teachers are comfortable talking about, students who advocate unpopular positions or raise controversial issues. Every teacher has experienced students who go too far in polemical wrangling and defensive posturing, but without the interjection of passionate argument into the classroom, learning would not be possible. Too many classes operate with gag rules, which squelch questions of ultimacy and confessional perspectives. Religious passion is particularly subversive in the classroom because it calls into question not only the teacher's ability to manage the discussion but also the very authority of secular education. Religious faith is, therefore, an independent pedagogical force in the classroom. Religious voices remind the

226

teacher (and other students) that there is no single understanding of rationality and no single authority in the process of becoming educated. Religious voices, in fact, can challenge those in education with the claim that there are authorities that transcend the educational system.

I have witnessed in the classroom a trend to which many of my colleagues also attest. My best students—those who are most independent in their thinking, most literate in their writing, and most devoted to their studies—are increasingly religious, theologically evangelical, and politically conservative. There are probably some socio-economic reasons to explain this. Perhaps religiously conservative parents raise their children in a more earnest atmosphere of greater expectations. These children are disciplined early to take seriously the power of written texts to shape their lives. Even more likely, religion today is giving our best students a way to break free from the pack of compulsive consumerists who are setting the pace for so many teenagers. Religion enables young people to choose a path that does not conform to the ways of shopping-mall America. It is awfully hard to mount any attack on secular society or even merely attain some critical distance from some of the worst aspects of contemporary culture. Religion helps young people differentiate themselves from their peer groups, so the factor that can be most uncomfortable to discuss in the classroom actually contributes to the independent thinking of some of our brightest students.

In any case, the Internet is changing the position of the teacher as the source of all authority in the classroom. Students can access so many sources of information that it is no longer possible to control the content of a course as it unfolds over a semester. This can be confusing and counterproductive for the teacher, who does not know what the students are reading and where they are getting their information. But it can be liberating for the students. Students who do not feel comfortable talking in the classroom can have alternative ways of communicating. And students can challenge teachers with alternative authorities.

227

I have had several students track down the E-mail addresses of the authors whose works we were reading to establish a direct line of communication with them and ask them the same questions we raised in class. These students then brought the author's comments into class as a kind of supplemental text to the one we were reading, expanding and challenging my views of the book. Of course, I try to suggest that the author of a text is not always the one who knows the most about how to interpret the ideas in that text, but the students have succeeded in opening up the text to multiple readings that escape my control. Situations like this will become more common in the future. Rather than discourage students from such "transgressions," we need to encourage them to find their voices wherever they can, even if that means outside the classroom and away from our influence.

Allowing students to speak their mind makes for a most difficult pedagogical situation. The skills to orchestrate a discussion must be finely tuned to avoid the twin faults of chaos and compliance. Too often, once a class gets too emotional teachers quickly begin to slow things down, afraid that real arguments will break out and feelings will get hurt. This is when teachers become the most involved in their classes and when they have to be the most careful about their own prejudices and desires. Students who get real in the classroom by saying it as they see it can become suddenly too real to teachers, annoying them by stepping outside the role of the "good student" to become more truly themselves. Teachers also are afraid that students might complain to the dean that they have let things get out of hand, or that other teachers will hear the noise in their classrooms and think they have lost control. Yet these are precisely the moments when the students feel they have the most at stake. They need to be given the space to work through their disagreements and figure out how the class should come to terms with conflict.

The religion classroom should not try to assimilate disparate religious views into one coherent picture. It is not the job of the teacher to dissolve religious friction into an agreeable mush of sentimental conformity. Saying that we all believe in the same

228

God, or that all religions teach the same values, or that it is not a matter of what one believes but how one acts, or that people are, deep down, all alike, is to pronounce specious generalizations that hardly stand up to the scrutiny of reason. Besides, even when students are being polite and smiling at such platitudes, few believe them. Every religious faith is responsive to its own revelational ground, and the essence of most religions is to resist such tempting assimilation.

Rethinking the Confessional Classroom Once More

We teachers guard our classes against testimony about religious experience just as we guard them against too much pleasure or any reference to embodiment. We think classes must be abstract to be productive, and we fear we will lose our students' respect if we permit discussions that do not conform to an academic norm. We want the classroom discourse to feel different from their other conversations, because how else can we justify being paid to be there guiding the discussion? If the class turned into the kind of rancorous but stimulating religious debate that could take place in any dorm on a late night, we would feel awkward and useless, because our authority would not be the focus of the classroom. Yet we complain about sullen and passive students who, before they enter our regimented classrooms, have precisely these kinds of debates back in their living units—debates that we cannot manage to engineer in class.

To be sure, personal experience must be handled with care. It can close down discussion rather than opening it up. Personal experience should mark the beginning of a discussion, not the end. Otherwise, the discussion ends up with identity politics, students claiming a special place for themselves that protects them from outside engagement. Personal experience of religion does not necessarily confer a privilege to speak that others, without such experiences, are denied. It also does not guarantee depth of insight or accuracy of the information conveyed. It does, however, show a student's willingness to risk connecting material to life outside the classroom.

Many theological resources exist to help the religion teacher personalize the classroom without taking herself or himself too seriously. The theologian knows that the classroom is about the personal in some ways, but in other ways it is not because, for Christians, the personal is never solely identical to the individual. Being a person means being created in the image of the triune God, who is communal in nature and whose identity is established in an overflowing of goodness that is relational and creative. The personal classroom, from the perspective of theo-pedagogy, will not revert to blind and arbitrary subjectivism. Instead, it will encourage students to give of themselves to each other as they give attention to the texts, ideas, and arguments presented by the teacher.

The Enlightenment viewed objectivity as a kind of selflessness that brackets every personal desire and need, so that objectivity is possible only when nothing personal is at stake. Theo-pedagogy does not oppose this notion of objectivity with an attitude of anything goes, allowing students to occupy their own positions without being challenged to change or grow. Instead, theo-pedagogy offers a new way of construing objectivity, in which rigor does not mean neutrality but a kind of selflessness that gives space for other views and even for truth. Simone Weil, a modern-day mystic, explicates the religious understanding of objectivity in an important essay, noting, "The key to a Christian conception of studies is the realization that prayer consists of attention."[26] No effort at attention is useless, because attention demands and creates a disciplined desire that is humble and contemplative.

The act of attending also reminds us of our limitations and inadequacies, the sin of selfishness that distracts us from the focus necessary for work. Attention is work, but it is not full of will power; it is a clarity of the soul that opens onto what is other with gratitude and trust. For Weil, the faculty of attention makes us more vulnerable to God and more able to be present to those who suffer. Suffering is something we might talk about in the classroom, but we rarely think of suffering as occurring in the classroom. Yet the struggle to find the courage to speak the right words can involve not a little pain and anguish.

230

There are certainly worse kinds of suffering, but this is the suffering that is presented to us in the classroom, and we must be ready to attend to it. Attention is a matter of emptiness and waiting; translated into pedagogical practice, it means that listening is what the teacher learns by teaching, and as the teacher learns to listen, that is what the teacher teaches.

What is usually called teaching, then, is a sign of failure, a recognition of an interruption in the process of learning. Just as some philosophers have argued that arguments occur only when conversations break down—so that the purpose of an argument should be to repair, not replace, a conversation—I want to suggest that "teaching" happens where the learning event, structured by a mutual conversation, falters. Hermeneutical philosophers long have suggested that dialogue is the model for all authentic communication, whether between two people or between a person and a text, idea, or work of art. Learning is a process that requires commitment, participation, and change. Only in a give-and-take conversation are those virtues habitually practiced. When two or more people talk about a text, for example, the subject of the text confronts them with a demand for understanding that can be worked out only over time, that is, in conversation. A conversation is an attempt to put into play the ideas of the text, and a classic text, with complex and provocative ideas, will never be exhausted by even many conversations. Of course, conversations do get interrupted. Something has to be checked; some information is needed. More important, a disagreement occurs, and the readers of the text must stand back from it to more closely listen to each other. An argument, then, is a moment within a conversation, a means of restoring the conversation—a way of keeping the conversation going, not bringing it to an end.

Similarly, teaching emerges through breaches in communication. Inevitably, the conversation of teaching reaches a spot where something needs to be explained. When I teach about Martin Luther's position on the Eucharist, I usually need to stop and explain the doctrine of transubstantiation so we can go on to discuss what Luther disliked about it. My explanation is useful and important to the extent that it serves the need of

231

the students to make a judgment about an important historical controversy. At such moments, the teacher must intervene as the teacher, telling the students what they do not know so the conversation can continue. But such telling is not an end in itself. Lecturing is thus an emergency response to some crisis, no matter how small—an attempt to fix a problem so learning can continue. When I hear myself teaching, no matter how pleasing my voice is or how well-shaped my words, no matter how impressive I think I sound, I feel I have failed in some fundamental way. Teaching at its best is thought in action, and that action is conversation. Teaching in the sense of a lecture, an informative aside, an expansive meditation on some complex issue, an authoritative explanation of what is really the case, or a moral declamation about how students should act is a dangerous temptation if it involves more than a necessary detour to get back to the true path. Teaching that goes beyond responding to a crisis within conversation becomes a disaster. All teaching comes perilously close to being this kind of disaster: an act of communication that tells rather than shows.

Of course, some classes, due to their size, inevitably include a lot of lecturing, but even then the point of the course should be to get students talking about issues, either among themselves outside the classroom or in small groups within it. The lectures become a context for a lot of conversations the students could not have otherwise. Too much of the resistance to lecturing among faculty stems from leftover sixties leftism, a misplaced desire to liberate students from external authority. I am not suggesting that all lecturing is wrong or bad because teachers have too much authority. On the contrary, the authority of teachers is in decline and needs to be strengthened, not weakened. Teachers often have to present material that is new, difficult, and demanding, and there is no easy way to do that without assuming a high degree of authority. Nevertheless, the goal of teaching is to broaden, not replace, the experiences the student brings to the classroom. The teacher's primary material is not the curriculum but the students. The teacher, then, is most responsible to the students, not the textbooks. Covering the syllabus is secondary to listening to what the students need to learn.

To teach, then, is to lose one's self in a conversation that flows just out of reach of any control or manipulation. It is the wager that a new personality can be formed through submission to the discipline of a guiding set of questions. Such teaching is an exercise in hope, faith, and charity. The teacher must hope that an event of learning takes place, because it cannot be planned or designed. The teacher, then, is thrown into a state of faith, waiting for something like grace to occur. Grace, in the Christian tradition, is the power of powerlessness, the experience of uplift from a combination of forces that includes the mysterious aid of God. To walk into a classroom is to take a stand on faith, to proclaim that there are no final answers except for the movement of truth through our attempts at those answers. If teaching depends on what I do as the teacher, then teaching will be a matter of my merit, worth, and pride. Such efforts might be impressive if well developed, but they will result in very little learning, because they will not give or risk anything. Effort alone never reaches its goal until it gives way to something else.

Why We Are All Theologians Now

One description of universities is that they foster unrestricted conversation. Such conversations have a civic mission to teach the habits of tolerance and openness that make democracy possible. Thus, indoctrination is the gravest pedagogical sin. As Robert Maynard Hutchins, president of the University of Chicago, argued in a book published during the McCarthy era, in the University of Utopia the professor "is supposed to have convictions, the deeper the better. He is not supposed to pound them into his students, even though his opinions are shared by the overwhelming majority of the population."[27] The problem with Hutchins's idealism is twofold. First, it is not clear that the university can have unrestricted conversations anymore, because it is not clear that such a concept is logically coherent. Every institution privileges certain kinds of speech and restricts

233

others, as demonstrated by the efforts of the government to legislate against hate speech and by the universities to draw up speech codes. Second, the dividing line between professing (passion, advocacy) and indoctrination no longer is clear. Indeed, advocacy teaching has become the norm in many disciplines, especially when issues of multiculturalism are at stake.

When the university becomes politicized, it should drop its pretensions of being a place for unrestricted conversations. The university should admit it is composed of competing discourses and quit using the banner of tolerance to suppress views that depart from the norm. As literary theorist Geoffrey H. Hartman has stated, "In the new political culture a rhetoric of sympathy for otherness is still accompanied by an intolerance of dissent and the creation rather than elimination of yet another 'hegemonic discourse.' "[28] Groups that are "in" are allowed to make wild and unsubstantiated charges against groups that are "out," while criticism of the politicization of academic discourse is dismissed as politically incorrect. There is no solution for this situation except to become more—not less—radically pluralistic. But questions remain. Can claims be made for any social group without the risk of excluding and denigrating others? How can teachers and students alike speak from their own situations without restricting the views of others?

In a talk at a workshop on teaching religion, I once suggested that, given the new emphasis on a personalized classroom, all of us who teach religion must be sensitive to theological issues. Indeed, I grandly exclaimed, in the postmodern world, we are all theologians. A historian of religion immediately objected that I was making a totalizing claim that left no room for him. He did not want to be squeezed underneath that umbrella, no matter how wide I envisioned it to be. I was trying to illuminate the ways in which religious faith is inevitably a dimension of every act of teaching religion, but my formulation was threatening to him. He saw me as trying to subsume his specialty, thus erasing his contributions to the study of religion. If I had been doing that, it would have been narrow-minded and offensive. He was not appeased when I said that all religion teachers are also historians, ethicists, comparativists, and exegetes. It was okay if

I, a theologian, also wanted to be a historian, but he, a historian, did not want to have anything to do with theology.

I was not asking my colleague to become a theologian. I do not think that only religious people make good teachers of religion, although I believe that, all things being equal, the religious person will have better insights into religion than the nonreligious person. However, I want to acknowledge that some religious people are too close to their faith to be able to teach religion effectively, while some nonreligious people have a sensitivity toward faith that is nearly equal to that of a religious insider. What I was asking my colleague to reflect on is the fact that all teachers of religion function, at times and in various ways, as theologians. When facing the particular situation of the classroom, where the participants bring their beliefs to the table and where people speak to each other and not to the universal audience of all rational agents, we all become constructive thinkers, not just descriptive or critical thinkers. We all come to the religion classroom with deep beliefs and try to combine those beliefs with strategies of critique and suspicion, based on the voices we hear from others as well as the voice within. We all construct ways in which reason and faith hang together. In this way, we are all theologians.

Returning theology to our schools, then, is not just a matter of changing the curriculum to include Aquinas, Augustine, and Karl Barth. It is also a matter of changing our pedagogy so students feel they can bring their faith to the classroom and have it challenged in ways that will help them to grow as spiritual beings. Of course, most teachers try to respect the voices of their students and take it for granted that students should be allowed to express themselves in class, but unless they are themselves products of a marginalized group, they will often miss the inward struggle of the evangelical students who come to school assuming they must keep their beliefs to themselves.

Is there room today for a truly pluralistic approach to religion, one that would recognize not only that religious studies draws students with a passion for the subject but also that questions of truth and belief cannot be ignored in the religion classroom? At the risk of oversimplification, let me suggest that there

235

are three main ways to teach religion. One is to examine religions as social structures that utilize power in the same ways as any other institution. Religions are treated as ideological systems that need to be analyzed and explained, and they are subjected to categories and theories that derive from the social sciences. The point of studying religions is to demystify their power and authority by showing how they work. The problem with this model is that it treats religion as a byproduct of more fundamental social or psychological factors, rather than as a phenomenon that has its own identity and integrity. It does not directly engage the religious beliefs of the students. At its worst, this approach lapses into a vulgar Marxism of conspiracy theories, dutifully hunting down the self-interest that hides behind every human endeavor. No room is left for anything that transcends human greed and desire. The grace and poetry of religion are turned into recipes for domination and exploitation.

The second way to teach the many religions is to treat them as variations of a single religious experience. Thus, the religion classroom drives toward generalizations, comparisons, and abstractions in an effort to develop categories that can account for an incredible amount of religious diversity. Religion is respected as a unique way of organizing knowledge and motivating believers, but no single religion is treated as unique. All religions basically do the same thing, orienting people of faith toward ultimate mystery. The problem here is that this religious way of teaching religion honors only two religious perspectives, that of ecumenical Christianity (and the ecumenical elements within other traditions) and New Agers who treat religions as tools necessary to achieve personal goals. More worrisome, this approach portrays the life of faith as a capitalistic market where religions provide goods and services for individual consumption. Religions are reduced to useful commodities, subjected to the vagaries of personal preference. The differences among the religions are minimized, and the question of religious truth is rendered irrelevant.

The third way is to teach religious traditions, in all of their density and complexity, as unique responses to divine revelation. Here religions are taken with the utmost seriousness as

236

viable responses to ultimate reality that cannot be reduced to social forces or to some common understanding of God. Studying religion involves not only a personal quest but also an inescapable decision, because religions make demanding claims that are utterly comprehensive and mutually exclusive. Of course, students need not come to a religious decision in the classroom, but the study of religion should give students the intellectual tools to help with those decisions when they are ready to make them. The problem with this strategy is that it looks like you are trying to sell the religious traditions to the students. Moreover, it raises the question of which traditions you teach. With limited time, and with a diverse student body, aren't you forced to teach all religious traditions as diverse examples of one common thing?

A pluralistic approach to the study of religion would include elements of all three pedagogical methods. Indeed, on Christian theological grounds alone, there is justification for some variants of the first two, not just the third. Christianity, with its debt to the prophetic tradition in Judaism, long has acknowledged the complicity of religion and power and has argued that it is a religious duty to distinguish between the two. And there are warrants internal to Christian theology to try to envision the religious truth and power of extra-biblical revelations of God. My argument here is that the third option should not be excluded merely because it invites a confessional attitude from teachers and students. Every approach to religion is grounded in a personal risk and a tradition of inquiry. No approach should be excluded merely because it is open to the risk of faith and the tradition of the church.

To permit the third way of teaching religion would mean treating theology as a necessary component in every religious studies classroom. This would be a boost to a discipline that no longer has much of an intellectual, national, or ecclesial audience. During the middle of the twentieth century, theologians tried to adjust to their declining status by appealing to common religious experience, but the Civil Rights movement and feminism shattered that ideal. Most scholarship today is based on the assumption that all experience is particular, so much so

237

that there is little left of anything held in common. The currently popular idea that theologians can become public intellectuals, as were Paul Tillich and Reinhold Niebuhr, seems optimistic at best. There is little national audience for the kinds of reflection that theologians generate. The best hope of theology, then, is to return to its roots and try to learn how to speak to the community that is most likely to listen.

Indeed, the argument can be made that national discourse about the sacred is so significantly shaped by nonacademics precisely because theologians have lost their one and true audience—the church. Too much academic theology is void of personal, emotional, and moral reflection.[29] Part of the problem is that, in an era of shrinking budgets, too many professors are concerned more about protecting their disciplinary boundaries than engaging in popular religious debates. Theologians, especially, are forced to spend a lot of time and energy justifying what they do in terms that are acceptable to their colleagues. Christian theologians are expected to apologize for the many wrongs the church has committed over the centuries, and many theologians do not really "do theology" but focus all of their energies on some field that constitutes a critique of religion. Theologians of a certain species have evolved into creatures adept at living on the margins of religious belief, joining with the large chorus of critics and reformers at the safe distance of alleged objectivity while never getting around to the question of what is left when the nay-saying has ended. Consequently, people do not look to scholars of religion for religious insight and, given the present state of such scholarship, they shouldn't.

One of the problems with any kind of writing is trying to identify your audience. Most academic writers solve this puzzle by imagining the widest and most general audience possible, a kind of universal or ideal audience, faceless but competent, vague but all knowing. Of course, scholarly tomes are not for universal audiences but for a very small community of like-minded colleagues. Nevertheless, while most scholars act as if they are writing for everybody, they end up writing for practically nobody. The professionalization of theology moved theologians out of the pulpit and into the classroom, so now few theologians publish their sermons and few church members can identify the leading theologians. This has resulted in a diminished audience for theology. What teaching can teach teachers is that there are no universal audiences: faces matter. Too often scholars teach like they write, driven by the goals of clarity, precision, complexity, and comprehensiveness. I now think it is becoming more and more important for all teachers, especially theologians, to write like they teach. One of the best aspects of teaching is that there is little space for footnotes in the classroom. Teaching is more direct and personal than writing. Teaching should be the means of finding our voices, not trying out our theories. Theology must be confessional, not in the technical sense that theology must not appeal to philosophy or other disciplines for aid and clarification but in the sense that theologians should be more willing to reveal themselves between the lines of even their most dense and theoretical works—just as teachers are drawn into such revelations in the classroom.

The purpose of such confessions is not to raise the personal for its own sake but to meet students where they are and to draw them into a past they did not know existed. Only by showing them where they came from can theologians make a claim to their plans for the future. For theologians to regain their public voices, then, theology again must become a kind of catechetical inquiry, probing Christian practices and beliefs, testing their implications and consequences, and applying them in consistent and comprehensive ways.[30] This does not preclude creative attempts to engage connections between Christianity and the wider culture, but it keeps the focus on introducing students to the thickness of Christian tradition.

For some academics, the teaching of theology always will represent a narrowing of religious studies, a sectarian focus that public institutions cannot tolerate, but there is another way of looking at this issue. The paradigm of liberal Protestantism connected religion to the vital issues of the public square, rather than the church proper. As a result, not only was the academic square left religiously naked, but the study of religion did not live up to the standards of professional competence and expertise. The study of religion was a way of learning the civic virtues of tolerance and openness, which are so necessary for our national democracy, but this meant that the topic of religion was treated as a means for conveying basic values rather than as an end in itself, worthy of the most careful elaboration. Even neo-orthodox theologians like Tillich and Niebuhr, who led a remarkable theological renaissance in mid-twentieth-century North America, were popular mainly because they translated theology into a cultural, political, and humanistic idiom. Theology made progress in education only by giving up its particular norms and vocabulary. The lesson to be learned from mainline Protestantism's attempt to sell religion to public education is that, if religious studies is to be a specialized discipline in the academy, religion cannot be treated as a generic category—a moral dimension of human experience without much intellectual content.

Indeed, theology has undergone a revival in recent years precisely because theologians are paying more attention to the specificities of Christian doctrine. The fragmentation and politicization of theology that began in the sixties—after the era of Tillich and Niebuhr—meant that theology was doing what other disciplines could do better. Theology became a redundant echo in a chorus of *isms,* but this trend is showing signs of reversing. The last decade has seen theologians recovering classic doctrines like that of the Trinity, with surprising results. A renewed orthodoxy is developing that is simultaneously radical and generous, enabling theologians to speak with more authority and openness. Theologians have discovered that they need not sacrifice their intellectual heritage to find their place in the academy. In fact, specialization in religious studies should lead to a greater awareness of doctrinal complexities and the fine points of theological argument. The demands of specialization suggest that a confessional approach to religion might be the only way to make progress toward greater religious knowledge and fuller mutual understanding.

Earlier in American history, the idea of catechetical theology in the public schools would have been anathema because it would have raised the insoluble question of which church and whose dogma should be taught. But now, as many scholars document,

240

denominations are becoming less important as embodiments of religious truth.[31] Denominational differences, therefore, are not nearly as disruptive as they once were, and, moreover, the ecumenical movement has drawn many denominations closer together as they grapple with the central tenets of the Christian faith. Indeed, denominations have been able to define themselves more clearly by entering into dialogue with each other, and such dialogues make progress only when they delve deeply into classical Christian themes. Asking students to ponder the full weight of religious belief, then, will raise differences, but those differences need not be divisive or destructive. Instead, discovering the reasons behind one's beliefs and evaluating the importance of religious differences can be liberating. Teaching theology in public education, then, will be sectarian only in the sense that sectarianism—rather than something to be feared and loathed in public education—is just the name for what results when theology in all of its particularity is taken seriously.[32] Catechetical theology thus will introduce students to the full range and depth of Christian belief.

Such breadth of instruction does not mean, however, that catechetical theology in the public schools should promote some notion of the church as a global institution.[33] Beginning with the hypothesis of one universal and common Christian experience risks repeating the ecumenical dream of one religious tradition, a dream inevitably defined in the terms of liberal Protestantism. Catechetical theology also assumes the unity of Christianity, but it does so by drawing students into the thickness of theological belief, not by replacing theology with morality or piety.[34] Rather than constructing an ideal Christianity that does not exist, catechetical theology would direct students back to their particular church experiences, if they have them, or, if not, teach students what it would mean to have an abiding religious commitment. Such instruction would honor the religious differences—as well as the lack of any religious background—that students bring with them to the classroom. Local religious traditions, represented by student beliefs, community standards, and regional history, as well as a sensitivity to

241

national religious trends and international developments, would become the focus of theological instruction.[35]

The answer, then, to the question of which church and whose dogma should be favored in the religion classroom is the students' church (or mosque or synagogue) and dogma. A religious education that is optional, local, and faithful should not cause alarm to secularists in education. Many disciplines, such as medicine, law, and art, have practical components to their studies. Teaching art without having an adequate studio where students can practice art would be unacceptable at any school or educational level. It should be equally unacceptable to teach religion without providing students with some forum for practicing the religious life. Indeed, all secondary and postsecondary schools should have a time and place set aside to honor the religious needs of students. High schools do this by letting students form religious groups, and colleges have various chaplaincy programs and religious ministries, whether officially supported or merely tolerated. The religion classroom must be sensitively attuned to these organizations, framing discussions so that they pick up on practical religious issues and carry over into the students' religious lives. True, religion cannot be practiced explicitly in most religion classrooms, but there can be attention to the ways in which the study of religion is a rehearsal for the students' exercise of their religious beliefs once they leave their schooling behind.

Craig Dykstra has argued that the notion of practice should be understood as "participation in a cooperatively formed pattern of activity that emerges out of a complex tradition of interactions among many people sustained over a long period of time."[36] Studying religion is a practice sustained by a long tradition of teaching, but it cannot be completely separated from the intellectual and devotional habits that sustain interest in religion in the first place. When we teach students religion, we are engaging them on a level that solicits and influences their religious practices. We must be honest with them about our own habits of mind and action, and we must encourage them to integrate their learning and their religious way of life. Anything short of that would not count as an instance of the prac-

242

NOTES

Chapter 1: Confessions of a Theologian

1. Since my high school years, Congress has made it easier for students to form religious clubs with the passing of the Equal Access Act in 1984, which protects student-initiated and student-led meetings and organizations. The U.S. Department of Education also has issued guidelines about granting students permission to distribute religious literature in school, saying that schools may not single out religious literature for special regulation.

2. Jane Tompkins, *A Life in School: What the Teacher Learned* (Reading, Maine: Perseus Books, 1996), 128.

3. Mark Edmundson, "My First Intellectual," *Lingua Franca* (March 1999): 59.

4. Ibid.

5. See the fine essay by Paul A. Marshall, "Religious Toleration and Human Rights," in *Should God Get Tenure? Essays on Religion and Higher Education,* ed. David W. Gill (Grand Rapids: Eerdmans, 1997).

6. For a more nuanced portrait of evangelicals, see Christian Smith, *Christian America? What Evangelicals Really Want* (Berkeley: University of California Press, 2000).

7. For a sympathetic critique of the limitations of some evangelical theology, see Mark Noll, *The Scandal of the Evangelical Mind* (Grand Rapids: Eerdmans, 1994). For a good survey of the history and the potential of evangelical theology, see Gary Dorrien, *The Remaking of Evangelical Theology* (Louisville: Westminster John Knox Press, 1998).

8. See George M. Marsden, *The Outrageous Idea of Christian Scholarship* (New York: Oxford University Press, 1997).

Chapter 2: Religion Lost and Found in Public Education

1. *The Bible and Public Schools: A First Amendment Guide* (1999) is published by the National Bible Association and the First Amendment Center. Although this pamphlet does a competent job of summarizing the conditions that would make the return of the Bible to the classroom acceptable, it is still in debt to simplistic distinctions between the academic and objective vs. sectarian and devotional approaches to the Bible. If the academic study of the Bible is itself up for grabs—that is, if scholars have not yet determined how religion can be taught most effectively and what constitutes good religious instruction—it is impossible to refer to terms like "objectivity" and "academic" to rule out of court "devotional" or "confessional" pedagogical strategies. Indeed, the strongest justification for teaching the Bible in public schools rests on the devotion that Jews and Christians pay to it, so teaching the Bible can never be separated completely from religious norms and concerns.

2. See Robert S. Michaelson, "Constitutions, Courts, and the Study of Religion," *Journal of the American Academy of Religion* 45 (1977): 291–308 and W. Royce Clark, "The Legal Status of Religious Studies Programs in Public Higher Education," in *Beyond the Classics? Essays in Religious Studies and Liberal Education,* ed. Frank E. Reynolds and Sheryl Burkhalter (Atlanta: Scholars Press, 1990). The distinction between teaching "about" and the teaching "of" religion is artificial because it has no theoretical basis (such a simplistic view of objectivity is nowhere to be found in pedagogical theory today) and is impossible to implement (except in the most grievous cases where a teacher advocates a religious position in ways that are insensitive to students and incongruent with the topic being discussed). In fact, the Supreme Court's insistence on objective pedagogy has been developed as dicta (statements by the Court that are not necessary to the decision and therefore are not binding and have no precedential value) in cases that do not directly concern religious studies in public schools. Nonetheless, such language has had a significant impact on the ways in which educators think religion must be approached in public classrooms. For example, in an attempt to help schools think through these complex issues, President Clinton issued a directive through the Department of Education in 1995 that, while clarifying the right of students to discuss religious belief in the classroom, forbade teachers from advocating any religious doctrine or belief. The problem with such well-intended

guidelines is that objectivity in pedagogy is not such a simple thing. Many public educators use the language of the Court to limit the teaching of religion to purely historical issues, so that any theological, philosophical, or comparative examination of the truth claims of religion is ruled impermissible. Of course, the Court is not primarily concerned with outlining the most effective way of teaching religion, but with interpreting the Constitution. The problem is that by ignoring the pedagogical implications of its rulings, the Supreme Court is causing unintended and unhelpful consequences in the classroom.

3. See Frank Guliuzza III, *Over the Wall: Protecting Religious Expression in the Public Square* (Albany: SUNY Press, 2000). Neutrality should not mean that the government must exclude religion from all public institutions. If church and state are thought to be completely separate, then, given the broad reach of the state into nearly every aspect of modern existence, the church will be left with very little room to express itself. A narrow interpretation of neutrality would result in hostility toward religion. Instead, religious viewpoints should be given the same opportunity for reasonable expression as other viewpoints. This position is sometimes called benevolent neutrality or nonpreferential accommodation. For a good critique of the notion of neutrality and objectivity in education, see Stanley Fish, *The Trouble with Principle* (Cambridge: Harvard University Press, 1999). Fish focuses on the ways in which liberal principles of neutrality involve substantial moral claims, rather than just being matters of procedural fairness. He demonstrates how these very principles are often used to exclude religious viewpoints from the public domain.

4. Stephen L. Carter, *The Culture of Disbelief: How American Law and Politics Trivialize Religious Devotion* (New York: Basic Books, 1993), 12.

5. Warren Nord, "Religion-free Texts: Getting an Illiberal Education," *The Christian Century* (July 14–21, 1999): 711–715. Also see Nord's comprehensive and groundbreaking work, from which I have learned much, *Religion and American Education* (Chapel Hill: University of North Carolina Press, 1995).

6. Leo Reisberg, "Enrollments Surge at Christian Colleges," *The Chronicle of Higher Education* (March 5, 1999): A42–A44.

7. For an excellent analysis of hypocrisy, see James S. Spiegel, *Hypocrisy: Moral Fraud and Other Vices* (Grand Rapids: Baker Books, 1999).

8. Mary Field Belenky, et. al., *Women's Ways of Knowing* (San Francisco: Harper Collins, 1986), 227. For an instructive book on women and religious education, see Mary Donovan Turner and Mary Lin Hud-

son, *Saved From Silence: Finding Women's Voice in Preaching* (St. Louis: Chalice Press, 1999). Also see Jane McAvoy, "Hospitality: A Feminist Theology of Education," *Teaching Theology and Religion* 1/1 (February 1998): 20–26.

9. *Women's Ways of Knowing*, 217.

10. Robin Lovin, "Confidence and Criticism: Religious Studies and the Public Purposes of Liberal Education," in *Beyond the Classics? Essays in Religious Studies and Liberal Education,* ed. Frank E. Reynolds and Sheryl Burkhalter (Atlanta: Scholars Press, 1990), 81.

11. Quoted in Scott Heller, "The New Jewish Studies: Defying Tradition and Easy Categorization," *The Chronicle of Higher Education* (January 29, 1999): A21.

12. Julie A. Reuben, *The Making of the Modern University: Intellectual Transformation and the Marginalization of Morality* (Chicago: University of Chicago Press, 1996), 19. Also see Jon H. Roberts and James Turner, *The Sacred and Secular University* (Princeton: Princeton University Press, 2000), ch. 1.

13. Stanley Hauerwas makes this point in many influential books and articles. See, for example, *Sanctify Them in the Truth: Holiness Exemplified* (Nashville: Abingdon Press, 1998).

14. For a portrait of morality that emphasizes the spiritual practices necessary to sustain any pursuit of the good, see William C. Spohn, *Go and Do Likewise: Jesus and Ethics* (New York: Continuum, 1999).

15. This position has been developed by postliberal theologians like George Lindbeck, William C. Placher, Stanley Hauerwas, and others, who have been influenced by the work of Hans Frei.

16. Alasdair MacIntyre, *Whose Justice? Which Rationality?* (Notre Dame, Ind.: University of Notre Dame Press, 1988), 382.

17. Alice Kaplan, *French Lesson: A Memoir* (Chicago: University of Chicago Press, 1993), 209.

18. Ibid., 134.

19. I have learned much about this topic from Pamela L. Caughie, *Passing and Pedagogy: The Dynamics of Responsibility* (Urbana and Chicago: University of Illinois Press, 1999) and Amy Robinson, "It Takes One to Know One: Passing and Communities of Common Interest," *Critical Inquiry* 20 (Summer 1994): 715–36.

Chapter 3: The Theology of Teaching and the Teaching of Theology

1. Ms. hooks does not capitalize either her first or last name. This departure from the usual capitalization practice will be respected in the following pages.

2. Parker J. Palmer, *The Courage to Teach: Exploring the Inner Landscape of a Teacher's Life* (San Francisco: Jossey-Bass Publishers, 1998), 31.

3. Ibid., 24.

4. Peter C. Hodgson, *God's Wisdom: Toward a Theology of Education* (Louisville: Westminster John Knox Press, 1999).

5. Gabriel Moran, *Showing How: The Act of Teaching* (Valley Forge, Pa.: Trinity Press International, 1997), 18.

6. *God's Wisdom,* 6.

7. Ibid., 11.

8. Ibid., 106.

9. Ibid., 70.

10. Ibid., 71.

11. Ibid., 77.

12. bell hooks, *Teaching to Transgress: Education as the Practice of Freedom* (New York: Routledge, 1994), 13.

13. Ibid., 19.

14. Ibid., 3.

15. Ibid., 6.

16. For a fine development of Freire's work in the context of compositions studies, see Bradford T. Stull, *Amid the Fall, Dreaming of Eden: Du Bois, King, Malcom X, and Emancipatory Composition* (Carbondale: Southern Illinois University Press, 1999).

17. *Teaching to Transgress,* 29–30.

18. Jake Ryan and Charles Sackrey, eds., *Strangers in Paradise: Academics from the Working Class* (Lanham, Md.: University Press of America, 1996), 205.

19. *Teaching to Transgress,* 187.

20. Ibid., 181.

21. Wayne Booth, *The Company We Keep: An Ethics of Fiction* (Berkeley: University of California Press, 1988).

Chapter 4: Classroom Confessions

1. Although, as James Duke points out, to say that there is no creed but Christ is not the same thing as saying there is no creed. See his "The Question of Confession Among Disciples," *Impact* (1990): 16–28.

2. See Martin L. Cook, *The Open Circle: Confessional Method in Theology* (Minneapolis: Fortress Press, 1991).

3. George Lindbeck, *The Nature of Doctrine* (Philadelphia: Westminster Press, 1984).

4. Michel Foucault, *The History of Sexuality, Vol. 1: An Introduction,* trans. Robert Hurley (New York: Vintage Books, 1980), 21.

5. For a thorough overview of the history of this sacrament, see Joseph Martos, *Doors to the Sacred: A Historical Introduction to Sacraments in the Catholic Church* (Liguori, Mo.: Triumph Books, 1991), ch. 9.

6. Foucault exaggerates the importance of the Lateran Council of 1215 for the codification of penance and confession. See Pierre J. Payer, "Foucault on Penance and the Shaping of Sexuality," *Studies in Religion* 14 (1985): 313–320.

7. *The History of Sexuality, Vol. 1,* 59.

8. Ibid.

9. Ibid., 57.

10. For a sound defense of confession as therapy, see Sharon Hymer, "Therapeutic and Redemptive Aspects of Religious Confession," *Journal of Religion and Health* 34 (Spring 1995): 41–54.

11. Miroslav Volf, *After Our Likeness: The Church as the Image of the Trinity* (Grand Rapids: Eerdmans, 1998), 149.

12. Ibid., 150.

13. Richard B. Miller, *Casuistry and Modern Ethics* (Chicago: University of Chicago Press, 1996), 208–9.

14. Ibid., 288.

15. Ibid., 217.

16. Miriam Peskowitz, "Identification Questions," *Journal of the American Academy of Religion* 65 (Winter 1997): 711.

17. Ibid., 721.

18. Ibid., 716.

19. Notice, however, how confession has returned to Protestantism with the growth of the Christian counseling movement. See Kenneth L. Faught, "Catholic Issues for Protestant Pilgrims," *The Theological Educator* 51 (Spring 1995): 9–17.

20. John Murray Cuddihy, *No Offense: Civil Religion and Protestant Taste* (New York: The Seabury Press, 1978).

21. Kimberley C. Patton, "Stumbling Along Between the Immensities: Reflections on Teaching in the Study of Religion," *Journal of the American Academy of Religion* 65 (Winter 1997): 847.

22. Friedrich Nietzsche, *Beyond Good and Evil,* trans. R. J. Hollingdale (New York: Penguin Books, 1990), 37.

23. Quoted in David Wisdo, "Kierkegaard on Confession and Understanding a Life," *Journal of Religious Studies* 17 (1991): 92.

24. Søren Kierkegaard, *Philosophical Fragments,* ed. and trans. Howard V. Hong and Edna H. Hong (Princeton: Princeton University Press, 1985).

25. Ibid., 37. It is interesting that during the discussion, Johannes Climacus accuses himself of plagiarism, indicating that the possession of the truth is equivalent to stealing, because truth always belongs (philosophically speaking) to somebody else or (theologically speaking) to God.

Chapter 5: Religion Amid the Ruins of the Postmodern University

1. Bill Readings, *The University in Ruins* (Cambridge: Harvard University Press, 1996).

2. Gabriel Moran, *Showing How: The Act of Teaching* (Valley Forge, Pa.: Trinity Press, 1997), 3.

3. Immanuel Kant, *The Conflict of the Faculties (Der Streit der Fakult),* trans. Mary J. Gregor (Lincoln: University of Nebraska Press, 1992).

4. *The University in Ruins,* 63.

5. Ibid., 77.

6. Ibid., 165.

7. Paul J. Griffiths, *Religious Reading: The Place of Reading in the Practice of Religion* (New York: Oxford University Press, 1999).

8. For a less postmodern and therefore more straightforward account of obligation (rather than the traditionally touted "academic freedom") as the foundation of pedagogy, see Donald Kennedy, *Academic Duty* (Cambridge: Harvard University Press, 1997).

Chapter 6: The Mystery of the Disappearing Chaplain

1. Quotations that are not footnoted come from material housed in the Wabash archives. I want to thank archivist Johanna Herring for her help as well as correspondence and conversations with Dick Ristine and Hall Peebles.

2. Robert S. Harvey, ed., *These Fleeting Years: Wabash College, 1832–1982* (Crawfordsville, Ind.: Wabash College, 1982), 6.

3. See James Insley Osborne and Theodore Gregory Gronert, *Wabash College: The First Hundred Years* (Crawfordsville, Ind.: R. E. Banta, 1932). I rely on this text throughout this essay.

4. *These Fleeting Years,* 18.

5. Ibid., 31.

6. See Julie A. Reuben, *The Making of the Modern University: Intellectual Transformation and the Marginalization of Morality* (Chicago: University of Chicago Press, 1996), 23. My account of the history of education is also informed by Conrad Cherry, *Hurrying Toward Zion: Universities, Divinity Schools, and American Protestantism* (Bloomington: Indiana University Press, 1995), Robert Shepard, *God's People in the Ivory Tower: Religion in the Early American University* (New York: Carlson Publishing, 1991), W. Clark Gilpin, *A Preface to Theology* (Chicago: University of Chicago Press, 1996), and George Marsden and Bradley J. Longfield, eds., *The Secularization of the Academy* (New York: Oxford University Press, 1992).

7. The most reliable history of religion at Wabash is "The History of Religious Education at Wabash College," by Edgar H. Evans, Wabash College archives.

8. Byron K. Trippet, *Wabash on my Mind,* ed. Paul Donald Herring (Crawfordsville, Ind.: Wabash College), 35–6.

9. In 1860, less than 1 percent of the college-age population pursued higher education. By 1930, that number had risen to 12.4 percent.

10. See *The Making of the Modern University.*

11. This point is persuasively documented in D. G. Hart, *The University Gets Religion: Religious Studies in Higher Education* (Baltimore: The Johns Hopkins University Press, 1999).

12. Douglas Sloan, *Faith and Knowledge: Mainline Protestantism and American Higher Education* (Louisville: Westminster John Knox Press, 1994), 22.

13. George Marsden, *The Soul of the American University: From Protestant Establishment to Established Nonbelief* (New York: Oxford University Press, 1994), 337.

14. George Marsden, *The Outrageous Idea of Christian Scholarship* (New York: Oxford University Press, 1997).

15. Martin E. Marty, *Second Chance for American Protestants* (New York: Harper & Row, 1963). I am grateful to Mark Toulouse for this citation.

16. This report, entitled "Report of Hans Frei to Faculty-Trustee Committee on Educational Programs, January 19, 1953," which has never been published, is in the Wabash College archives.

17. Ibid., 3.

18. Ibid., 7.

Chapter 8: Theology and Religious Studies

1. Robert Wuthnow, in Steve Moore, ed., *The University Through the Eyes of Faith* (Indianapolis: Light and Life, 1998), 149–50.

2. *A Preface to Theology*, 149.

3. *Hurrying Toward Zion*, 123.

4. Erik J. Sharpe, "Religious Studies, the Humanities, and the History of Ideas," *Soundings* 71 (1988): 251 (italics are the author's).

5. Ibid., 251.

6. Ronald Knox, *The Hidden Stream* (London: Burns, Oates, 1952), 105.

7. Eric J. Sharpe, *Comparative Religion: A History,* 2d ed. (La Salle, Ill.: Open Court, 1986), 2.

8. Ibid., 3.

9. Steven M. Wasserstrom, *Religion After Religion: Gershom Scholem, Mircea Eliade, and Henry Corbin at Eranos* (Princeton: Princeton University Press, 1999), 3.

10. Donald Wiebe, *The Politics of Religious Studies: The Continuing Conflict with Theology in the Academy* (New York: St. Martin's Press, 1999), 9.

11. Ibid., x.

12. Ibid., 142.

13. Ibid., 143.

14. Ibid., 155.

15. Ibid.

16. Ibid., 166.

17. See Daniel L. Pals, "The Faith of the Scholars," *The Christian Century* (September 8–15, 1999): 859.

18. See Eldon Eisenach, *The Next Religious Establishment: National Identity and Political Theology in Post-Protestant America* (Lanham; Md.: University Press of America, 2000).

19. Russell T. McCutcheon, *Manufacturing Religion: The Discourse of Sui Generis Religion and the Politics of Nostalgia* (New York: Oxford University Press, 1997).

20. Gerald Graff, *Beyond the Culture Wars: How Teaching the Conflicts Can Revitalize American Education* (New York: Norton, 1992).

21. Robert J. Nash, *Faith, Hype, and Clarity: Teaching About Religion in American Schools and Colleges* (New York: Teachers College Press, 1999).

22. Ibid., 91.

23. Ibid., 56–7.

24. Ibid., 193.

25. *The Culture of Disbelief,* 16.

26. Simone Weil, *Waiting for God,* trans. Emma Craufurd (New York: Harper & Row, 1973), 105.

27. Robert Hutchins, *The University of Utopia* (Chicago: University of Chicago Press, 1953), 96.

28. Geoffrey H. Hartman, "Higher Education in the 1990s," *New Literary History* 24 (Autumn 1993): 734.

29. For analysis of and solutions to the problem of theology's lack of a broad audience, see two articles by William C. Placher, "Helping Theology Matter: A Challenge for the Mainline," *The Christian Century,* (October 28, 1998): 994–98, and "Taking Risks to Reach a Popular Audience," *Religious Studies News,* (November 1998): 20.

30. For the argument that academic theology is essentially pastoral, see Ellen T. Charry, *By the Renewing of Your Minds: The Pastoral Function of Christian Doctrine* (New York: Oxford University Press, 1997). Also see the seminal work of Edward Farley on the history and nature of theological education, especially his *Theologia: The Fragmentation and Unity of Theological Education* (Philadelphia: Fortress Press, 1983).

31. See Roberth Wuthnow, *The Restructuring of American Religion: Society and Faith since World War II* (Princeton: Princeton University Press, 1988).

32. Any serious rhetorical analysis of the use of *sectarian* as a charge against an opponent will confirm my observation. Somebody is being sectarian when raising an intellectual issue concerning religious belief that cannot be assimilated into a liberal and ecumenical paradigm. A sectarian approach to religion, then, insists on the honest admission that religious disagreements cannot be resolved without the intellectual issues at stake being clear. Religious dialogue must pass through, rather than around, the complexities of theological argument before it can result in some kind of accord.

33. See, for example, the recent proposal by Joseph C. Hough and John B. Cobb, *Christian Identity and Theological Education* (Chico, Calif.: Scholars Press, 1985).

34. For a good example of the position I am defending, which emphasizes the church as having a particular way of life that should not be subsumed into patriotic talk about the American way of life, see Rodney Clapp, *A Peculiar People: The Church as Culture in a Post-Christian Society* (Downers Grove, Ill.: InterVarsity Press, 1996).

35. See James F. Hopewell, "A Congregational Paradigm for Theological Education," in *Beyond Clericalism: The Congregation as a Focus for Theological Education,* ed. Joseph C. Hough Jr. and Barbara Wheeler (Atlanta: Scholars Press, 1988).

36. Craig Dykstra, "Reconceiving Practice," in *Shifting Boundaries: Contextual Approaches to the Structure of Theological Education,* ed. Barbara G. Wheeler and Edward Farley (Louisville: Westminster John Knox Press, 1991), 43.

Stephen H. Webb is associate professor of religion and philosophy at Wabash College (Crawfordsville, Indiana). His other books include *On God and Dogs: A Christian Theology of Compassion for Animals* and *The Gifting God: A Trinitarian Ethics of Excess*.